critical race counterstories
along the chicana/chicano
educational pipeline

The *Teaching/Learning Social Justice* Series
Edited by Lee Anne Bell, Barnard College, Columbia University

Critical Race Counterstories along the Chicana/Chicano Educational Pipeline
Tara J. Yosso

Understanding White Privilege: Creating Pathways to Authentic Relationships across Race
Frances E. Kendall

critical race counterstories along the chicana/chicano educational pipeline

tara j. yosso

Routledge
Taylor & Francis Group

New York   London

Published in 2006 by
Routledge
Taylor & Francis Group
270 Madison Avenue
New York, NY 10016

Published in Great Britain by
Routledge
Taylor & Francis Group
2 Park Square
Milton Park, Abingdon
Oxon OX14 4RN

© 2006 by Taylor & Francis Group, LLC
Routledge is an imprint of Taylor & Francis Group

Printed in the United States of America on acid-free paper
10 9 8 7 6

International Standard Book Number-10: 0-415-95195-X (Hardcover) 0-415-95196-8 (Softcover)
International Standard Book Number-13: 978-0-415-95195-1 (Hardcover) 978-0-415-95196-8 (Softcover)
Library of Congress Card Number 2005010409

Library of Congress Cataloging-in-Publication Data

Yosso, Tara.
    Critical race counterstories along the Chicana/Chicano educational pipeline / by Tara J. Yosso.
        p. cm. -- (Teaching/Learning Social Justice)
    Includes bibiographical references.
    ISBN 0-415-95195-X (hb : alk. paper) -- ISBN 0-415-95196-8 (pb : alk. paper)
    1. Mexican Americans--Education.   2. Racism in education--United States.   3. Educational equalization--United States. I. Title. II. Series.

LC2683 .Y67   2006
71.829′680773′11--dc22   2005010409

Taylor & Francis Group
is the Academic Division of Informa plc.

Visit the Taylor & Francis Web site at
http://www.taylorandfrancis.com

and the Routledge Web site at
http://www.routledge-ny.com

Para la familia Gutierrez,
whose struggles inspired me more than they know

And to all those along the Chicana/o educational pipeline,
those whose stories are part of this book, and those whose stories
have yet to be told. Que sigan siempre adelante…

Contents

Acknowledgments

Just as it takes a village to raise a child, it took a community to complete this book. Thank you to Danny Solórzano for your mentorship and support—for helping me brainstorm, graciously sharing data, research insights, and for your encouragement. After 12 years of working together, I continue to deeply admire you and I appreciate the ways you act justly and walk humbly.

Thank you to those who in small and big ways have been a source of encouragement and support to complete this project. Much appreciation and thanks to supportive *colegas*: Dolores Delgado Bernal, Octavio Villalpando, Augustine Romero, Irene Vasquez, and Dave Stovall. Thanks to William A. Smith, for helping me break through writer's block with phone calls of brainstorming and encouragement. Very special thanks to Rebeca Burciaga, Tara Watford, Gloria Sanchez, and Veronica Velez for offering research insights, commenting on drafts, and helping me prepare seemingly endless references. To the Latina Equity in Education Project *mujeres* at UCLA who provided helpful research data. To Laura Telles for your personal and professional support and patience with my usually dramatic phone calls to track down Danny. To my UCSB colleagues Ralph Armbruster-Sandoval and Yolanda Broyles-Gonzales—*gracias por todo*. Thank you Marisela Marquez, for continued support. Heartfelt appreciation to Martha Alcantar, Diane Mercado, and the students of *El Congreso de UCSB*.

Thank you to those whose paths have crossed mine and who have positively influenced my journey and this book. To teachers from Pioneer High School: Mr. Padilla, Mr. D (Lou DeLaRosa), Mr. Church, and Mr. Anaya. At UCLA, to Concepción Valadez, Chon Noriega, Peter McLaren, Vilma Ortiz, Raymond Rocco, Bob Land, and thank you to the Academic Advancement Program, for working to retain, empower, and graduate me along with thousands of other first generation, low income, underrepresented students. Thank you to Richard Valencia, Richard Delgado,

Margaret Montoya, Rudy Acuña, and Juan Goméz-Quiñones for inspiring scholarship and insightful advice. To Anita Tijerina Revilla, Marcos Pizarro, Miguel Ceja, Rita E. Urquijo-Ruiz, Irene Serna, Hector Alvarez, Jill Pinkney-Pastrana, Carlos Tejeda, John Fernandez, Valerie Talavera-Bustillos, Rachel Raimist, Armida Ornelas, Michelle Knight, Corina Benavides, Carlos Haro, Nadine Bermudez, and Marisabel Ortiz-Lopez *y familia*. To Carlos San Miguel, thanks for working through my computer problems as if they were your own and for your efforts in the Peace on Berryman Project. Thanks to Lee Anne Bell and to Catherine Bernard and Brook Cosby at Routledge, Julie Spadaro at Taylor & Francis, and Scott Suckling at MetroVoice Publishing.

Gracias a la familia Garcia de Oxnard. Abrazos and a sincere thank you to David G. Garcia for your friendship, humor, and encouragement. Thanks also for your critical editing and amazing cover design. Thank you to my parents, Kathleen and Joe, for the love and sacrifices that allowed your children to achieve beyond what we could imagine and to keep dreaming. To Mom, for your prayers and genuine efforts to understand and accept all of me. To Dad, for nurturing my imagination and humor. To Jason, for medical advice, computer assistance, and encouraging energy that can be felt across the long distance, and to David, for reminding me to pursue stories I have a passion to tell.

In 1970, Thomas P. Carter's book explained that Mexican Americans suffered *A History of Educational Neglect*. In 1979, Carter and Roberto D. Segura examined the continued systemic failures of the educational system, while they analyzed individual and institutional reform efforts representing *A Decade of Change* for Mexican Americans in school. I am deeply grateful to these scholars and other trailblazers whose work documents injustice and inequality and demands justice and equality. Now twenty-six years later, I present this book in an effort to examine and challenge the racism and structural inequality that continues to limit educational opportunities for Chicana/o students. The cover of the book offers a representation of a multigenerational yearbook of Chicanas/os struggling and succeeding in U.S. schools. *Mil gracias* to each of you who offered your photos to humanize the statistical realities and possibilities presented by the Chicana/o educational pipeline.

Though a community helped create this book, I take responsibility for any errors herein. Thank you to those who I've forgotten to mention.

And as a student's words eloquently add to Jose Antonio Burciaga's Stanford mural *The Last Supper of Chicano Heroes*, to "all the people who died, scrubbed floors, wept, and fought," so that Chicanas/os could pursue higher education and social change—*gracias*.

Series Editor's Introduction

This series explores the many ways people engage diversity, democracy, and social justice in classrooms and communities. The term "social justice" is the umbrella for texts that address broad concerns of democracy, equality, diversity, and justice. "Teaching/learning" emphasizes the essential connections between theory and practice that books in this series will examine. The series addresses both popular education as well as education in formal institutions. Central are the stories and lived experiences of people who struggle both to critically analyze and challenge oppressive relationships and institutions, and to imagine and create more just and inclusive alternatives. My hope is that the series will balance critical analysis with images of hope and possibility in ways that are accessible and inspiring to a broad audience of educators and activists who believe in the possibility of social change through education and who seek stories and examples of practice, as well as honest discussion of the barriers and struggles in challenging oppressive institutions.

The goals of this series are beautifully realized in Tara Yosso's *Critical Race Counterstories along the Chicana/Chicano Educational Pipeline*. This timely book by a critical race theorist addresses an issue that is prominent in the news as colleges and universities, as well as public K–12 educators committed to social justice, reflect on the recent Supreme Court decision providing a twenty-five-year window to remedy the underrepresentation of students of color in higher education. The pressure of this deadline has made educators at all levels pay more attention to the entire pipeline from kindergarten through higher education and to reducing the barriers that block movement through the pipeline.

Through critical race counterstories, Yosso represents the various stages in the educational pipeline for Chicanas/os and brings to life the qualitative, often hard-to-see dimensions of the struggle for equal education in Chicana/o communities. Through these stories the reader gets a more vivid and complex picture of the dimensions of the problems Chicana/o students face at all levels of schooling and the barriers put in place by schools and the dominant society. Yosso's counterstories also invoke and develop the multiple possibilities for challenging these barriers, imagining alternative scenarios for success through schooling in Chicana/o communities and holding schools accountable to all young people in this country. In so doing, Yosso makes a powerful contribution to theory and practice aimed at opening up the educational pipeline to disenfranchised communities and to bringing the rhetorical promise of education as a path to equality and opportunity closer to reality.

Lee Anne Bell
Professor and Barbara Silver Horowitz Director of Education,
Barnard College, Columbia University

1

WHY USE CRITICAL RACE THEORY AND COUNTERSTORYTELLING TO ANALYZE THE CHICANA/O EDUCATIONAL PIPELINE?

I shed tears of anguish
as I see my children disappear
behind the shroud of mediocrity
never to look back to remember me
I am Joaquin. ...

I have endured in the rugged mountains
    of our country.
I have survived the toils and slavery
    of the fields.
        I have existed
in the barrios of the city,
in the suburbs of bigotry,
in the mines of social snobbery,
in the prisons of dejection,
in the muck of exploitation
and
in the fierce heat of racial hatred. ...

I am the masses of my people and
I refuse to be absorbed.
    I am Joaquin
The odds are great
But my spirit is strong
    My faith unbreakable[1]

1

The above excerpts of Rodolfo "Corky" Gonzales' 1967 epic poem "I am Joaquin" are part of a Chicana/o[2] counterstory. A counterstory recounts experiences of racism and resistance from the perspectives of those on society's margins.[3] In the spirit of Gonzales—whose life's work expressed the same defiance and hope of his poem—this book offers Chicana/o counterstories that challenge social and racial injustice along the educational pipeline.

Gonzales' Joaquin endures a legacy of social and racial inequality. Likewise, Chicana/o communities struggle to survive a history of institutional neglect in U.S. public schools. Abysmal statistical realities pervade today's Chicana/o educational pipeline. Fifty-six percent of Chicana/o students do not graduate high school and only 7% graduate from college. Chicanas/os suffer daunting schooling conditions throughout the educational pipeline. Most Chicana/o students attend overcrowded, racially segregated schools, which lack sufficient numbers of trained faculty, updated textbooks, and even desks.

Despite seemingly insurmountable odds, Gonzales' Joaquin maintains his faith. In the same way, Chicana/o youth and their families continue to challenge an educational system that has consistently failed them. Indeed, their counterstories carry on Joaquin's legacy and demonstrate hope and possibility all along the Chicana/o educational pipeline.

DEMOGRAPHIC CONTEXTS OF THE CHICANA/O EDUCATIONAL PIPELINE

Chicana/o communities have long experienced the explicit and implicit effects of racism through social institutions such as schools.[4] To frame this discussion, I begin with a brief demographic overview of the Chicana/o, Latina/o community in the United States. Latinas/os[5] comprise the largest and fastest growing racial/ethnic "minority" group in the United States. According to the 2000 U.S. Census, at least 35.3 million Latinas/os reside in the United States, and account for about 13% of the total U.S. population. Projections indicate Latinas/os will make up 18% of the U.S. population by 2025. People of Mexican descent—Chicanas/os—represent the youngest, the largest, and the fastest growing Latina/o population subgroup. Chicanas/os comprise an estimated 66% of the total Latina/o population. The remainder of the Latina/o population includes Central or South Americans (14%), Puerto Ricans (11%), Cubans (5%), and other Latinas/os (7%).[6]

Historically rooted and indigenous to the southwestern United States, Chicanas/os now represent the largest single "minority" group in almost every major metropolitan area west of the Mississippi River. In addition, Chicanas/os are moving in large numbers to major metropolitan areas in the Pacific Northwest, the Midwest, the East Coast, and the South. The median age of the Chicana/o population is 24 years old, and one of every two Chicanas/os under the age of 18 lives in poverty. The educational opportunities made available to these young Chicanas/os will yield societal repercussions as major cities across the nation exhibit demographic patterns already evident in California and the Southwest. To address some of these contemporary contexts, I begin with a critical examination of the Chicana/o educational pipeline at the turn of the 21st century (figure 1.1).

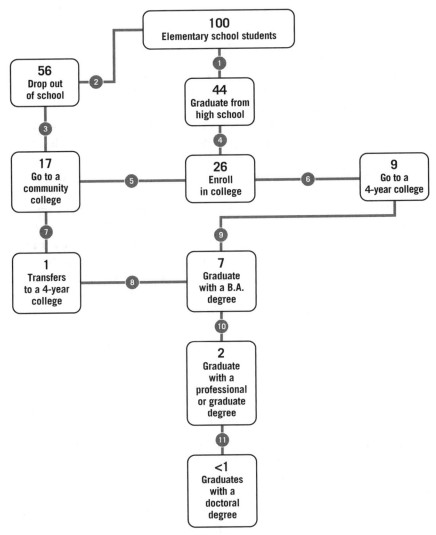

Figure 1.1. The Chicana/o Educational Pipeline[7]

The pipeline represents a system of connecting educational institutions. Schooling structures, practices, and discourses facilitate the flow of knowledge, skills, and students along the educational pipeline. However, at any given point in the pipeline—no matter how one measures educational outcomes—Chicanas/os do not perform as well as Whites and attain less than other racial or ethnic groups in the United States.[8] Figure 1.1 demonstrates these very serious leaks in the Chicana/o educational pipeline.[9] Utilizing 2000 U.S. Census data and information from the National Center for Educational Statistics, we begin with 100 Chicana and Chicano students at the elementary level, noting that 56 drop out of high school and 44 continue on to graduate. Of the 44 who graduate from high school, about 26 continue on toward some form of postsecondary education. Of those 26, approximately 17 enroll in community colleges and nine enroll at 4-year institutions. Of those 17 in community colleges, only one will transfer to a 4-year institution. Of the nine Chicanas/os attending a 4-year college and the one community college transfer student, seven will graduate with a baccalaureate degree. Finally, two Chicana/o students will continue on to earn a graduate or professional school degree and less than one will receive a doctorate.

In order to humanize some of these statistical realities along the Chicana/o educational pipeline, I utilize a method of presenting research called counterstorytelling. Indeed, social scientists offer at least two types of stories to explain unequal educational outcomes—majoritarian stories and counterstories.[10] A majoritarian story implicitly begins from the assumption that all students enjoy access to the same educational opportunities and conditions from elementary through postsecondary school. From this premise, and utilizing seemingly neutral and objective standard formulae, the majoritarian story faults Chicana/o students and community cultural traditions for unequal schooling outcomes.

A counterstory, on the other hand, begins with an understanding that inadequate educational conditions limit equal access and opportunities in Chicana/o schooling.[11] Pointing out the biased and subjective formulae of the majoritarian story, the counterstory reveals that Chicanas/os usually attend overcrowded, run-down, and racially segregated schools.[12] Too often, these schools provide low per-pupil expenditures, few well-trained teachers, and limited access to a quality, college-bound curriculum.[13] Instead of blaming Chicana/o students or community cultural traditions, a counterstory addresses the structures, practices, and discourses that facilitate high dropout (pushout)[14] rates along the Chicana/o educational pipeline.

Counterstorytelling as used in this book draws directly from scholarship in critical race theory (CRT). CRT refers to a framework used to examine and challenge the ways race and racism implicitly and explicitly shape social structures, practices, and discourses.[15] This book utilizes critical race counterstorytelling to theorize, examine, and challenge the ways race and racism implicitly and explicitly effect Chicanas/os in the United States educational system.

Below, I briefly define the terms race, racism, and White privilege for this book, and further introduce readers to CRT as a conceptual, theoretical, pedagogical, and methodological framework in education. Next, I extend on the description of majoritarian storytelling. I then outline the methodology of counterstorytelling in CRT and for this book in particular. Finally, I address some of the critics of critical race counterstories, and propose four functions of counterstorytelling.

RACISM, WHITE PRIVILEGE, AND CRITICAL RACE THEORY

Race is a socially constructed category, created to differentiate groups based primarily on skin color, phenotype, ethnicity, and culture for the purpose of showing the superiority or dominance of one group over another.[16] The social meanings applied to race find their justification in an ideology of racial superiority and White privilege—an ideology of racism. I draw on the work of Audre Lorde,[17] Chester Pierce,[18] and Manning Marable[19] to define racism as (1) a false belief in White supremacy that handicaps society, (2) a system that upholds Whites as superior to all other groups, and (3) the structural subordination of multiple racial and ethnic groups. With its macro, micro, interpersonal, institutional, overt, and subtle forms, racism entails institutional power. Communities of Color[20] in the United States have never possessed this form of power.

Racism—the systemic oppression of People of Color—privileges Whites. Drawing on the work of Beverly Tatum,[21] Zeus Leonardo,[22] Peggy McIntosh,[23] and Devon Carbado,[24] I define White privilege as a system of advantage resulting from a legacy of racism and benefiting individuals and groups based on the notions of whiteness. Whiteness intersects with other forms of privilege, including gender, class, phenotype, accent, language, sexuality, immigrant status, and surname. As a very light-skinned Latina of mixed race, people either assume that I am White, refer to me as *Güera*,[25] or ask, "What are you?" Born in northern California to working-class, monolingual English-speaking parents, without a Spanish surname, I learned Spanish as a second language and have come to identify as a Chicana. Though I suffer various forms of oppression, I also enjoy multiple layers of White privilege, both in my daily activities (e.g., being served pleasantly at a restaurant, talking my way out of traffic citations, traveling internationally without border patrol harassment), and in my life-trajectory (e.g., being tracked in college preparatory courses, having my offer to purchase a home accepted over other financially qualified potential buyers, receiving quality healthcare). For the most part, White privilege seems invisible. Those who experience everyday benefits and other unearned White privileges may not recognize that the systemic oppression of People of Color enables these institutionalized racial preferences.

In order to address the historical and contemporary realities of race, racism, and White privilege, I draw on a dynamic analytical framework called critical race theory. Critical race theory (CRT) originated in schools of law in the late 1980s with a group of scholars seeking to examine and challenge race and racism in the United States legal system and society. Feeling limited by work that separated critical theory from conversations about race and racism, these legal scholars sought "both a critical space in which race was foregrounded and a race space where critical themes were central."[26] Specifically, they argued that critical legal studies scholarship did not listen to the lived experiences and histories of People of Color. Scholars such as Derrick Bell and Alan Freeman asserted that without analyzing race and racism, critical legal scholarship could not offer strategies for social transformation.[27] This argument had also been taking place in social science and history circles, specifically in ethnic and women's studies scholarship.

Rooted in the scholarly traditions of ethnic studies, U.S./third-world feminisms, Marxism/neo-Marxism, cultural nationalism, and internal colonialism, CRT scholarship initially focused its critique on the slow pace of civil rights legislation. Much of the early CRT literature pointed out the unrealized promise of civil rights legislative efforts for Black and White communities. Some CRT scholars challenged this tendency toward a Black/White binary,[28] explaining that oppression in the law and society could not be fully understood in terms of only Black and White. While acknowledging that African Americans endure a unique and horrendous history of racism and other forms of subordination in the United States,[29] these scholars noted that other People of Color inherit histories likewise shaped by the intersections of racism. As a result of these self-reflective discussions, CRT's family tree expanded to recognize these histories and experiences.[30] Almost 20 years after its inception, CRT and its branches of FemCrit, LatCrit, TribalCrit, AsianCrit,[31] and WhiteCrit[32] evidence an ongoing search by socially and racially marginalized communities for a framework "grounded in the particulars of their social reality and experience."[33]

Latina/o critical race (LatCrit) theory scholarship in particular brought a Chicana/o, Latina/o consciousness to CRT in examining racialized layers of subordination based on immigration status, sexuality, culture, language, phenotype, accent, and surname.[34] This LatCrit consciousness extended critical race discussions to address the layers of racialized subordination that comprise Chicana/o, Latina/o experiences within and beyond U.S. borders.[35] I engage CRT informed by this LatCrit consciousness.

CRT's roots and branches inform the critical race movement in education.[36] Over the last 10 years, CRT scholars in education have theorized, examined, and challenged the ways race and racism shape on schooling structures, practices, and discourses. Education scholar Daniel Solórzano[37] identified at least five tenets of CRT.[38] Below I describe these tenets as they apply to education.

1. **The *Inter*centricity of Race and Racism.** CRT starts from the premise that race and racism are endemic and permanent in U.S. society.[39] Discussions of race within CRT begin with an examination of how race has been socially constructed in U.S. history and how the system of racism functions to oppress People of Color while privileging Whites. A CRT in education centralizes race and racism, while also focusing on racisms' intersections with other forms of subordination, based on gender, class, sexuality, language, culture, immigrant status, phenotype, accent, and surname.[40]

2. **The Challenge to Dominant Ideology.** Critical race scholars argue that traditional claims of race neutrality and objectivity act as a camouflage for the self-interest, power, and privilege of dominant groups in U.S. society.[41] A CRT in education challenges claims that the educational system offers objectivity, meritocracy, color-blindness, race neutrality, and equal opportunity.[42] A critical race praxis (practice informed by CRT) questions approaches to schooling that pretend to be neutral or standardized while implicitly privileging White, U.S.-born, monolingual, English-speaking students.[43]

3. **The Commitment to Social Justice.** CRT is dedicated to advancing a social justice agenda in schools and society.[44] Acknowledging schools as political places and teaching as a political act,[45] CRT views education as a tool to eliminate all forms of subordination and empower oppressed groups—to transform society.[46]

4. **The Centrality of Experiential Knowledge.** CRT finds the experiential knowledge of People of Color legitimate, appropriate, and critical to understanding, analyzing, and teaching about racial subordination.[47] Critical race research in education views this knowledge as a strength and draws explicitly on the lived experiences of Students of Color by analyzing "data," including oral traditions, *corridos*,[48] poetry, films, *actos*,[49] and humor. CRT scholars may also teach or present research findings in unconventional and creative

ways, through storytelling, chronicles, scenarios, narratives, and parables.[50]

5. **The Interdisciplinary Perspective.** CRT analyzes racism, classism, sexism, and homophobia from a historical and interdisciplinary perspective.[51] As Matsuda explains, "…the desire to know history from the bottom has forced [CRT] scholars to sources often ignored: journals, poems, oral histories, and stories from their own experiences of life in a hierarchically arranged world."[52] A CRT in education works between and beyond disciplinary boundaries, drawing on multiple methods to listen to and learn from those knowledges otherwise silenced by popular discourse and academic research.[53]

Individually, these five tenets are not "new." The scholarly and activist traditions of ethnic and women's studies found in the roots and branches of CRT embody aspects of these tenets, as do multicultural education and critical pedagogy.[54] CRT draws on the strengths these traditions bring to the study of race and racism in and out of schools. CRT also learns from blindspots exhibited by some of these academic traditions (e.g. the tendency to de-center race and racism in multicultural education and critical pedagogy).[55] With the power of historical hindsight and the strength of multiple intellectual and community traditions, CRT's five tenets comprise a unique framework that challenges existing modes of scholarship in education. CRT scholars and practitioners seek to understand how Communities of Color experience and respond to racism as it intersects with other forms of subordination in the United States educational system. They also search for ways CRT might inform research, curriculum, policy, the study of knowledge (epistemology), and teaching (pedagogy).[56] In short, they look to develop critical race praxis—practice informed by CRT. Guided by this CRT framework, the counterstories in this book ask at least four questions:

1. How do racism, sexism, classism, and other forms of subordination shape the Chicana/o educational pipeline?
2. How do institutions of education and educational structures, practices, and discourses maintain race-, gender-, and class-based discrimination?
3. How do Chicanas/os respond to and resist racism, sexism, classism, and other forms of subordination in education?
4. How can education become a tool to help end racism, sexism, classism, and other forms of subordination?

MAJORITARIAN STORYTELLING IN EDUCATION

Majoritarian storytelling is a method of recounting the experiences and perspectives of those with racial and social privilege. Traditionally, mainstream storytelling through mass media and academia rely on "stock" stereotypes if and when they discuss issues of race. Gordon Allport defined a stereotype as "an exaggerated belief associated with a category. Its function is to justify (rationalize) our conduct in relation to that category."[57] The term "stock stereotype" emphasizes that these exaggerated beliefs associated with a category draw on a virtual stockroom of stereotypes developed through history and distributed through individuals, groups, and institutions such as schools and media.

Everyday majoritarian narratives—embedded with racialized omissions, distortions, and stereotypes—perpetuate myths that darker skin and poverty correlate with bad neighborhoods and bad schools.[58] This "good" versus "bad" narrative portrays working class people and People of Color as irresponsible and less intelligent while depicting White middle- and upper-class people as just the opposite.[59] Majoritarian narratives tend to silence or dismiss people who offer evidence contradicting these racially unbalanced portrayals.

Majoritarian stories along the Chicana/o educational pipeline often feature Chicana/o parents who supposedly do not care about educating their children, or Latina/o and Black students who ostensibly receive "racial preferences" in college admissions. The majoritarian story asserts: if Chicana/o students perform poorly in school, then their parents probably do not "value" education enough to inculcate academic excellence in their children. If White students are denied admission to a university, then an undeserving Black or Latina/o student likely "took" their rightful spot. Yet research shows that Chicana/o parents have higher aspirations for their children than White parents.[60] In addition, the dismally low numbers of Students of Color admitted to colleges and universities nationally, challenge the myth that universities regularly deny admission to qualified White students to make way for unqualified Students of Color.[61]

The legacy of racism and White privilege determine whose stories are recounted as historical and whose experiences are dismissed as merely anecdotal. Majoritarian stories center layers of race, gender, class, and other forms of privilege as the point of reference.[62] This means, majoritarian stories exhibit the racialized assumptions and perspectives of White men and women—particularly those considered to be middle/upper class and heterosexual.

Although Whites most often tell majoritarian stories, People of Color often buy into and even recite majoritarian stories.[63] Often, "minority" majoritarian storytellers receive social benefits for recounting these stories.[64]

Two examples of minority majoritarian storytellers include Linda Chavez, a Latina author and head of a conservative think tank who advocates for cultural and linguistic assimilation, and African American Supreme Court Justice Clarence Thomas, whose judicial record demonstrates staunch opposition to the civil rights of People of Color and women.[65] Whether told by People of Color or Whites, people rarely question majoritarian stories. Like White privilege, majoritarian stories seem invisible. Instead of stories, they appear to be "natural" parts of everyday life.

CRITICAL RACE COUNTERSTORYTELLING

Critical race counterstorytelling is a method of recounting the experiences and perspectives of racially and socially marginalized people. Counterstories reflect on the lived experiences of People of Color to raise critical consciousness about social and racial injustice.[66] Indeed, Communities of Color cultivate rich and continuing traditions of storytelling.[67] Recognizing these stories and knowledges as valid and valuable data, counterstorytellers challenge majoritarian stories that omit and distort the histories and realities of oppressed communities. Drawing also on academic research, social science and humanities literature, and judicial records, counterstories question racially stereotypical portrayals implicit in majoritarian stories.

Yet counterstories do not just respond to majoritarian stories. As Lisa Ikemoto and Gloria Anzaldúa explain, merely reacting to the stories of racial privilege actually re-centers those stories.[68] Likewise, counterstories do not focus on trying to convince people that racism exists. Instead, counterstories seek to document the persistence of racism from the perspectives of those injured and victimized by its legacy. Furthermore, counterstories bring attention to those who courageously resist racism and struggle toward a more socially and racially just society. So while counterstories challenge mainstream society's denial of the ongoing significance of race and racism, they do so by offering a critical reflection on the lived experiences and histories of People of Color. In its multiple forms, counterstorytelling can strengthen traditions of social, political, and cultural survival and resistance.

The CRT literature evidences at least three types of counterstories: autobiographical,[69] biographical,[70] and composite.[71] For this book, I focus on composite stories. Composite counternarratives draw on multiple forms of data to recount the experiences of People of Color.

Through memorable characters such as Geneva Crenshaw[72] and Rodrigo Crenshaw[73] Bell and Delgado introduced thousands to their composite counterstories. These characters engage in lively analyses of legal decisions, historical events, and current debates about racial realities in U.S.

society. Because they document these discussions with hundreds of footnotes, Bell and Delgado provide insights into how social scientists might create composite characters and counternarratives. Composite counterstories integrate at least four data sources: (1) empirical research data (e.g., findings from surveys, focus group interviews, etc.); (2) existing social science, humanities, legal, or other literature on the topic(s) evidenced in the research; (3) judicial records (court filings, rulings, oral arguments, etc.); and (4) authors' professional and personal experiences.[74] Methodologically, authors may begin with these data sources and create composite characters who embody the patterns and themes evidenced in the research. Then, authors write these composite characters into social, historical, and political situations that allow the dialogue to speak to the research findings and creatively challenge racism and other forms of subordination.

COUNTERSTORYTELLING METHODOLOGY FOR THIS BOOK

To create the critical race counterstories for this book, I analyzed findings from multiple research projects and followed the composite counterstory methodology described above. I began by finding and unearthing sources of data. My first form of data came from primary sources, namely from Chicanas/os themselves, in the form of individual and group interviews and national survey data. My primary sources also included judicial records and court filings. I outline specific data sources within each chapter.

Next, I analyzed secondary data from social science, humanities, and legal studies scholarship, addressing the education of People of Color generally[75] and Chicana/o education specifically.[76] In sifting through this literature, I began to draw connections with the relevant primary data. This grounded theory approach starts with the data and, as its name insinuates, builds theory from the ground up.[77] Yet this systematic process of sifting through data to identify themes and patterns in social science research is neither neutral nor objective. Data cannot "speak" without interpretation, so I try to bring *theoretical sensitivity*[78] to this research process while I draw upon my *cultural intuition*[79] to interpret and analyze findings.

Barney Glaser and Anselm Strauss assert, "The generation of theory requires that the analyst take apart the story within his [/her] data."[80] To recover and recount the story evidenced in the patterns and themes of the data, I also include my own experiences as a source of data.[81] This data entails personal reflections and experiences of family, friends, colleagues, and acquaintances, as well as Chicana/o oral traditions, cultural expressions, and collective history.[82]

After compiling and analyzing these various sources of data, I created Chicana/o composite characters to engage the themes, patterns, and concepts that surfaced in the research process.[83] I set each counterstory in a location that would provide further social and historical context to the data. The composite characters personify the research in an effort to humanize the numbers along the Chicana/o educational pipeline.[84]

Though each of the characters and counterstories in this book certainly exhibit fictional elements, counterstorytelling differs from fictional storytelling. Counterstories present academic research creatively, but serve the purpose of critically examining theoretical concepts and humanizing empirical data. Each of the following four chapters begins with a more standard academic narrative to overview the research at elementary, secondary, postsecondary, and graduate school levels of the pipeline, respectively. The counterstories then investigate how some Chicana/o students, parents, teachers, and faculty respond to the everyday forms of racism, sexism, and classism they face in and outside schools. Grounded in the statistical reality that Chicana/o communities are part of the largest and fastest growing population in the United States, the four counterstories take place in locations throughout the Southwest and Midwest regions of the United States now reflecting these demographic trends. In the tradition of Freire,[85] each chapter's counterstory speaks to the others thematically so that readers might engage in the dialogue about Chicana/o education through sharing, listening, challenging, and reflecting along with the characters.

CRITIQUES OF CRT AND COUNTERSTORYTELLING

To date, the education literature features only one critique of CRT. In *After Race: Racism After Multiculturalism*, education scholars Antonia Darder and Rodolfo Torres[86] interrogate CRT's use of "race" as an analytical concept, and assert that instead, class inequality and capitalism merit analytical focus.[87] They explain, "The empire is not built on 'race' but on an ideology of racism—this being one of the primary categories by which human beings are sorted, controlled, and made disposable at the point of production."[88] The authors do not suggest how we might address this ideology of racism without first understanding its roots in the socially constructed concept of race. Darder and Torres seem to ignore that race—even as a social construction—constitutes a very real part of the daily lives of People of Color. Downplaying the intercentricity of race also supports majoritarian stories that insist race and racism no longer matter.[89] This theoretical approach to challenging social inequality without listening to the lived experiences of People of Color is, in Cherríe Moraga's words, "dangerous."[90]

Darder and Torres' critique is not particularly new. In fact, CRT's genealogy reveals that this theoretical blindspot—this tendency to dismiss race—led in part to scholars separating from critical legal studies and forming CRT 20 years ago. While acknowledging the inextricable links between race and class oppression, CRT scholars maintain that a theory based on one form of inequality cannot sufficiently address racism as it intersects with multiple forms of subordination and shapes the lives of People of Color in U.S. society.[91] A CRT approach holds that both Marx *and* the lived experiences of People of Color can and should illuminate our understandings of savage social and racial inequalities.[92]

Daniel Farber and Suzanna Sherry specifically critique CRT's methodology of counterstorytelling. In their 1997 book, *Beyond All Reason: The Radical Assault on Truth in American Law*, Farber and Sherry argue that critical race counterstories (1) recount atypical and therefore unrepresentative experiences of People of Color; (2) overemphasize the unique perspective of the author and/or "the voice of color," and therefore reduce the generalizability of counterstories; (3) lack clarity, analysis, and academic rigor; and (4) distort the truth.

These critiques, however, reveal more about the paradigm of White privilege rather than provide substantive questions of critical race scholarship.[93] For example, counterstories do not aim to resurrect one Person of Color's experience as representative of all or to generalize about all Communities of Color.[94] Actually, majoritarian stories tend to essentialize, tokenize, and stereotype based on generalizations. Too often, these stories overemphasize one Person of Color as representative of all People of Color. Counterstories, on the other hand, illuminate patterns of racialized inequality by recounting experiences of racism both individual and shared. Furthermore, the argument that counterstories lack academic rigor and clear analysis suggests that critics either have not read the meticulously footnoted sources informing CRT counterstories, or purposefully dismiss critical race scholars' interpretations of these data.

Moreover, Farber and Sherry claim counterstories distort "truth." Here, critical race critics profess to know the "truth" and ostensibly judge when someone else distorts it. This argument affirms the power of counterstories as tools that reveal perspectives long silenced. Indeed, numbers, images, and events do not speak for themselves. People who have personal histories, experiences, and knowledges interpret numbers, images, and events. Farber and Sherry's arguments against counterstorytelling actually demonstrate that challenging racism from the perspectives of racism's victims threatens the status quo. Richard Delgado explains, "Majoritarians tell stories too. But the ones they tell—about merit, causation, blame, responsibility, and social justice—do not seem to them like stories at all, but the truth."[95] Counterstories challenge this facade of the "truth" by showing the perspective of racialized power and privilege generating this "truth."[96]

Derrick Bell argues that in listening to and recounting the stories of racially marginalized groups, critical race theorists "are attempting to sing a new scholarly song—even if to some listeners our style is strange, our lyrics unseemly."[97] Bell concedes, "We do not expect praise for our legal scholarship that departs from the traditional. We simply seek understanding and that tolerance without which no new songs will ever be heard."[98]

Finally, some CRT critics believe the scholarship has not gone far enough in posing practical solutions to the problems it outlines.[99] Bell responds to this critique by affirming that CRT offers a tool to examine, better understand, and therefore more effectively challenge racism. He assures, "For us, this writing is not some idle vogue. Nor are we willfully confrontational. Rather we feel we must understand so as better to oppose the dire forces that are literally destroying the many people who share our racial heritage."[100] Bell's explanation resonates with Freire, whose legacy reminds that as each of us challenge racialized oppression through our daily work, we tranform our world.[101] Delgado also remarks that academics tend to look "for interesting problems to solve and theories to critique, rather than coming to grips with real-world problems of the community of color."[102] He admonishes academics who seem to analyze racial discourse without an explicit critique of the structures of inequality shaped and rationalized by such discourse.[103] For educators, a parallel goal of CRT is critical race praxis.[104] Critical race praxis refers to our work toward the transformation of education inside and outside classrooms.

FUNCTIONS OF COUNTERSTORIES

Keeping these critiques in mind, this book joins the continuous struggle to ensure counterstories challenge and transform institutionalized racism. Framed by the tenets of CRT in education, the counterstories in the following chapters can serve at least four functions in the struggle for educational equality.

1. **Counterstories can build community among those at the margins of society**. Because they bring a human and familiar face to empirical research, counterstories remind us that as we navigate through the educational pipeline, we do not struggle alone. In addition, counterstories can serve as a tool of empathy among marginalized communities. A counterstory can open new windows into the realities of those "faces at the bottom of society's well"[105] and address society's margins as places of possibility and resistance.[106]

2. **Counterstories can challenge the perceived wisdom of those at society's center.** As they expose the White privilege upheld in majoritarian storytelling, counternarratives provide a context to understand and transform established belief systems. Delgado explains, "Our social world, with its rules, practices, and assignments of prestige and power, is not fixed; rather we construct it with words, stories, and silence."[107] To challenge those who benefit from maintaining silence about the injuries inflicted by racism, counterstories listen to the voices and experiences of racism's victims.

3. **Counterstories can nurture community cultural wealth, memory, and resistance.** Counterstories shatter oppressive silences created through the omission and distortion of Outsider histories.[108] Mari Matsuda explains, "...the stories of those who have experienced racism are of special value in defeating racism."[109] In affirming pedagogies and knowledges[110] cultivated in Communities of Color, counterstories also preserve community memory of the history of resistance to oppression.

4. **Counterstories can facilitate transformation in education.** Because counterstories embed critical conceptual and theoretical content within an accessible story format, they can serve as pedagogical tools. Margaret Montoya asserts, "Stories must move us to action and inform our praxis... storytelling and other critical tools must refashion our curricula and pedagogies."[111] Through a combination of elements from both the story and the current reality, counterstories teach us that construction of another world—a socially and racially just world—is possible.

The counterstories in the following chapters correspond to each level of the Chicana/o educational pipeline. Chapter 2 analyzes Chicana/o community cultural knowledges in elementary schools. In chapter 3, the counterstory addresses the historical contexts of racialized inequality in high schools. Chapter 4 proposes a model describing how Chicana/o students navigate through college. The counterstory in chapter 5 reflects on the struggles of Chicana/o graduate students. Finally, a brief counterstory in the Epilogue looks toward the future of the Chicana/o educational pipeline.

NOTES

1. "I am Joaquin." © 1967 Rodolfo Gonzales, used with permission.
2. The term Chicana/o has been used synonymously with Mexican American, and I utilize it here to refer to women and men of Mexican descent residing in the United States regardless of immigration status. Chicana/o is a political term, referring to a people whose indigenous roots to

North America and Mexico date back centuries. For more discussion of the origins of this term, see Acuña, 1972, 2004; Chapa & Valencia, 1993.

3. Gonzales passed away on April 12, 2005 but his legacy lives on. Gonzales grew up in Denver Colorado in the 1930s. Because he could not afford the cost of college, Gonzales began a career in boxing, and became one of the best featherweight boxers in the world (though he was never granted an opportunity for a title fight). In 1966, Gonzales founded the Crusade for Justice—an urban civil rights cultural movement. Throughout the late 1960s and 70s, Gonzales became nationally known as a political activist and leader in the Chicana/o Movement. For example, Gonzales led the Chicana/o contingent in the Poor People's March on Washington in 1968 and articulated the need for Chicana/o communities' political, economic, and educational self-determination. He collaborated with others to organize the National Chicano Liberation Youth Conference (1969, 1970) and develop *El Plan Espiritual de Aztlan* (1969). In 1970, he helped organize the Chicano Moratorium against the Vietnam War in East Los Angeles, and that year he also founded the Colorado Raza Unida Party (See Vigil, 1999). Gonzales also founded a Chicano-centric school in Denver Colorado—*Escuela Tlatelolco*. His obituary on the school's website concludes, "As long as there are injustices, double standards, racism, and apathy, Corky's dedication, loyalty, and love of struggle against these diseases of society will serve as an inspiration to for all people to act." See http://escuelatlatelolco.org/corky_bio.html (Retrieved April 17, 2005).

4. Garcia, E. E., 2001; González, 1990, 1997; Menchaca, 1995, 1998; Moreno, 1999

5. The term Latinas/os refers to women and men of Latin American origin or descent (e.g., Salvadoran, Guatemalan, Puerto Rican), residing in the United States, regardless of immigrant status. Latina/o is an umbrella term that includes women and men of Mexican origin or descent. When data refers to Hispanics, I replace that term with Latina/o. Whenever data are disaggregated by the Latina/o subgroup, I focus on and use the term Chicana/o.

6. It should be noted that some Latinas/os identify as Chicanas/os to acknowledge the shared struggles they engage in as marginalized U.S. groups. Furthermore, socioeconomic diversity within Latina/o groups, resulting from different U.S. immigration policies and racialization processes, means that Central Americans and Puerto Ricans may experience the educational system in ways more similar to Chicanas/os than with other Latinas/os, such as Cubans or South Americans.

7. U.S. Bureau of the Census, 2000

8. See Solórzano & Solórzano, 1995

9. See Chapa & Valencia, 1993; Rumberger, 1991; Solórzano, 1994, 1995; Solórzano & Solórzano, 1995; U.S. Bureau of the Census, 2000; Valencia, 1991, 2002a

10. See Richard Delgado, 1989

11. See Pizarro, 2005; Solórzano & Solórzano, 1995

12. See Valencia, 1991, 2002b; for environmental concerns see also http://www.arb.ca .gov/research/indoor/pcs/pcs.htm and http://www.arb.ca.gov/research/ej/ej.htm?PF=Y.

13. See Oakes, 1985; Oakes & Lipton, 2004; *Williams v. State of California*, 2000

14. See the 1971 U.S. Commission on Civil Rights Mexican American Education Study Report I, p. 102. A push out refers to a student who is not retained during a given course of study and not graduated as a result of ineffective schooling structures and practices. In other words, the burden of retention and graduation lies with the school, rather than the student (see Solórzano, Ledesman, Pérez, Burciaga, & Ornelas, 2003).

15. See Crenshaw, Gotanda, Peller, & Thomas, 1995; Delgado, 1995a; Wing, 1997, 2000; Valdes, McCristal Culp, Harris, 2002

16. Haney López, 1994

17. Lorde (1992) defines racism as "the belief in the inherent superiority of one race over all others and thereby the right to dominance" (p. 496).

18. Pierce (1975) defines racism as a "public health and mental health illness," based on the delusion or false belief, in spite of contrary evidence, that innate inferiority correlates with dark skin

color. Pierce asserts that given this massive public and mental health crisis, "Everyone in the U.S. is handicapped by racism" (pp. 97–98).

19. Marable (1992) defines racism as "a system of ignorance, exploitation, and power used to oppress African-Americans, Latinos, Asians, Pacific Americans, American Indians, and other people on the basis of ethnicity, culture, mannerisms, and color" (p. 5). Marable's definition of racism shifts the discussion of race and racism from a discussion about Black and White to one that includes multiple faces, voices, and experiences.

20. People of Color, Communities of Color, and Students of Color are all terms referring to African American, Native American, Chicanas/os, Latinas/os, and Asian Americans, also referred to as racial "minorities" or underrepresented groups.

21. Tatum (1997) explains, "Despite the current rhetoric about affirmative action and 'reverse racism,' every social indicator, from salary to life expectancy, reveals the advantages of being White" (p. 8). She offers an example where a Person of Color is discriminated against and denied an equal opportunity to find housing, so the apartment ends up being rented to a White person. As a result of the racism that denied access to the Person of Color, this White person is "knowingly or unknowingly, the beneficiary of racism, a system of advantage based on race" (p. 9).

22. Leonardo (2004) finds that White privilege is too often discussed without an analysis of those violent acts of colonization and conquest, which created those privileges enjoyed by Whites.

23. McIntosh (1989) addresses multiple everyday instances wherein she as a White woman benefits from White privilege.

24. Carbado (2002) begins to complicate the discussion of White privilege by addressing privileges that intersect with whiteness, such as sexuality and gender.

25. Light-skinned girl, woman with a fair complexion. For example, when initially meeting me, I've had high school and college students comment on my skin color, saying: "*Estás blanca, blanca*...you're Latina, no?" (You're white, white...you're Latina right?).

26. Crenshaw, 2002, p. 19

27. A critical analysis of the CRT literature reveals that CRT scholars incorporate many of the strengths of each of these theoretical models, while learning from some of their blindspots (e.g. Marxisms' blindspots regarding race and gender, cultural nationalisms' blindspots in addressing gender, class, and sexuality) See Solórzano & Yosso, 2001 for more description of CRT's family tree. See also Delgado, 1995a; Ladson-Billings, 1998

28. Perea, 1998, pp. 211–247

29. Espinoza & Harris, 1998

30. See Crenshaw, 1989, 1991; Wing, 1997, 2000; Valdes, McCristal Culp, Harris, 2002

31. For FemCrit see Caldwell, 1995; Wing, 1997, 2000; For TribalCrit see Brayboy, 2001, 2002; Williams, R., 1997; For Asian Crit see Chang, 1993, 1998; Chon, 1995; Ikemoto, 1992; For WhiteCrit see Delgado, 1997.

32. Delgado & Stefancic, 1997

33. Matsuda, 1989, pp. 2323–2324

34. See Espinoza, 1998; Johnson, 1999; Montoya, 1994; Valdes, 1997; See also Arriola, 1998; Stefancic, 1998; and the LatCrit organizational website: http://personal.law.miami.edu/~fvaldes/latcrit/

35. Arriola, 1997; Valdes, 1998. October, 2005 marks the tenth annual LatCrit Symposium. The papers presented at each symposia become part of a special issue of a university law review. See for example symposium issues of the *Harvard Latino Law Review* (Cabrera, 1997); UCLA *Chicano-Latino Law Review* (Martínez & Reyna, 1998); and the joint symposium issue of UC Berkely's *California Law Review* and *La Raza Law Journal* (Oakland & Valenzuela, 1998).

36. See for example, Dixson & Rousseau, 2005; Lynn & Adams, 2002; Ladson-Billings & Tate, 1995; Lopez & Parker, 2003; Lynn, Yosso, Solórzano, & Parker, 2002; Parker, Deyhle, Villenas, & Crossland, 1998; Solórzano, 1997, 1998; Solórzano & Delgado Bernal, 2001; Solórzano & Villalpando, 1998; Tate, 1994, 1997, Taylor, 1998; for WhiteCrit in education, see Marx, 2003.

37. Solórzano, 1997

38. See also Matsuda, Lawrence, Delgado, & Crenshaw, 1993 for discussion of CRT tenets outlined in the legal field.
39. Bell, 1987
40. Arriola, 1997; Espinoza, 1998; Harris, 1994; Perea, Delgado, Harris, & Wildman, 2000; Valdes, 1997
41. Calmore, 1992
42. Ladson-Billings, 2000; Solórzano, 1997
43. Ladson-Billings, 1998; Oseguera, 2005; Solórzano & Yosso, 2002a
44. Bell, L. A., 1997; Matsuda, 1991
45. Freire, 1970, 1973; see also hooks, 1994
46. Pizarro, 1998; Solórzano, 1989; Solórzano & Delgado Bernal, 2001; Lopez, 2003
47. Bell, 1987, 1992; Carrasco, 1996; Delgado, 1989, 1993, 1995a, 1995b, 1996; Olivas, 1990
48. A Mexican oral musical tradition that offers a narrative historical account of individual experiences and events, similar to a ballad (see Paredes, 1958).
49. A Chicana/o performance tradition created collectively to represent social reality, and performed as a one-act play (see Valdez, 1971).
50. Hurtado, 1996; Solórzano & Delgado Bernal, 2001; Solórzano & Villalpando, 1998; Solórzano & Yosso, 2000, 2001, 2002a, 2002b
51. See Delgado, 1984, 1992; Garcia & Baker, 1995; Olivas, 1990; Valdes, McCristal Culp, & Harris, 2002
52. Matsuda, 1989, pp. 2323–2324
53. This is an interdisciplinary/transdisciplinary approach. See Solórzano & Yosso, 2001a, 2002a.
54. See Parker & Stovall, 2004
55. See Sleeter & Delgado Bernal, 2004
56. See for example, DeCuir & Dixson, 2004; Duncan 2002a, 2002b, 2005; Fernandez, 2002; Jay, 2003; Lynn, 1999, 2002; Revilla, 2001; Yosso, 2002b
57. Allport, 1979, p. 191
58. See Bell, L. A., 2003; Council for Interracial Books for Children 1977; Gutierrez-Jones, 2001
59. For example, California's Proposition 187 attempted to deny "suspected" undocumented persons access to public schools and health facilities. Governor Pete Wilson funded numerous commercials repeating false claims about undocumented immigrants supposedly draining California's economy and resources. California voters passed the initiative in Spring 1994. In 1997, California's Supreme Court declared Proposition 187 unconstitutional, but popular discourse (through both news and entertainment media) continues to perpetuate racially offensive and blatantly false stories about undocumented immigrants (see also Arriola, 1997; Garcia, R., 1995). In December 2003, Ron Prince (the principal author of Proposition 187) started to gather signatures to put a new Proposition 187 initiative on the California ballot, which would charge state-employees with a misdemeanor for offering services to persons without documents (see Hernandez, 2003).
60. See Espinosa, Fernández, & Dornbusch, 1977; See also Solórzano, 1992; Valencia & Black, 2002
61. Bowen & Bok, 1998
62. Richard Delgado and Jean Stefancic (1993) assert that majoritarian stories include the "bundle of presuppositions, perceived wisdoms, and shared cultural understandings persons in the dominant race bring to the discussion of race" (p. 462).
63. Similarly, misogynistic stories are often told by men, but can also be told by women, and while these women may receive some individual benefits, the stories they tell reinforce patriarchy.
64. For an example of this within a counterstory, see the character of Professor Gleason Golightly in Derrick Bell's (1992) *Faces at the Bottom of the Well*, chapter 9: The Space Traders (pp. 163–164).
65. Chavez, 1992; see Higginbotham, 1992
66. Freire, 1970, 1973
67. For example, see African American (DuBois, 1920/2003; Ellison, 1952/2002; Humez, 2003), Chicana/o (Paredes, 1958; Villaseñor, 1991), Native American (Deloria, 1969; Darby & Fitzgerald, 2003), and Asian American (Hong Kingston, 1976; Wakatsuki Houston & Houston, 1973).

68. Ikemoto (1997) writes, "By responding only to the standard story, we let it dominate the discourse," (p. 136). Anzaldúa (1987) asserts "it is not enough to stand on the opposite river bank, shouting questions, challenging patriarchal, white conventions....the possibilities are numerous once we decide to act and not react" (pp. 78–79).

69. Espinoza, 1990; Lawrence, 1992; Montoya, 1994; Williams, 1991

70. Fernandez, 2002; Lawrence & Matsuda, 1997

71. Bell, 1987, 1992, 1996; Solórzano & Yosso, 2000, 2001a, 2001c, 2002b; Delgado, 1989, 1995b, 1996, 1999; 2003; Delgado Bernal & Villalpando, 2002; Solórzano & Delgado Bernal, 2001; Solórzano & Villalpando, 1998

72. See Bell, 1987, 1992

73. See Delgado, 1989, 1995b, 1996, 1999, 2003a, 2005

74. Solórzano & Yosso, 2002a

75. See for example Lewis, 2003; Lomotey, 1990; Nakanishi & Nishida, 1995; Parker, Dehlye, & Villenas, 1999

76. See Carter, 1970; Carter & Segura, 1979; Darder, Torres, & Gutierrez, 1997; Gandara, 1995; Solórzano & Solórzano, 1995, Gonzalez, 1990; Menchaca, 1995; Moreno, 1999; Tejeda, Martinez, & Leonardo, 2000; Valencia, 1991, 2002a

77. Glaser & Strauss, 1967

78. Strauss & Corbin (1990) assert "Theoretical sensitivity refers to the attribute of having insight, the ability to give meaning to data, the capacity to understand, and capability to separate the pertinent from that which isn't" (pp. 41–42).

79. Dolores Delgado Bernal (1998) defines cultural intuition as "a complex [research] process that is experiential, intuitive, historical, personal, collective, and dynamic" (pp. 567–568).

80. Glaser & Strauss, 1967, p. 108

81. Delgado Bernal (1998) explains that cultural intuition "extends one's personal experience to include collective experience and community memory, and points to the important of participants' engaging in the analysis of data" (pp. 563–564).

82. For example, collective experiences include union struggles such as the Justice for Janitors movement, student-initiated struggles such as Youth Organizing Communities, as well as countless community actions and vigils against war, racism, police brutality, and unjust deportations. While not usually documented by mass media, these experiences remain part of community memory. Oral traditions, music, art, and poetry nurture this community memory. Public expression of these traditions, through murals, performance, or puppets and signs held up during marches also becomes part of collective experience.

83. A few of the characters were initially developed as part of previously published counterstories (e.g., For "Professor Sanchez" and "Lupe" see Solórzano & Delgado-Bernal, 2001; For "Claudia Vasquez" and Leticia Garcia" see Solórzano & Yosso, 2000, 2001a, 2001c, 2002b, 2002c.

84. See Bernal, 1988; Cuádraz, 1992; Cuádraz & Pierce, 1994; Espin, 1993; Gandara, 1982, 1995; Montoya, 1994; Rendon, 1992; Solórzano, 1998

85. Freire, 1973

86. Darder & Torres, 2004; see also Darder & Torres, 2000

87. See Darder & Torres, 2004, Ch. 5, "What's so critical about critical race theory: A conceptual interrogation."

88. Darder & Torres, 2004, p. 100

89. Cornel West's (1993) work reminds that *Race Matters*.

90. Cherrie Moraga (1983) writes, "The danger lies in ranking the oppressions. The danger lies in failing to acknowledge the specificity of the oppression. The danger lies in attempting to deal with oppression purely from a theoretical base. Without an emotional, heartfelt grappling with the source of our own oppression, without naming the enemy within ourselves and outside of us, no authentic, non-hierarchical connection among oppressed groups can take place (p. 29).

91. See Stovall, 2005

92. Kozol, 1991

93. See Delgado, 1993, pp. 665–666

94. See Delgado, 1990

95. Delgado, 1993, p. 666. Delgado also responds to Farber and Sherry and other CRT critics in his 1999 book, *When Equality Ends: Stories About Race and Resistance.*

96. In his 1992 book *Faces at the Bottom of the Well: The Permanence of Racism*, Bell questions the "standards" by which CRT scholarship is deemed "nontraditional" and lacking the merit to grant employment or tenure in academia. He states, "The presentation of truth in new forms provokes resistance, confounding those committed to accepted measures for determining the quality and validity of statements made and conclusions reached, and making it difficult for them to respond and adjudge what is acceptable" (p. 144).

97. Bell, 1992, p. 144

98. Bell, 1992, p. 146

99. See Gee, 1997, 1999; Litowitz, 1997

100. Bell, 1992, p. 145

101. Freire, 1970, 1973; See also Malaquias Montoya's print series, "*Trabajo y así transformo el mundo*" (I work, and that's how I transform the world).

102. Delgado, 1999, p. 232

103. For example, in a critique of some of Charles Lawrence's work that addresses "unconscious racism," Delgado (2001) writes, "ideal factors—thoughts, discourse, stereotypes, feelings, and mental categories—only partially explain how race and racism work. Material factors—socio-economic competition, immigration pressures, the search for profits, changes in the labor pool, nativism—account for even more especially today" (p. 2280). See also Delgado, 2003b. For a response to Delgado's critique of the idealist v. the materialist, see Kevin Johnson, 2004.

104. See Parker & Stovall, 2004

105. See Bell, 1992, p. v

106. See hooks, 1990

107. Delgado, 1995a, p. xiv

108. See Collins, 1986

109. Matsuda, 1989, p. 2380

110. See Delgado Bernal, 1998

111. Montoya, 2002, p. 246

2

MADRES POR LA EDUCACIÓN
Community Cultural Wealth at Southside Elementary[1]

INTRODUCTION

A recent report from the American Association of University Women found
that Latinas represent the largest "minority" group of girls in the United
States K–12 system.[2] In the 2003–2004 school year, Latinas comprised over
50% of California's public school kindergarten, first-, and second-grade
classes.[3] Latinos did not lag too far behind, making up over 50% of the
kindergarten and first grades. Because people of Mexican descent account
for the majority of Latinas/os, these numbers reflect the growth pattern
of Chicana/o populations. While evidently present at the primary school
level, numerous structural barriers continue to hinder Chicana/o access to
the ensuing levels of the educational pipeline.

Chicanas/os usually attend underfinanced, racially segregated, overcrowded elementary schools that lack basic human and material resources.[4]
The least experienced teachers tend to be placed in the most low-income,
overcrowded schools.[5] Indeed, schools comprised predominately of low-
income Students of Color evidence a higher proportion of uncertified
and less-experienced teachers, more unfilled teacher vacancies, and a
high teacher turnover rate.[6] Few Chicanas/os have access to a well-trained
teacher who appropriately implements bilingual/multicultural education
by drawing on the cultural and linguistic knowledge students bring from
their homes and communities to the classroom.[7]

Because elementary school serves as an important prerequisite to
later educational attainment, one would expect to find a high-quality academic curriculum available to all students.[8] This is not the case. Compared
to White schools, elementary schools comprised of low-income Students

of Color rarely offer high-quality programs.[9] Most often, the elementary schools Chicanas/os attend stress academic remediation and a slowing down of instruction, rather than academic enrichment or an acceleration of the curriculum.[10] The common practice of rigid ability grouping in these early grades also leads to lower academic achievement for Chicana/o students.[11] Moreover, English Language Learners (ELLs) tend to find a shortage of quality programs.[12]

Well before high school, most schools do not nurture a college-going culture for Chicanas/os. Low per-pupil expenditures exacerbate the lack of a quality, academically enriched curriculum in Chicana/o elementary schools.[13] For instance, Gifted And Talented Education (GATE) and magnet programs severely under-enroll Chicanas/os.[14] This disproportionate access corresponds with discriminatory school-based structures and practices as opposed to a lack of student or parent interest in academic enrichment. For example, teachers tend to hold low educational expectations for Chicana/o students, school staff may assume less responsibility for educating Chicana/o students, and school boards usually place quality academic enrichment programs outside Chicana/o neighborhoods.[15] Too often, educators perceive Chicana/o students' culture and language as deficits to overcome instead of strengths to cultivate.[16] Furthermore, primary curricula often exclude or minimize Chicana/o social and historical experiences and reinforce negative stereotypes.[17]

To explain unequal conditions or discriminatory practices, social science researchers most often use deficit models. Deficit models blame Chicana/o students and communities for lacking certain attributes and therefore causing low academic outcomes. Little empirical evidence exists to support deficit models.[18]

Even so, researchers rely on at least two main deficit models—genetic and cultural.[19] The genetic determinist models traces the low educational attainment of Chicana/o students to deficiencies in their genetic structure.[20] This scenario features few social policy options—lacking genetic transformation or total neglect—to raise the educational attainment of Chicana/o students. The works of Lloyd Dunn,[21] the Minnesota Twin Studies,[22] Frederick Goodwin,[23] and Richard Herrnstein and Charles Murray[24] evidence a renewed interest in the genetic model. Meanwhile, in everyday classroom situations, this genetic deficit thinking continues to inform an over-reliance on aptitude tests and other inappropriate standardized assessments.[25]

The culture deficit model is the most widely used in the deficit tradition. The cultural deficit model finds dysfunction in Chicana/o cultural values and insists such values cause low educational and occupational attainment.[26] These supposedly deficient cultural values include a present versus future time orientation, immediate instead of deferred gratification, an emphasis on cooperation rather than competition, and a tendency to mini-mize the importance of education and upward social mobility.[27] Cultural deficit models assert that Chicana/o families also exhibit problematic in-ternal social structures. They claim these social structures—large, disor-ganized, female-headed families; Spanish or nonstandard English spoken in the home; and patriarchal or matriarchal family hierarchies—cause and perpetuate a culture of poverty.[28] Cultural deficiency models also argue that since Chicana/o parents fail to assimilate and embrace the educational val-ues of the dominant group, they continue to socialize their children with values that inhibit educational mobility.[29]

Informed by racial stereotypes, the cultural deficit model enjoyed widespread popularity in the 1960s and 1970s, but remains the theory of choice (hidden and overt) at many elementary schools,[30] teacher education departments,[31] professional meetings, and settings where people discuss the topic of Chicana/o educational inequality.[32] Indeed, the revival of the cultural deficit model over the last 20 years features a rubric of the cul-tural "underclass" and terms such as "at risk" and "disadvantaged."[33] Joseph Kretovics and Edward Nussel explain, "At the highest levels of educational policy, we have moved from deficiency theory to theories of difference, back to deficiency theory."[34]

Schools driven by deficit models most often default to methods of bank-ing education critiqued by Paulo Freire.[35] As a result, schooling practices usually aim to fill up supposedly passive students with forms of cultural knowledge deemed valuable by dominant society. Scholars Shernaz García and Patricia Guerra find that such deficit practices overgeneralize family background and fail to acknowledge the ways personal views of educa-tional success shape "sociocultural and linguistic experiences and assump-tions about appropriate cultural outcomes."[36] Ironically, while schools may perceive numerous cultural deficiencies originating in Chicana/o homes, they increasingly claim to want more parental involvement in education. Of course, Chicanas/os again face the blame in this scenario because educa-tors insist low educational outcomes result from parents' supposed, "lack of involvement." Educators most often assume that schools work and that stu-dents, parents, and communities need to change to conform to this already effective and equitable system.

Indeed, deficit thinking permeates U.S. society, and both schools and those who work in schools mirror these beliefs. García and Guerra argue that this reality necessitates a challenge of personal and individual race, gender, and class prejudices expressed by educators, as well as a "critical examination of systemic factors that perpetuate deficit thinking and repro-duce educational inequities for students from nondominant sociocultural and linguistic backgrounds."[37] The counterstory in this chapter attempts to offer such a challenge to specifically address the elementary school level of the Chicana/o educational pipeline.

The counterstory below recounts perspectives of some of the most marginalized yet important voices in Chicana/o elementary education— Chicana/o parents. Drawing on national, state, and district level data from the Office of Civil Rights, social science scholarship presenting ethnographic accounts of Chicana/o communities, and the work of actual parent organizations, this counterstory offers a conceptual discussion of community assets. A Chicana graduate student, Paula Guevara, serves as our narrator during three meetings with a parent group from Southside Elementary School. She and the parents meet in the downtown district of a city in the southwestern United States.

MEETING LAS MADRES

I felt a little anxious walking into the parents' meeting that first night, but a warm welcome from a woman named Guillermina calmed my nerves right away. I apologized for being late, telling her my graduate seminar ran longer than I had expected, so I got stuck in a lot of traffic. Guillermina reminded me to call her Mina, saying, *"así me llaman todos."*[38] She introduced me to the childcare volunteers and to her own kids, who were already engaged in an arts and crafts activity. Mina reminded her youngest child that the paste was for sticking things to her paper, not for eating, and proceeded to guide me into the room where about 20 parents had gathered their folding chairs into a discussion circle.

As I learned, the woman who organized most of the meetings, Barbara Johns,[39] made sure to schedule around parents' work responsibilities and she also coordinated transportation and childcare activities. Ms. B, as she preferred to be called, had worked as a grassroots organizer for almost 30 years, and had been mobilizing with this Southside group since its inception about 2 years prior. An African American woman who grew up in the segregated South, Ms. B. moved to our southwestern city in the 1980s with her husband and they opened a café/art gallery dedicated to artwork by and about Black Native Americans. She regularly offered the gallery space to host progressive events such as the parent group.

I had met Mina the month before, while doing some participant observation research at Southside Elementary. The front office secretary called me over from my post, supervising children on the playground at recess. She asked me to facilitate a conversation between her and Mina. Although Mina understood a lot of English, she was a relatively recent immigrant and felt much more comfortable expressing herself in Spanish. Mina had dark skin, long hair that she wore in a beautiful braid, and a very quick wit accompanied by an infectious laugh. She volunteered in the Head Start program and her third grader, Jazmin, attended Southside Elementary.

After finishing with the secretary, Mina walked with me back out to the playground and began to tell me the story about how she and other parents came together to challenge the ongoing inequalities occurring at Southside Elementary. Demographically, Southside Elementary's student population includes about 70% Chicanas/os, 20% Whites, 5% African Americans, and 5% Native Americans. Southside offers a magnet school and the regular school on the same campus. Designed to attract students through academic enrichment, the magnet program specifically caters to students designated "Gifted and Talented Education" (GATE). White students from the Northside of the city account for 75% of the magnet/GATE program's enrollment. Chicanas/os comprise less than 20% of the magnet/GATE program, and African Americans or Native Americans represent less than 5% of the magnet/GATE students. Approximately 95% of the students in the "regular" program at Southside Elementary qualify for free lunch.

Mina explained that 2 years ago, while picking up her kindergartener from school, she saw some Chicana/o students stomping on boxes in the trash dumpster. Shocked to see them physically in the dumpster, Mina asked the students why they were not in class. Apparently, their teacher had asked for volunteers and they had been working in the cafeteria serving lunch and cleaning up since the beginning of the school year. Upon further investigation, Mina learned that this practice of having Chicana/o students "volunteer" for cafeteria duty was not new. In fact, 30 minutes before lunch everyday, the fifth grade teacher excused his Chicana/o fifth graders from math so they could report for work in the cafeteria while their White peers remained in class, learning fractions. The school did not inform any of the parents about their children working in the cafeteria during class time.

Mina spoke with her neighbor, Ms. B., and together they informed the Chicana/o parents about what had been happening. They delivered a petition with parents' signatures to the principal, insisting that their children did *not* have permission to leave the classroom to work in the cafeteria. When Mina told me initially, I thought, "If those children volunteered for having a 2-hour recess, would the teacher have allowed that and never told their parents?"

Mina said this was not an isolated incident and it exemplified the complete lack of *respeto*[40] the school shows Chicana/o parents and students. She explained that the school did not provide a translator or transportation for Parent Teacher Association (PTA) meetings, and did not send home notices to students in Spanish outlining PTA proposals. Chicana/o parents who had attended PTA meetings reported feeling very intimidated. PTA members tended to speak condescendingly to Chicana/o parents and regularly dismissed their concerns. Mina and the other parents felt frustrated that the PTA depended on Chicanas/os to make food for the school fundraisers, but that money usually went to the magnet program. Beyond bake sales and tamale fundraisers, the PTA did not seek out Chicana/o parents' input when organizing events or proposing school activities.

As she recounted the other parents' concerns and her own experiences, it struck me that Mina did not use victim language to describe their situation. Historically, the city's Southside communities suffered from lack of access to quality education, healthcare, and housing. But in response, these survivors worked to mobilize and change ongoing inequalities. They named their group "*Madres Por la Educación*," usually abbreviated as *Las Madres*. Listening to Mina, I began to wonder if this group might allow me to observe and participate as a graduate student researcher. When I asked Mina if I could volunteer and learn from *Las Madres*, she seemed surprised, but also a little skeptical. She said she would have to ask the other parents.

A few weeks later, I received a phone call from Ms. B., who asked if I would be available for translation at one of the meetings. It took a few months of volunteering and being a good listener at the meetings for the women to begin to trust me. Ms. B. explained that the Southside community was all too familiar with the tendency for academics to conduct "drive-by" research. She remarked, "They barely slow down the car, let alone park, look around, and listen to what's really going on." I thought about a few scholarly readings I had done about other grassroots organizations such as the *Comité de Padres Latinos*[41] in Carpinteria, California and the *Mothers of East Los Angeles*.[42] In addition, I looked at some of the methods other Chicanas used in their work to ensure a respectful and reciprocal research process.[43] Through my actions, I tried to assure the women of my commitment to be there and to learn.

Over the first year of monthly meetings, I noted that *Las Madres* began their evening sessions with an update on the list of ongoing grievances and actions pending or in progress. They conducted all of the meetings bilingually in Spanish and English, providing all materials in both Spanish and English, and designating at least one translator as needed.[44] Some of the major concerns parents expressed focused on issues of language and culture in the classroom.[45] They wanted to know whether their children needed to take the "mandatory" standardized tests in English if they had not yet transitioned into English. On one occasion, a teacher gave out a practice exam, and one of the parents made copies for the group. The women realized none of the exam questions addressed the cultural experiences of their children. Many parents wanted to know why their students could not gain access to any extra academic enrichment activities like those in the GATE/magnet program. Some parents suggested that the whole concept seemed a little backward. They remarked that it makes more sense to offer enrichment activities to 'regular' students as opposed to those already identified as gifted. Diane, a young woman who usually wore tailored suits with her hair slickly pulled into a bun, repeatedly asked: "Why not label the whole school *gifted*?"[46]

EDUCACIÓN CON CORAZÓN:[47] FREIRE FOR PARENTS

That first night at our meeting in the Art Gallery, Mina gave me a few of the bilingual handouts and I proceeded to read through them while listening to the discussion already underway. One of the pamphlets offered a mission statement, which read:

> *We are concerned parents and community members working to change our school system so students have equal educational opportunities. We are inspired by the work of Brazilian educator, Paulo Freire,[48] and we believe all education is political. Since schools are not neutral institutions, we will not be neutral parents or community members. We will be advocates for change.*

The lower half of the paper had two sketches: one showing "knowledge" deposited from the teacher down to the student, and titled "Banking Approach" (figure 2.1). I read a list of main points evident in the banking approach to education noted along with the sketch.

Parallel to this sketch, another drawing, titled "Problem-Posing Approach" (see figure 2.2), indicated "knowledge" flowing from the student

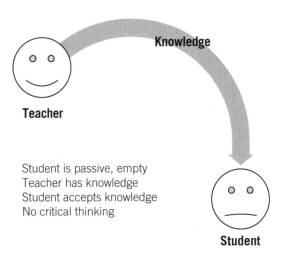

Figure 2.1. Banking Approach

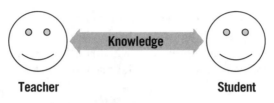

Teacher   Student

Student is active
Teacher/student communicate in dialogue
Student creates/holds/challenges knowledge
Critical thinking

Figure 2.2.   Problem-Posing Approach

to the teacher and from the teacher to the student. Again, I read the main points featured in the problem-posing approach to education listed underneath this sketch.

The back of the handout (figure 2.3) showed "problem-posing" as a cyclical method with four phases: (1) naming/identifying the problem, (2) analyzing causes of the problem, (3) finding solutions to the problem, and (4) reflecting on the process.[49]

A short description of the process also accompanied the sketch. It read:

> In the naming phase, we dialogue with our community to identify and name the problems we face. In the analysis phase, we engage with the community to describe and analyze the causes of the problem. In the solution phase, we collaborate with community members to find and carry out solutions to the problem. We then reflect on the process, and begin to ask more questions to again start the naming phase. This is the process of liberatory education.

WOW! I thought to myself, this group is…wow! I don't think anyone in my graduate seminars could ever imagine working-class Parents of Color—let alone recent Mexican immigrant and Chicana/o parents—engaging critical pedagogy in this way.

The second handout entailed a packet of information, stapled together, including a calendar of upcoming meetings, the contact numbers for some of the parent coordinators, minutes from the previous meeting, and the current meeting agenda. I looked up from my reading and listened in more carefully to the conversation in progress.

Diane, a woman in a tailored navy suit, was explaining, "Through the problem-posing process, we found that Southside Elementary seems to expect failure from our children." I soon learned that Diane worked downtown as a legal secretary and had a son in the third grade. Some parents'

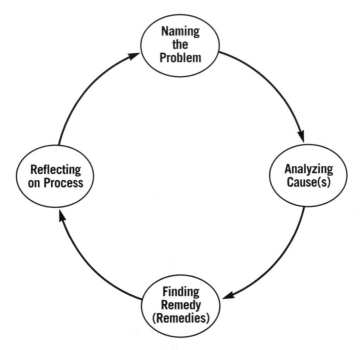

Figure 2.3.   Problem-Posing Methodology

side comments revealed a strong sentiment that schools did not really prioritize education for youth on the predominately Mexican Southside of the city because of racial discrimination.[50] A woman named Carmen, who had light skin and medium brown straight hair, spoke as she gave a bottle to her 6-month-old son. Rocking back and forth, Carmen explained that *Las Madres* shared a connection to a history of struggles against racism in Chicana/o communities. She offered an example of this history with the *Committee de Los Vecinos de Lemon Grove*, who successfully challenged an all-White school board's decision to racially segregate schools in California in 1931.[51] She also noted that multiple organizations (including Black, Jewish, Japanese, and Latino groups) joined the *familia Mendez*, who successfully sued the California Westminster School District in 1946 for racial segregation. She suggested that the group think about what they can learn from this history to inform their current struggle against racially segregated schools.[52]

In response, Sylvia, an older woman with medium brown skin and short black and gray hair who worked as an administrative assistant at the university across town, remarked, "*Sí Carmen, gracias por sus palabras y esa breve historia. Podemos aprender mucho de esas luchas. Por ejemplo, no nos importa si nuestros hijos están o no están sentados a un lado de los Americanos, queremos que tengan las mismas oportunidades.*[53]

Carmen nodded in agreement and as we all paused and reflected for a moment, I thought to myself about the irony of referring to White people as Americans while identifying everyone else by their skin color or their ancestors' national origin. I recalled the song by Los Tigres Del Norte, *America*, which lists all the countries south of the U.S.–Mexico border and asserts with a soft cumbia rhythm that *"los del norte dicen que soy Latino, no me quieren decir Americano ...America es todo el continente, el que nace aquí es Americano. El color podrá ser diferente, más como hijos de Dios, somos humanos."*[54] Mina tapped my shoulder to show me some *pan dulce*[55] and *champurado*[56] that I hadn't seen at the back of the room. I thanked her and humming the song to myself quietly, I walked to the back table and served myself an evening snack.

Long after the meeting that night, I continued to reflect on Carmen's comments about the historical racism Chicana/o communities endure and challenge.

CAN LEGAL REMEDIES CHANGE UNEQUAL SCHOOLING?

I took a break in July to visit with family, travel, and try to renew my energies after what had been another tough year of graduate school. Ms. B. left me a phone message in mid-August, asking if I could assist with one of the night courses *Las Madres* offered. Later that month, a legal team comprised of various civil rights and advocacy organizations, including the American Civil Liberties Union (ACLU), the National Association for the Advancement of Colored People (NAACP), and the Mexican American Legal Defense and Education Fund (MALDEF), asked *Las Madres* to speak about some of their experiences with inadequate facilities and lack of basic educational needs. These organizations had recently put together a case against another state and wondered if *Las Madres* could help them to document the short- and long-term impacts of such overt educational neglect here.

Diane, the young legal secretary, worked for the ACLU and had mentioned her involvement with *Las Madres* to her boss. She believed Southside Elementary offered a clear example of uneven distribution of resources between the regular and magnet school, both housed on the same campus. A series of portable classrooms without air conditioning housed the "regular" school and its predominately labeled English Language Learners (ELLs). Most of the teachers for the regular school had not yet earned their credentials or were in their first years of teaching. On the other hand, the new building with air-conditioning and a technology center including 40 new computers, housed the "magnet" school's GATE-designated students. Most of the magnet school faculty had earned advanced degrees beyond the credential and were veteran teachers. Although these issues seemed quite unfair to the parents, they also knew that a number of other Southside schools suffered years of institutional neglect under even worse conditions.

The lawyers explained that across the state and here in our city, schools "overwhelmingly populated by low-income and nonwhite students and students who are still learning the English language" are "being deprived of basic educational opportunities available to more privileged children."[57] They shared with us some of their statewide documentation, showing that most Chicana/o students "go to school without trained teachers, necessary educational supplies, classrooms, or seats in classrooms…schools that lack functioning heating or air conditioning systems, that lack sufficient numbers of functioning toilets, and that are infested with vermin, including rats, mice, and cockroaches."[58] They thanked us for helping add depth to their documentation.

Some of the parents expressed doubt that a court mandate would create equal opportunities for their students. They gave an example from the parent-initiated "create a garden" day for Southside Elementary. While volunteering, Mina's husband Armando learned that the city had a parks ordinance mandating a certain number of parks per square foot of the city. The mandate did not stop developers from putting most of those parks on the Northside of the city. And the parks' programs on the Southside were not maintained at the same level as programs in other parts of the city. Ms. B. added that the scarcity of sports and other extracurricular activities available to Southside communities reflected a pattern evident in many urban communities. She pointed out that the slow pace of civil rights legislation made her more cynical that legal reforms could effectively change schools, but she always maintained hope because folks continued to fight for change.

Others mentioned that the lawsuit failed to discuss issues of air pollution. They noted that their children suffered from asthma, likely exacerbated or even caused by breathing in the toxins in the Southside portable classrooms.[59] In addition, parents believed that when the state finally settled the suit, the pressure would remain on parents and communities to make sure the agreements on paper converted into actual change in the schools. In general, the lawsuit seemed like an important step, but most parents felt something lacking. I think this feeling became more obvious at the following month's meeting, when Las Madres challenged deficit thinking with a discussion about community cultural wealth. A bit of mystery still surrounds that night, but it was truly an unforgettable, inspiring meeting.

A SPIRITED DISCUSSION: A FREIREAN CHALLENGE
TO CULTURAL DEFICIT SCHOOLING

I arrived late to the gallery for that evening's meeting because my room-mate Eva felt sick. Because of her high fever, I took her to the student health center, where we waited for hours until a nurse practitioner finally sent us home with some medication. Embarrassed about my tardiness, I sat down quietly in the circle of folding chairs and silently waved to a few of the parents on the other side of the room. One of the mothers, Debbie, who was already raising her hand, waved to me as the coordinator acknowledged her. Debbie said, "Last month we were talking about how Freire developed the problem-posing method to teach educational skills, while also helping develop critical consciousness. But we didn't get a chance to finish our discussion in terms of connecting it to the list of school-based problems we've encountered. I see it here on the agenda, but am hoping we can get to it sooner rather than later because my daughter is sick and I need to get home early tonight. Can we move it up on the agenda?" The meeting coordinator, Nancy, smiled and replied, "Well, I think we were heading right in that direction. Does everyone think this is OK?" Most folks nodded in agreement and Carmen leaned over to Debbie to share some *consejos*[60] about easing the coughing of her sick child. I made a mental note to myself to take some extra zinc before going to bed tonight.

"OK, thank you. And I'm sure Debbie thanks you too," said Nancy. While jotting down a soup recipe, Debbie looked up and nodded with a big smile of appreciation. Debbie had long brown hair pulled loosely back in a ponytail with dangling, brightly painted *calavera*[61] earrings. We considered her the artist of the group and some of us teasingly nicknamed her Frida.[62]

Nancy continued, "So, according to Freire, students may move through different stages of consciousness[63] including magical, naive, and critical consciousness. In our initial discussions, we discussed these stages and we came up with working definitions as well as examples from our own experiences, *verdad*?[64] So tonight we printed out these definitions on your handout to refresh our memory briefly, especially for a few of us who are new to the group."

I looked around the circle, nodding slightly to acknowledge the new faces, and surprisingly saw an elderly man sitting next to Nancy with his hands folded neatly on his lap. Although fathers and uncles supported our efforts in different ways, men rarely participated in the monthly meetings. I had not slept much the night before with my roommate being ill, so I felt kind of dazed and caught myself staring at this elderly man for a minute. He looked so familiar. He returned my gaze with a nod and a smile. Startled and a little embarrassed, I smiled briefly and looked away.

Nancy paused as we each read over the three short definitions on the handout. I marveled at how Nancy kept up her energies and seemed to not have any white hairs. She must be in her late 40s, I thought to myself, how does she do it? Nancy was from a working-class Irish family, but she grew up on the Southside so she knew a lot of Spanish. She and her husband Carlos had been foster parents for many years and she was very committed to Southside Elementary and the parent group. She had short brown hair and wore stylish reading glasses. Nancy reminded everyone where to find the Spanish version on the bottom of the page, as she put her glasses on and read in English out loud:

"*Magical*: At the magical stage, we may blame inequality on luck, fate, or God. Whatever causes the inequality seems to be out of our control, so we may decide to not do anything."

"*Naive*: At the naive stage, we may blame ourselves, our culture, or our community for inequality. A naive response to experiencing inequality may be to try changing ourselves, assimilating to the mainstream culture, or distancing ourselves from our community."

"*Critical*: At the critical stage, we look beyond fatalistic or cultural reasons for inequality to focus on structural, systemic explanations. A critically conscious response to experiencing inequality would be working to change the system."

Nancy reminded the group that transitioning from the magical stage to the naive stage and then to the critical consciousness stage corresponds with the literacy process and provides the foundation for the adult literacy classes *Las Madres* sponsors twice a week there at the gallery. She also discouraged us from judging or belittling anyone regardless of which stage we might feel they are in. Nancy admitted that for many years she tended to blame fate or luck for most problems. She said her own process of shifting away from the magical stage might look different from someone else's process.

Sylvia asserted that sometimes people seem very critical about class issues but respond naively when confronted with racial inequality and even respond almost from a magical consciousness regarding sexism. I made myself a mental note to ask her more about that later. I wondered if she was also drawing on her experiences interacting with university faculty and administrators. I recalled reading in the paper that just last month, some university employees had gone on strike for a living wage and yet some of the supposedly progressive professors did not support the workers' demands. In my graduate program, I had certainly come across a few professors who seem very critical of the way schools reproduce socioeconomic inequality, but express great discomfort in addressing racism. They can talk about poverty in theory, using big three-syllable words, but feel uneasy dealing with the reality that class intersects with race.[65] While they write about Freire and empowerment, in their classes and hallway interactions, these professors silence Chicanas/os in general and Women of Color in particular. Maybe Sylvia had some insights about the uneven development of critical consciousness.

Mina took a sip of her coffee and explained, "In this process we have been discussing that our schools tend to work from a naive consciousness. At Southside, *casi siempre los maestros culpan a los estudiantes o a las familias*[66]—they blame Mexican or Chicana/o culture, and the Southside community when our students' scores are low. Maybe they should ask why the teachers have such low expectations of students, or what's wrong with those tests, or why the teachers don't have much training."

Debbie then added that her concern came from a visit to the local library. She explained, "My daughters go every other week to the storybook hour, where a volunteer reads a book and then the children act out the book using puppets." I nodded as she spoke, remembering that though she remained quite humble about her contributions, Debbie facilitated the creation of the puppet theater a few years back. She continued, "Well, I was looking in the education section and I came across a book titled, *Cultural Literacy: What Every American Needs to Know*. The author, E. D. Hirsch, has been in the news lately because a local elementary school just adopted his 'Core Curriculum' in their effort to raise the standardized test scores of 'disadvantaged children.'[67] Have any of you seen this book?" Debbie answered her own question. "Hirsch's curriculum is dedicated to having students memorize a list of 'essential names, phrases, dates, and concepts' so they can be culturally literate, and then have social and economic success."

Diane commented that the anti-bilingual education initiative[68] used the same argument a few years back—that since Latina/o parents want economic stability and success for their children, they should vote for English-only.[69] Debbie nodded and continued, "*Sí, sí, es horrible!*[70] As I looked closer at Hirsch's book, I found that in his list of '5,000 essential names, phrases, dates, and concepts that every American needs to know,' students might only have access to 27 terms that relate with Chicanas/os.[71] Debbie began listing the terms for us and Nancy wrote them with a brightly colored marker on a large piece of poster paper (figure 2.4).

Ms. B. added, "Wow, thank you for sharing this with us, Debbie. I didn't realize Hirsch and company were still advocating that schools organize their curriculum around these 'essential' phrases and concepts.[72] In the 1970s, as part of the research team supporting the Council for Interracial Books for Children,[73] I worked to uncover and challenge similar racial and gender

1492	Conquistadores	Maestro	Señor
Adiós	Diego Rivera	Mañana	Señora
Alamo	Fiesta	Mayan Civilization	Señorita
Alto	Gracias	Mexican War	Siesta
Aztecs	Gringo	Mexico	Wetback
Basta	Hector	Mexico City	Zapata
Chicanos	Macho	Rio Grande	

Figure 2.4. E. D. Hirsch's 27 Chicana/o-related terms

stereotyping in school curriculum. We focused more on U.S. History high school textbooks, and we found an elitist emphasis on Europe. These nationally used texts either ignored or distorted Black, Chicana/o, Native American, and Asian American experiences."

Carmen remarked, "I guess racism changes forms, but the message is still the same. Mexicans were seen as biologically inferior and then culturally deprived.[74] So instead of calling us the uncivilized savages or genetically unintelligent, now they're calling us culturally illiterate?" Debbie nodded and sarcastically noted, "Supposedly, we're at a cultural disadvantage because we don't know all these phrases, dates, and names!" She continued in a more seriously concerned tone, "Looking at the books on the shelf, I saw that Hirsch also published grade-by-grade lists of what students should know."

Nancy pointed at the words on the poster paper as she asked the group almost rhetorically, "Looking at this list, what do Chicana/o elementary students learn about who they are and what their history means in the context of the United States? What do White students learn about Chicanas/os in the United States?" Diane made a guttural noise, showing her annoyance as she pointed to the terms on the poster paper and responded, "Hirsch sees Chicanas/os as a conquered people who have parties (*fiestas*), take naps (*siestas*), and put off work for tomorrow (*mañana*)." Debbie added flatly, "I didn't find any other racially derogatory words besides *wetback* in the over 5,000 terms. Apparently, Hirsch feels that all Americans need to be familiar with the word *wetback* in order to be culturally literate."

MOVING FROM DEFICITS TO ASSETS

The elderly man's gentle voice interrupted the silence in the gallery. He said, "Hirsch's idea of literacy domesticates and socializes students to accept the status quo and accept their subordinate position. It doesn't help students critically understand the power relationships of their world in order to challenge inequality."

Perhaps surprised that no one else responded to this insightful observation, Mina asserted, "This discussion is helping me process a meeting I had last week with one of my daughter's teachers. First of all, the teacher scheduled the meeting at 10:00 AM last Monday, during the in-service day, but didn't ask if that was a good time for me!" Mina added this comment because the group had repeatedly asked the school to schedule parent–teacher conferences at times when parents were not working and when there was a translator available. The district provides a translator for parent–teacher meetings scheduled from 3:00–7:00 PM and only with plenty of advanced notice. Mina told the group that she felt privileged to at least understand English and to have a flexible job, but the teacher should not have assumed anything without making an effort to communicate with her in advance.

"Last year, my daughter Jazmin read on grade level," she continued, "But this year, the teacher placed her in the slow reading group. Right away in our conference it became clear to me that this teacher hadn't noticed *todo lo que sabe mi hija y todo lo que ella puede hacer*."[75] Mina told the group that at the laundromat, her daughter recites impromptu poems as a way to study for her vocabulary tests. Sometimes, she even creates melodies to sing the poems. Mina added, "But the school 'sees' my daughter as lacking in language skills! Well, if the *maestra*[76] can't see these types of abilities in Jazmin, she's probably not seeing the abilities in the other students either. I think this follows up on some of the comments made earlier." Debbie nodded in agreement.

At this point, the elderly man offered, "Perhaps the naive consciousness of our schools is based on the banking method. Since the school does not see that our students bring any knowledge with them to the classroom, they see our communities as empty places too. So instead of 'seeing' the cultural assets and wealth we have in our communities, they 'see' deprivation."

I almost thought it seemed odd that no one responded directly to this comment, but the discussion kept flowing, obviously informed by the elderly man's words. Consuelo, who worked as a seamstress in the garment district downtown, raised her hand and shared that her son had been recently labeled Educable Mentally Retarded (EMR) after scoring poorly on the standardized test.[77] On the verge of tears, she asked how this could be possible if at home, her son helped translate the bills and write out checks. An older woman with a cane shared that her granddaughter was very quick when it came to thinking on her feet and negotiating prices for fruit and vegetables at the farmer's market, but at school she did not excel in math and the teacher said she was "slow." Why couldn't the school see her granddaughter's abilities? Soon, each of the parents began offering examples of their own children's skills and strengths that the school either did not see or saw as weaknesses.

The elderly man said, "Listening to you share about the multiple talents and skills of your children brings me great joy." Many of us must have looked confused at such an optimistic comment. I know I probably looked puzzled, but then again, I had a slight headache from lack of sleep. The elderly man continued, "The school is really just telling you whose knowledge counts and whose knowledge is discounted in an already unequal U.S. society."[78]

This comment reminded me of French social theorist Pierre Bourdieu,[79] so I shared this idea with the group, describing Bourdieu's assertion that our hierarchical society considers the knowledges of the upper and middle classes valuable capital. I said, "His work explains that if we are not born into a family whose knowledge is already deemed valuable, we need formal schooling to help us access the knowledges—the cultural capital—of the middle and upper class." I then described to the group the way Bourdieu's theoretical insight about how a hierarchical society reproduces itself has been repeatedly used to rationalize the deficit model we were discussing earlier. I summed up, "The assumption follows that People of Color 'lack' the social and cultural capital required for social mobility. So, schools often structure ways to help 'disadvantaged' students whose race and class background has left them lacking necessary knowledge, social skills, abilities, and cultural capital." The elderly man asked the group: "Are there other forms of capital that racially marginalized groups bring to the table that are not recognized or are not acknowledged by this interpretation of social capital theory?"

Sylvia asked for clarification. She turned to me, saying: "OK, so it sounds like in that argument, some communities are culturally wealthy while others are culturally poor? Hmmm, so does that mean we are all compared to some sort of White, middle-class culture? They don't recognize our forms and expressions of culture, so they say we're culturally poor?" She paused and then motioned to one of the women who spoke earlier, saying, "Doesn't that sound familiar? It's like the standardized tests they give our students. Whose standard? Which group do they build the standard around?"[80] Carmen added, "So cultural capital includes knowledge and skills that the White middle class already has. And White middle-class kids inherit those specific forms of cultural knowledge and skills that schools turn around and say are valuable."

Mina offered, "A middle- or upper-class student may have access to a computer at home and can learn computer vocabulary or skills before arriving at school. This student may have what you called, what? Cultural capital?" I nodded in agreement, wondering why she didn't direct her question to the elderly man who sat patiently listening to the ensuing discussion.

Debbie continued, "Yes, computer-related vocabulary and technological skills are valued in the school setting, so that would be cultural capital. And, on the other hand, a working-class Chicano student whose mother works in the garment industry, like Consuelo, may bring a different vocabulary, probably in two languages (English and Spanish), to school, along with skills of conducting errands on the city bus and translating phone calls, reading mail and bills for his mother."[81] Consuelo blushed as she heard her name and her child's experiences described for the group. Mina put her arm around Consuelo to ease her embarrassment and added, "This cultural knowledge is very valuable to Consuelo, to her son Jaime, and to the whole *familia*,[82] but it isn't necessarily considered valuable, or a form of capital in the school context."

Ms. B. remarked, "This seems to connect with some of our questions about the long-term effectiveness of that lawsuit." Debbie added, "You're right, it's easy to just say, 'Oh those Chicana/o students lack cultural capital,' or what E.D. Hirsch[83] terms 'cultural literacy,' because that's the popular thing to do, right? Even that lawsuit focused on all the things we're lacking. It's important to focus on how schools are structured so that we are not given access to equal conditions or what the lawyers were calling opportunities to learn, *verdad*? But then what? We have new textbooks and new buildings but no *corazón*[84] inside those buildings that listens to and appreciates our kids?"

The elderly man remarked, "If, like you've noted, schools are working with a naive lens and they don't 'see' our communities as bringing resources to the classroom, then they would likely continue to teach from that deficit perspective in a new building. New textbooks continue to distort the histories and lives of Chicana/o communities. So now students will have an extra book to take home with them, but whose knowledge does that book value? Whose history does that book dismiss?"[85]

Finally, it seemed like some of the other women responded more directly to this elderly man who had made some very insightful comments. In reference to the lawsuit, Diane admitted that the law appeared limited in its ability to "see" community resources.

We took a 15-minute break so we could visit the restroom, check in on the children, and grab a snack from the cafe. I called the apartment to check on Eva's status and was relieved to find out she felt better. She thanked me for making her some *fideo*[86] before I left. I tried to splash some water on my face in the bathroom and swallowed a couple pain relievers I had in my purse, hoping that my headache would ease up soon. I grabbed an *oreja*[87] and cup of chamomile tea before taking my seat again. The elderly man dunked some bread into what looked like a cup of *café con leche*.[88] He smiled at me and I lifted my teacup slightly, acknowledging him with a silent toast. I wondered if anyone had greeted him during the break and I hoped he felt welcome. I was about to walk over and introduce myself to him and thank him for his comments, but Nancy called us back to order and the discussion rapidly picked up where we had left off before the break.

REVEALING CULTURAL WEALTH IN CHICANA/O COMMUNITIES

Nancy put her reading glasses back on and referred to the poster paper, "OK, how do we get the school and teachers to 'see' our community resources?" The elderly man remarked, "Maybe the teachers can conduct community case studies with their students?"[89] I nodded in agreement and added, "A community case study could connect this back to Freire[90] and engage students in the problem-posing approach to education.[91] With this approach, students actively discover and develop their own knowledge. Students could create knowledge with their teacher and others."

Mina added, "And students would not just be talked down to, but they would be more in *una plática*[92] with their teacher. A community case study would encourage students to feel that their thoughts and ideas are important enough to engage the teacher in a dialogue. And then teachers would be more like facilitators as opposed to the know-it-alls, *verdad*? So students can challenge the teacher? Not in a disrespectful way, of course, but you know what I mean, like questioning the ideas and values of the dominant group—asking why *los Americanos*, the White students, are seen as the norm and Chicanas/os have to always try to fit that standard. *Porque nunca van a ser como ellos, aun con 'hooked-on-phonics,' con su ingles bien pronunciado. Siempre van a ser Mexicanos. Y como dicen, hablando se entiende la gente. Asi es que, ojalá ya no se vayan a sentir tan despreciados siendo de herencia Mexicana, no?*"[93] Debbie took advantage of the natural pause in the discussion to say goodnight. She commented that this dialogue about the Southside as a place with valuable cultural resources offered an exciting start to bringing a Freirean approach into the school.

I waved good-bye to Debbie and thought about Mina's code-switching hooked-on-phonics remark. It seems so ridiculous the way mass media and too many educators misunderstand literacy reform efforts that seek to help students acquire high levels of comprehension across subjects and real-world analytical skills, while learning to speak English.[94] Instead of empowering students with Freirean literacy, reactionary policies trashed "whole language" in order to "get back to basics" with phonics, and then threw out bilingual education altogether. I also thought about the arguments that Richard Rodriguez made in his book *Hunger of Memory*.[95] His embarrassment of his parents' Spanish-accented English connected to his feeling humiliated, defenseless, and without options in a society that did not value what his *familia* offered. I wonder how dramatically different Rodriguez' schooling experiences may have altered if his teachers had been trained to value his community's assets. Anti-bilingual education folks and mass media probably would not cite him so frequently if his writings did not support the deficit view of Chicana/o communities as places of cultural poverty and disadvantage. Ironically, a real scoop for the media would be stories featuring cultural assets in Communities of Color.[96]

The elderly man interrupted my thoughts by asking, "This connects to some of your undergraduate sociology readings, no?" I paused briefly, confused as to how this man may have had a casual conversation during the break where my sociology major came up as a topic. I must have looked like a light bulb went on over my head though, because Nancy looked at me expectantly. I wiped my mouth of the remaining pastry crumbs and decided to ignore the awkwardness of the man's interjection. I said, "Yes, maybe some of my work from college can help us here with the concept of community resources. Sociologists Melvin Oliver and Thomas Shapiro[97] argue that *income* includes our wages or salary over a typical year. So income is one single source of *capital*, right? On the other hand, they argue that *wealth* includes the total extent of an individual's accumulated assets and resources, like ownership of stocks, money in the bank, owning a home or business, etc. A broad range of resources and diverse forms of capital account for part of wealth."[98]

Nancy wondered out loud, "So maybe cultural capital can be seen like income? It's one source of capital, which White, middle-class students have, and that's the form of capital schools value.[99] Then maybe wealth could include our community's cultural assets and resources added together over time? And different forms of capital would add together to create cultural wealth, *verdad*?" She drew some circles on the poster paper to help create a visual aid for the dialogue (see figure 2.5). The room began to buzz with excitement. Our late-night sugary treats probably helped raise our energies, but in any case, the group began a fast-paced discussion of various forms of capital that might comprise cultural wealth.

Aspirational Capital

Carmen, balanced her baby on her lap and started the dialogue, asking, "What would we call the dreams I have for *mis hijos*, the hopes I have that my children will go to college and do all the things I never had the chance to do? I don't have a college degree, yet. I've been at the community college

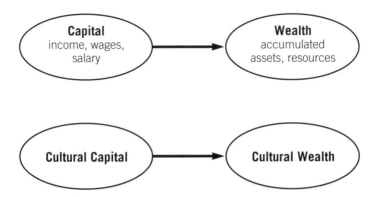

Figure 2.5. Cultural Capital versus Cultural Wealth

for 2 years, taking the classes I should have had in high school. I might not have a lot to give my kids in terms of money, but I always talk with them about my dreams for them. My mom had a lot of dreams for me too. She worked in a *maquila* and came to the U.S. alone, raising her own *hijos* and working as a nanny, raising other people's children at the same time. My mom held onto her hopes for a better future and always encouraged me to dream. And now I have dreams for my kids."[100]

Sylvia responded, "That is so beautiful, Carmen. I think those hopes and dreams are also like aspirations. Even without the personal experience of going to college, or even finishing high school, we can still hold high aspirations for our children and we can support them to reach those dreams."[101] Nancy nodded excitedly, "Should I write *aspirational capital* as we continue to talk about this?" She drew a circle on the poster paper (figure 2.6).

Most of the group nodded and Ms. B. commented that maybe the working definition could read: *"Aspirational capital: the ability to maintain hopes and dreams for the future even in the face of barriers."*[102] I thought to myself about farm worker union activist and human rights organizer Dolores Huerta, who is also a mother. Huerta has held onto hope for her own *familia* and works tirelessly to make dreams of social justice for thousands of *familias* a reality. Out of the corner of my eye, I saw the elderly man

Figure 2.6. Aspirational Capital

nodding and smiling. I smiled to myself and refocused my attention on the women's discussion.

Linguistic Capital

In reflecting on the experiences Mina shared earlier, Diane asserted that maybe we could have a category for language or *linguistic capital*. She explained, "Even though our state doesn't 'see' or doesn't want to 'see,' or recognize the benefits of bilingual education."[103] Nancy agreed this reflected the idea that Chicana/o students arrive to school with multiple language and communication skills. She said, "By kindergarten, Chicana/o children have usually already experienced community traditions of storytelling. So they have listened to and probably retold some *cuentos*,[104] *dichos*,[105] and oral histories of their family.

Mina added, "And in storytelling, they learn memorization, how to pay attention to details, how to take dramatic pauses." Sylvia chimed in, "They learn how to tell jokes, and that making faces when you speak can change the meaning of the words. Or changing your tone or the volume of your voice." Mina nodded, made a funny face, and went on, "And if they are anything like my daughter, who tries to play drums on everything she comes across, they also learn rhythm with their words." I laughed at Mina's facial expression and thought about her daughter's poems at the laundromat. That reminded me of my niece, who made up little rhymes and she twirled around like a dancer at the end of each phrase. I said, "Yes, and they learn how to rhyme." Mina continued, "And as we sit here in this art gallery, isn't visual art also a form of communication?" Diane remarked, "Even graffiti is a form of language, right?" Ms. B. admitted, "And I might not understand it or even like it too much, but the hip hop my grandkids listen to does speak through music and, well, poetry."[106] Nancy added, " And just like we learn to whisper, whistle, or sing, our children often develop and draw on various language styles to communicate with different audiences."

Diane said, "The school should 'see' that because bilingual children often translate for their parents or other adults, they actually gain all kinds of vocabulary. They start becoming more aware of how to communicate with different audiences and across cultures.[107] They may also have developed math,

Figure 2.7. Linguistic Capital

teaching, and tutoring skills. And certainly, these translating experiences give children a sense of family and community responsibility, and even social maturity.[108] Aren't those all important tools for school success?"

Nancy prompted us again for what she should write on the poster paper. The group agreed to a working definition for linguistic capital as those *intellectual and social skills learned through communication experiences in more than one language and/or style.* She again drew a circle with the term inside (figure 2.7).

Navigational Capital

Mina reminded the group of what Consuelo shared earlier about her son helping run errands on the city bus. She said, "*Navegando por la ciudad es difícil, pero tambien navegando por el sistema de educación!*[109] Diane exclaimed, "Yes, that's it—*navigational capital.*" Nancy began writing it on the poster paper (figure 2.8) as Diane continued, "Maybe it's like what we talked about earlier in terms of the limits of the legal system. Navigational capital is the ability to make our way through social institutions not created with Chicanas/os in mind."

Sylvia added, "Of course, that makes so much sense, like Consuelo was saying too, our students can achieve even while they struggle through really stressful conditions and events."[110] She went on, "So they're very vulnerable to all these forms of oppression and barriers, but at the same time, some are making it through and they are very—." Sylvia seemed to be at a loss for words, so Nancy interjected, "Resilient!" Nancy added, "Oh yes, with foster kids I've been amazed how resilient[111] children can be, even in extremely stressful environments."[112] She had shared with us on a couple of occasions her own experiences as a foster parent and the amazing resilience of children stuck in a system offering poor odds for their survival, let alone successful navigation. Thinking about this, I commented to the group that researchers call resilient students "academically invulnerable."[113] But I also noted that for students to navigate through school successfully—to be academically invulnerable or resilient—they needed individual, family, and community support. I added, "And schools could help nurture these students' social and psychological 'critical navigational skills.'[114] No?"

Figure 2.8. Navigational Capital

Ms. B. nodded in agreement, and remarked, "Academic invulnerability and resilience do not take place in a social vacuum, though." She reminded the group that working-class Women of Color experience layers of racialized privilege, so one's social location[115] influences one's navigational strategies. "For example," she said, "as a Black woman I experience layers of race and gender oppression, but I experience some privileges because I speak English and am relatively middle class." Nancy added that as a White woman raising Chicano foster kids, she sometimes felt limited in how many strategies she could teach them because her own experiences had been so layered with privilege. "They are still vulnerable even when they're invulnerable," she remarked. Through teary eyes she said, "They're resilient, and they find a way through the situation—through the racism—but the wounds of that stress stay with them."

Carmen reached over and rubbed Nancy's back soothingly and we all paused for a moment of reflection. Nancy took a deep breath and reworded the working definition she had already written on the poster paper, *"Navigational capital refers to skills of maneuvering through social institutions."* She took off her glasses again, wiped her eyes, and commented that she really liked this form of capital because it acknowledges that individuals have agency even though their decisions and actions take place within constraints. She said, "And it also connects to social networks that facilitate community navigation through places and spaces including schools, the job market, and the healthcare and judicial systems."[116]

Social Capital

Mina brought up the fact that many in the group had met through other community social activities outside of the school. She offered, for example, that she and Sylvia met because their daughters played on the same soccer team. Carmen added that she had met Diane at a church function. Many of the women nodded when she gave this example. Apparently, a lot of Southside families interacted at church. Carmen continued, again helping provide some historical context for the discussion.

She explained, "In my *Introduction to Chicana/o Studies* class last semester, the professor talked about the history of Mexican immigrant social networks—*mutualistas*, or mutual aid societies.[117] Thinking about how we each get and give information, we could probably draw out a whole social network for ourselves that we might not even realize we are part of." Many of the women nodded and a few remarked that *mutualistas* still play an important role for the neighborhoods on the Southside. They offered examples of holding fundraisers to assist families in need, helping recent arrivals find housing and employment, and organizing *tandas*[118] to save money without depending on a bank.

Sylvia added, "And from the brief examples we've just seen here, many of our social networks probably overlap! I'm thinking also about how our kids have their own social networks. And we are usually concerned about who is part of their peer group because of the types of information and resources they may share, *verdad*?[119] So Carmen, would you say it's *social capital*?" Carmen nodded in agreement and for a minute or two, many of the women talked to one another about social networks they and their children shared in common.

Nancy brought us back to the group discussion while drawing on the poster paper (figure 2.9), saying, "OK *mujeres*, so *social capital* can be understood as *networks of people and community resources*?"

Carmen asserted, "Yes, and historically Chicanas/os utilize their social capital to maneuver through the system, but they also turn around and give the information and resources they gained through the navigation process back to their social networks." Nancy remarked, "OK, so social capital can help us navigate through society's institutions. That's important because Sylvia mentioned that our social networks overlap, and it seems like these forms of capital, these types of community cultural wealth also overlap?" I nodded in agreement and said, "Yes, because social capital addresses the peer and other social networks developed to assist in the movement through social institutions, like schools."[120] I added, "And social capital speaks to the fact that we are not alone in our struggles. We develop social spaces rich in resources. Without social spaces to share information, our ability to help each other navigate would weaken. So these forms of cultural wealth do seem interdependent."

Ms. B. commented that this tradition of offering emotional support while sharing information and resources as part of a community reminded her that her aunt participated in one of the oldest African American women's organizations in the country, the National Colored Women's Association, and their motto is "lifting as we climb."[121] Carmen took a moment to thank the group for being a supportive social network for her family, especially in light of some difficult personal circumstances that she had shared with us in recent months.[122] I shared with the women that this reminded me

Figure 2.9. Social Capital

again of how they are conceptualizing cultural wealth very differently than cultural capital. I said, "Cultural capital is accumulated, like a deposit in the bank, but cultural wealth is meant to be shared."[123]

Familial Capital

Nancy asked, "Speaking of sharing, what about how our families model lessons of caring, coping, and providing? Family lessons help shape us emotionally and give us moral guidance.[124] Can there be *familial capital*?" At this point the room seemed to sigh collectively. So often, schools insist Chicana/o parents hinder their children's progress, and *Las Madres* were recognizing family as a source of community cultural wealth!

Consuelo explained that the lessons Nancy mentioned are taught not just within families, but also between families, and through church, sports, school, and other social community settings. She said, "*y nos demuestran la diferencia entre una persona con educación universitaria e una persona bien educada. Porque a veces tienen la escuela, pero no tienen la educación no tienen la educación para ser una persona con principios.*"[125]

Nancy interjected that traditional understandings of "family" tend to carry race, class, and heterosexual assumptions, so if we agree to call it familial capital, we should expand the concept of family to include a more broad understanding of kinship. Diane thanked Nancy for reminding the group about the power of words and the power to choose words.[126] Other women also nodded and commented supportively about this expanded notion of family. They remarked that immediate family as well as aunts, uncles, grandparents, and friends—living or long passed on—might all be considered part of our *familia*.[127] Nancy drew a circle indicating familial capital on the poster paper (figure 2.10).

Sylvia commented, "It seems that familial capital connects with a commitment to community well-being. We learn the importance of maintaining a healthy connection to our community and its resources. So we don't feel so isolated. Like with the social capital, families 'become connected with others around common issues' and realize they are 'not alone in dealing with their problems.'"[128] Mina nudged a woman sitting next to her, Elena. Mina exclaimed, "Yes! And helping each other find solutions. Like

Figure 2.10. Familial Capital

when Elena's oldest son wanted to drop out of school, she told him, '*está bien!*'" The women paused, looking at Elena expectantly. Elena had medium brown skin and light brown wavy hair. She had been listening intently but had not spoken. She said in a matter-of-fact tone, "*Pues sí. Plactiqué eso con Mina porque me daba tanta tristesa. Y luego, le dije a mi hijo, 'andale, si no quieres ir a la escuela, está bien mijo.'*" She paused and then remarked, "*Puedes trabajar conmigo en la K-Mar. Y así agarras todos los blue light specials.*" Most of the woman laughed out loud as others shook their heads, smiling at Elena's response. Mina added, "He's in his second year of college now?" Elena nodded and smiled.

Diane continued, "It sounds almost like familial capital includes some of the language we use in the law. On the one hand, families can give emotional support like what we've talked about. But then we can also give instrumental support.[129] Like when my son is trying to study, I have my husband turn off the TV, even if it's in the middle of his favorite program, and I make sure the house is totally quiet. And Sylvia also gives this support by buying enough detergent so her daughter can do her laundry when she's home from college." Sylvia smiled and said, "And buying her groceries she can take back to school when she leaves!"

Consuelo also noted that parents use multiple teaching strategies with their children that the school does not seem to notice. "*Dicen que no nos importa, que no estámos involucrados en la educación de nuestros hijas e hijos.*"[130] She told the group that like many of them, she had also tried to get involved with the PTA, but that the women did not welcome her, did not make Spanish translation available, and they set up a pretty intimidating environment where she felt almost invisible. Nancy suggested that perhaps the group could think about developing a list of ways they do engage their children's education. She gave an example of a family she knew. She said that on summer break and sometimes on weekends, the parents brought their children with them to work picking fruit in the fields. Apparently, four of their children now attend or already graduated from top universities and their youngest is set to graduate as the valedictorian from Southside High School this year. Knowing they could not help with algebra or reading in English, these parents taught about hard work and integrity while working alongside their children in the fields.[131] Nancy offered that maybe we could present these types of examples to the school at a later date. She explained this might help challenge the false and historically inaccurate idea that Chicanas/os are not "involved" in their children's schooling and therefore don't value education.[132]

I thought to myself that familial capital connected to aspirational capital, and I smiled, imagining the parents Nancy mentioned sharing their dreams with their children of a life with options, a life without back-breaking work.

Consuelo also shared with us that her husband—a carpenter—was in the process of making a desk for her son, Jaime. She believed the desk would give Jaime a consistent place to study and help him better organize his homework and develop good study skills. In addition, Consuelo saw the desk as a way to show her son that his education is important to his parents. Nancy jotted down a few more notes on the poster paper and read aloud the working definition of *familial capital* as those *"cultural knowledges nurtured among* familia *(kin) that carry a sense of community history, memory, and cultural intuition."*[133] She said, "Chicana/o students bring these teachings from home[134] with them to the classroom, but the schools ignore or can't 'see' these funds of knowledge."[135]

Resistant Capital

Sylvia said she hoped her daughters would carry some of those teachings even beyond high school. Through verbal and nonverbal lessons, Sylvia tried to teach her daughters to assert themselves as intelligent, beautiful, strong, and worthy of respect.[136] She emphasized her efforts to teach her girls to question society's distorted messages about beauty, success, love, and integrity. She explained, "I have been consciously 'raising resistors.'"[137] Another older woman agreed and added that it was very difficult to teach her daughter to *darse valor*[138] or *valerse por si misma*[139] within a racist, materialistic, and sexist society and perhaps even more difficult to raise a son who would resist the pressures of perpetuating patriarchy through stereo-typical *macho*[140] attitudes.

As Carmen reminded us in a past meeting, Ms. B. noted that Communities of Color have historically resisted racial and social injustice. She spoke about her own children's involvement supporting various community efforts for equity. Ms. B remarked, "Students' efforts to transform unequal conditions show us that this continuity of community resistance includes many forms of expressing opposition.[141] But of course, not all behavior that seems to go against the norm is motivated by a critical consciousness or a desire for social justice. Many of our young people today participate in what seem to be self-defeating or conformist strategies of resistance, like dropping out of school or trying to challenge racial and gender stereotypes through their individual actions to 'fit in.' Those forms of resistance feed back into the system and don't challenge the more structural causes of inequality. But, when students recognize and name the structures of oppression, and then are motivated to work toward social and racial justice—resistance takes on a transformative form."[142] Ms. B. pointed to the handout section on Freirean critical consciousness.

Nancy drew another circle on the almost filled-up piece of poster paper (figure 2.11), as she asked, "So should we say that *resistant capital* draws on

Figure 2.11. Resistant Capital

this legacy of resistance to oppression in Communities of Color and refers to those *knowledges and skills cultivated through behavior that challenges inequality?*[143]

Women nodded and some applauded in agreement, feeling the excitement in the air about resistance initiated by communities to transform society. Diane remarked, "Through this group, we are learning to recognize the structures of racism and we are definitely motivated to transform them. But how do we use transformative resistant capital to challenge what's happening at Southside Elementary?"

A Model of Community Cultural Wealth

Before anyone could answer her question, we paused to admire the fresh piece of poster paper where Nancy busily finished connecting the circles to reflect the discussion (see figure 2.12). She stepped back to reveal a visual model of cultural wealth! I sketched out the model on my own notepad and again smiled, thinking of how surprised most of my colleagues would be when I shared the ways these parents engage with theory. In all my graduate school reading, social theories seem too obtuse and difficult to apply in "real life." Yet here, I witnessed these working-class Parents of Color applying Freire[144] and Bourdieu[145] to their everyday experiences. I felt so humbled to listen and learn from these women. From their position at the margins of society, these women challenge the inequalities of the educational system. They develop and demonstrate *pedagogies of the oppressed.*[146] These women hold on to the belief that as bell hooks writes, the margin can be "more than a site of deprivation … it is also the site of radical possibility, a space of resistance."[147] As they question the forms of racism that shape their children's educational opportunities, they also offer a model that can transform the prevalent cultural deficit approach to elementary schooling.

Nancy noted that Diane asked a good question we had not addressed. Mina agreed and said, "I like the idea Nancy had, to make a list of the ways Chicanas/os are involved in education. Maybe we can show the principal this chart when we do that, so he can 'see' what our community brings to Southside Elementary." Carmen lit up and said, "I think the PTA and the teachers should be hearing this too, no? We could have a forum or something.

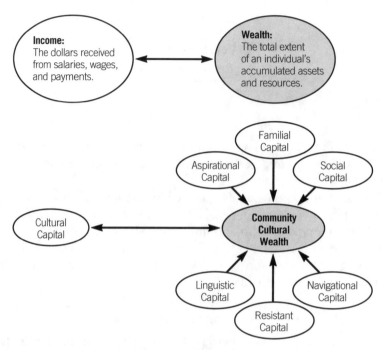

Figure 2.12. A Model of Community Cultural Wealth

Maybe before that, though, we should ask ourselves, what would Southside Elementary look like if it centered the curriculum on the community cultural wealth of Chicana/o students?"[148]

Though it had been a long night, the women exuded a clear feeling of excitement about the possibility of presenting the cultural wealth model to the principal, teachers, and the PTA. Mina took a deep breath and remarked, "*Sería una transformación completa.*"[149] Most of the women nodded in agreement, while some shook their heads with doubt that such a transformation could occur. Diane commented that to start, they could advocate for making the whole school a magnet school and designating all the students GATE. Pointing to the model on the poster paper, she exclaimed, "Look at all the ways our students are gifted and talented!" Diane's suggestion offered an example of school transformation that seemed to resonate with the group.

Putting community cultural wealth into practice required much more discussion, which would have to wait for another night. Ms. B. announced that the childcare volunteers were scheduled to leave at 9:00 PM and it was already 9:15. Nancy thanked the women for their patience through what had been a pretty long, but productive meeting. The women again applauded each other before saying goodnight, collecting their children and heading home in their own cars or in the vans that Ms. B. had arranged for transportation.

I stood to stretch and throw away my tea bag and napkin of *pan dulce* crumbs. I wanted to introduce myself to the elderly man who had offered such insightful comments earlier. In the fast-paced excitement of the discussion, I realized that my headache had eased up. I walked back over to the circle of chairs and began to help the women clear out the space for the cafe customers the next morning. As I picked up and stacked the folding chair where the elderly man sat, I asked Mina if she had seen him leave. She looked at me bewildered, "An elderly man was here tonight? *Ay mujer,*[150] I hope your *compañera*[151] gets over the flu soon, sounds like you need some rest." Sylvia asked if my headache was better or if I needed a ride home. She gave me a hug and said she would check on me later in the week because I looked a little pale, "Like you've seen a ghost."

Suddenly, I got chills realizing why the elderly man looked so familiar. Could it be? *Mi tocayo*[152] Paulo Freire? Instead of being pale by the time I got home, I felt flushed with excitement. I found Eva awake and enjoying leftovers from the refrigerator. Her fever had finally broken and she had not eaten much for a few days. I shared with her the details of the spirited discussion at the meeting and she laughed and said, "Paula, I hope Freire comes by again sometime soon. Our schools need him now more than ever. His legacy should never be forgotten." She paused and then jokingly chided me, "Should I leave some of this chicken for him in case he comes over for a late-night snack? Or maybe we can play Ozomatli's song, *Cumbia de los Muertos*[153] and he'll come dance with us?" I laughed as she began dancing with me in the kitchen. She obviously felt much better. I headed to bed, thinking about dancing with my loved ones who had passed on. I too hoped humbly that Freire's spirit would not be a distant memory.

NOTES

1. Mothers for Education. Southside is a composite elementary school located in an unidentified city in the Southwest region of the United States.
2. Ginorio & Huston, 2001
3. Office of Civil Rights, see http://205.207.175.84/ocr2000r/
4. Valencia, 2002b
5. Donato, Menchaca, & Valencia, 1991; Orfield & Monfort, 1992; Valencia, Menchaca, & Donato, 2002
6. Darling-Hammond, 1988
7. There is also a general shortage of teachers servicing minority communities, with the most severe involving Latina/o teachers, and specifically teachers in bilingual and special education fields (Darling-Hammond, 1988; Los Angeles County Office of Education, 1994; Tomas Rivera Center, 1993).
8. Orfield, 1996

9. Lockheed, Thorpe, Brooks-Gunn, Casserly, & McAloon, 1985
10. Levin, 1987; See also Solórzano, Ledesma, Pérez, Burciaga, & Ornelas, 2003
11. Oakes, 1985, 1990
12. Garcia, E. E., 1987/88, 1999; Willig, 1985
13. See Garcia, E. E., 1999
14. See Solórzano, Burciaga, Calderón, Ledesma, Ochoa, Rivas, Sanchez, Velez, Watford, Ortega, & Pineda, 2004
15. Baron, Tom, & Cooper, 1985; Persell, 1977; U.S. Commission on Civil Rights, 1973
16. Delgado-Gaitan, 1992
17. Council on Interracial Books for Children, 1977; Loewen, 1995; Pearl, 1991, 2002
18. Kretovics & Nussel, 1994; Persell, 1977; Solórzano & Solórzano, 1995; Valencia & Solórzano, 1997
19. See Valencia, 1997
20. Jensen, 1969; Kamin, 1974; Terman, 1916
21. Dunn, 1987; See Fernandez, 1988
22. Bouchard, Lykken, McGue, Segal, & Tellegen, 1990
23. See Breggin & Breggin, 1993
24. Herrnstein & Murray, 1994
25. For example, Louis Terman (1916) was a eugenicist and one of the main importers of the Stanford Binet Intelligence test, now called the SAT. See Valencia, 1999; Valencia & Aburto, 1991; Valencia, Villareal, & Salinas, 2002
26. For examples of cultural deficit writings, see Bernstein, 1977; Chavez, 1992; McWhorter, 2000; Ogbu, 1990
27. For further description and critique of cultural deficit models, see Barrera, 1979, 1997; Carter & Segura, 1979; Valencia, 1997
28. For culture of poverty argument, see Lewis, O., 1968; Sowell, 1981
29. See Banfield, 1970; Heller, 1966
30. Persell, 1977; Solórzano, 1997; Solórzano & Yosso, 2001b
31. See Lewis, A., 2003
32. See Kretovics & Nussel, 1994; Spring, 2001
33. Baca Zinn, 1989; Valencia & Solórzano, 1997
34. Kretovics & Nussel, 1994, p. x
35. Freire, 1973
36. García, S. B., & Guerra, 2004, p. 163
37. García, S. B., & Guerra, 2004, p. 155
38. That's what everyone calls me.
39. This character is inspired by Barbara Johns, the teenager who organized a student strike against Moton High School in Farmville, Virginia, and led 450 students to a walkout on April 23, 1951, to demand a new, updated, and quality school. Fearing for her safety, her parents sent Barbara to live in another city. Her leadership led to the *Davis v. the School Board of Prince Edward County* lawsuit, which was one of the five suits brought before the Supreme Court in *Brown v. Board of Education* in 1954. Ms. B.'s gallery also draws inspiration from the John Sayles film *Lone Star*, where an African American man living in Texas has a picture collection dedicated to the history of Black Native Americans (see Foster, Miller, & Renzi, prds., 1996).
40. Respect.
41. See Delgado-Gaitan, 2001
42. See Pardo, 1990, 1991, 1998
43. See Delgado Bernal, 1997
44. This format does not lend itself to fully translating the entire meeting bilingually. To remind readers of this and to emphasize certain points, I code-switch throughout.
45. See Donato, 1997
46. See Hopfenberg, Levin, Meister, & Rodgers, 1990
47. Education with Heart.

48. Freire, 1970, 1973
49. Alschuler 1980; Freire 1970, 1973; Smith & Alschuler, 1976
50. Edward Buendía, Nancy Ares, Brenda Juarez, and Megan Peercy (2004) detail the ways that notions such as "southside" or "westside" in cities across the U.S. take on racially coded, classed significance that are constructed and reconstructed by schools.
51. *Álvarez v. Lemon Grove School District*, Superior Court of the State of California, County of San Diego, 1931, Petition for Writ of Mandate, No. 66625. See also Espinosa, 1986; Montoya, 2001
52. *Mendez v. Westminster School District*, 64 F. Supp 544 (S.D. Cal 1946), affirmed 161 F. 2d 774 (9th Cir. 1947). See also Perea, 2004; Valencia, 2005
53. Yes Carmen, thank you for your words and that brief history. We can learn a lot from those struggles. For example, it's not important that our children sit next to the White students, we want them to have equal opportunities. See DuBois, 1935
54. People from the north say that I'm Latino, they don't want to call me American. America is the whole continent, whoever was born here is American. Skin color might differ, but just like we're all children of God, we are all human. See Los Tigres Del Norte, 1988
55. Sweet bread.
56. A hot drink with chocolate, cinnamon, flour, and milk.
57. *Williams v. State of California*, Superior Court of the State of California, County of San Francisco, 2000. No. 890221 (plaintiff complaint, p. 5).
58. *Williams v. State of California*, Superior Court of the State of California, County of San Francisco, 2000. No. 890221 (plaintiff complaint, p. 5). See also settlement conditions *Williams v. State of California*, Superior Court of the State of California, County of San Francisco, 2004, No. 312236 (settlement agreement).
59. See Donoso & Reyes (2002), p. 20, Table 5: Environmental Working Group: Air Pollution Inside California's Portable Classrooms, May 1999.
60. Advice.
61. Skeleton.
62. Frida Kahlo, Mexican artist and socialist.
63. See Freire, 1970
64. Right?
65. CRT and LatCrit scholars continue to work toward better understanding and articulating the intersection of race and class. See for example, Hutchinson, 2004; Revilla, 2001
66. The teachers tend to blame the students or the families.
67. See Hirsch, 1988, p. xiv
68. See Proposition 227 in California (1998), Proposition 203 in Arizona (2001).
69. The majority of Latinas/os voted against the "English-only" initiatives in both California (Prop 227) and Arizona (Prop 203).
70. Yes, yes, it's horrible.
71. See Hirsch, 1988, pp. 152–215
72. Ragland, 2002
73. See Council for Interracial Books for Children, 1977
74. See Solórzano & Valencia, 1997
75. Everything that my daughter knows and everything that she can do.
76. Teacher.
77. See Donato, 1997
78. See Delgado Bernal, 1998; Ladson-Billings, 2000
79. Bourdieu & Passeron, 1977
80. See Rosner, 2001
81. See Faulstich Orellana, 2003
82. Family.
83. Hirsch, 1988, 1996
84. Heart.
85. See Loewen, 1995

86. Similar to angel hair pasta, but prepared like chicken noodle soup with a spicy tomato base.
87. A type of *pan dulce*, pastry shaped like two *orejas* (ears) stuck together.
88. Coffee with milk.
89. Barnes, Christensen, & Hansen, 1994
90. Freire, 1970, 1973
91. See Smith-Maddox & Solórzano, 2002; Solórzano, 1989
92. A casual conversation.
93. Because they're never going to be like them, even with "hooked-on-phonics," with their well-pronounced English. They will always be Mexican. And like the saying goes, in dialogue, people develop a better understanding of one another. And that way hopefully they won't feel too humiliated because of their Mexican heritage, right?
94. Martinez, C., 2000
95. Rodriguez, 1982
96. Solórzano & Solórzano, 1995; Valencia & Solórzano, 1997; Villalpando & Solórzano, 2005; Yosso, 2005
97. Oliver and Shapiro (1995) differentiate between income and wealth to document ongoing racial inequality between Black and White communities. They explain that while the income of Blacks may be climbing and the Black/White income gap may be narrowing, their overall wealth, compared to Whites, is declining and the gap—the inequality between the two groups—is increasing.
98. In his 2004 book, *The Hidden Cost of Being African American*, Thomas Shapiro extends this discussion of wealth to address the role of schools in exacerbating racial inequalities.
99. After conducting and analyzing 44 interviews with African American youth ages 13–20 in Yonkers, New York, Prudence Carter (2003) found that "Blacks develop their own forms of cultural capital" (p. 150). The forms of "black" cultural capital these students exhibit "yield social benefits and rewards within their community, but within the school walls, students find that officials devalue precisely these cultural attributes" (p. 149). Carter asks, "Are there other forms of non-dominant cultural capital or even other forms of 'black cultural capital' (p. 151)? She calls for "a more nuanced understanding of the multifaceted processes affecting academic achievement," and for schools to acknowledge and value the "cultural capital portfolio" of Students of Color (p. 151).
100. See Espinosa, Fernández, Dornbusch, 1977; Solórzano, 1992
101. These stories nurture a culture of possibility as they represent "the creation of a history that would break the links between parents' current occupational status and their children's future academic attainment" (Gándara, 1995, p. 55). See also Gándara, 1982
102. These barriers may be real or perceived.
103. See anti-bilingual education Proposition 227 in California, 203 in Arizona. For benefits of bilingual education, see Cummins, 1986; Darder, 1991; García, O. & Baker, 1995; Gutierrez, 2002; Gutierrez, Rymes, & Larson, 1995; Macedo & Bartolomé, 1999
104. Stories.
105. Proverbs.
106. Thanks to UCSB undergraduate students, Pablo Gallegos, Moises Garcia, Noel Gomez, and Ray Hernandez, whose research conceptualizing graffiti and hip hop poetry as unacknowledged sources of community cultural wealth expanded the concept of linguistic capital.
107. See Carter, 2003; Castañeda, A., 1998
108. In her research, Marjorie Faulstich Orellana (2003) found that since they are regularly called upon to translate, bilingual children develop knowledge and skills, including "vocabulary, audience awareness, cross-cultural awareness, 'real-world' literacy skills, math skills, metalinguistic awareness, teaching and tutoring skills, civic and familial responsibility, [and] social maturity" (p. 6).
109. Navigating through the city is difficult, but also navigating through the educational system!
110. Sylvia Alva (1991) found that invulnerable, resilient Chicana/o students are able to "sustain high levels of achievement, despite the presence of stressful events and conditions that place them at risk of doing poorly at school and, ultimately, dropping out of school," (p. 19). See also Auerbach, 2001; Laosa, 1990

111. Resilience has been recognized as "a set of inner resources, social competencies, and cultural strategies that permit individuals to not only survive, recover, or even thrive after stressful events, but also to draw from the experience to enhance subsequent functioning" (Stanton-Salazar & Spina, 2000, p. 229).
112. See Carroll, 1998
113. Alva, 1995; Arrellano & Padilla, 1996
114. Solórzano & Villalpando, 1998
115. Zavella, 1991
116. Williams, P., 1997
117. Gómez-Quiñones, 1973, 1994; Sanchez, 1993
118. *Tandas* function like savings accounts. For example, a group of five people each contribute $100 per week and on a rotating basis one person receives the entire $500. Each week, one person receives the *tanda*. This would play an important role especially because formal banking practices may require photo identification such as a driver's license, or may be otherwise discriminatory. Undocumented immigrants may not have access to opening a bank account.
119. Right?
120. Stanton-Salazar, 2001
121. See Guinier, Fine, & Balin, 1997, p. 167
122. Concha Delgado-Gaitan's (2001) ethnographic research with the Mexican immigrant community of Carpinteria, California, found that "Families transcend the adversity in their daily lives by uniting with supportive social networks" (p. 105). Similarly, Myrna Jean Gilbert's (1980a, 1980b) ethnographic research with second generation Mexican American families in Santa Barbara and Fillmore, California, found that social networks offer forms of emotional and instrumental support, and cultivate a sense of *confianza* (trust). See also Vélez-Ibáñez, 1980
123. In the 2005 HBO film, *Lackawanna Blues*, this point is clear. Set during the preintegration 1950s and 1960s, this coming-of-age autobiographical tale of Ruben Santiago-Hudson, Jr. explains that "Jr.'s" parents are unable to care for him, so Nanny, a proprietor of a rooming house and mentor to countless down-on-their luck Blacks, unofficially adopts him. Nanny's place recreates a sense of community and family for these boarders and, in turn, each of the characters shares their cultural wealth—their knowledge of Black history, skills of navigation through a racist society, and lessons of love, trust, and hope—with young Ruben Jr. (See Nugiel, prd., 2005).
124. See Auerbach, 2004; See also Ricardo Stanton-Salazar (2001), who finds, "Through the bestowing of *consejos* and through exhortations, parents tried to morally obligate and thus motivate their children to forge ahead in their schooling" (p. 105).
125. And they demonstrate the difference between a person who has an education from school and a kind person with integrity. Because sometimes they have schooling, but they don't have any sense of being a person with principles. See Elenes, Gonzalez, Delgado Bernal, & Villenas, 2001 for more discussion on the layered meaning of being *una persona bien educada*.
126. bell hooks (1994) also notes the power of language as she quotes a poem by Adrienne Rich that acknowledges, "This is the oppressor's language, but I need it to talk to you" (p. 167).
127. Family.
128. Delgado-Gaitan, 2001, p. 54
129. See Gilbert, 1980a, 1980b
130. They say that we don't care. That we're not involved in the schooling of our children.
131. See Lopez, 2003
132. Black parents endure similar accusations of not caring about their students' education. For further discussion of this history of Black parent "involvement" in schools and the role of desegregation in disrupting communal bonds nurtured within African American school communities, see Foley, 1997; Morris, 1999.
133. See cultural intuition, Delgado Bernal, 1998
134. See "pedagogies of the home," Delgado Bernal, 2002
135. See Gonzalez, Moll, Tenery, Rivera, Rendon, Gonzales, & Amanti, 1995; Moll, Amanti, Neff, & Gonzalez, 1992; Olmedo, 1997; Rueda, Monzo, & Higareda, 2004; Vélez-Ibáñez & Greenberg, 1992

136. See Robinson & Ward, 1991; See also hooks, 2002
137. Ward, 1996
138. Value herself.
139. Be self-reliant, See Villenas & Moreno, 2001
140. Chauvinist.
141. See Solórzano & Delgado Bernal 2001; Delgado Bernal, 1997
142. See Solórzano & Yosso, 2002c
143. Giroux, 1983; Freire, 1970, 1973; McLaren, 1994
144. Freire, 1970, 1973
145. Bourdieu & Passeron, 1977
146. Freire, 1973
147. hooks, 1990 p. 149
148. See Pizarro, 1998; Villenas & Deyhle, 1999
149. It would be a complete transformation.
150. Oh woman.
151. Roommate.
152. My namesake.
153. Cumbia of the Dead. Ozomatli sings, "*Cierta gente solo puede ver espíritus bailando entre la gente*" (Only certain people can see spirits dancing among us). See Ozomatli Music, 1998

3
STUDENTS ON THE MOVE
Desegregation at Bandini High School[1]

INTRODUCTION

Out of every 100 Chicana and Chicano elementary school students, only 44 graduate high school. What happens at the secondary levels of the educational pipeline so that 56 of every 100 Chicana/o elementary school students do not earn a high school diploma? This chapter examines some of the educational structures, practices, and discourses that shape these outcomes.

High schools tend to reflect patterns of structural inequality evidenced at the primary levels of the pipeline. In urban, suburban, and rural communities across the United States, Chicana/o students usually attend racially segregated, overcrowded high schools in dilapidated buildings with an insufficient number of functioning bathrooms.[2] Within these poorly maintained schooling facilities, Chicanas/os are too often enrolled in classes where undertrained, uncredentialed faculty attempt to teach with a shortage of updated textbooks, library materials, and desks.[3]

It is not news that so many Chicana/o high school students attend schools with poor conditions.[4] Nor is it a novel idea to restrict, Chicana/o students to remedial and vocational courses of study within high schools. Historically, Chicana/o communities endured many such forms of racism, such as physical segregation into "Mexican schools" and exposure to differentiated curriculum within racially "integrated" schools.[5] Mainstream schooling practices for at least the first half of the 20th century presented knowledge to Chicana/o students with little regard for their language, culture, or potential to think critically. For example, schools insisted Chicanas/os needed lessons on "proper" hygiene, "standard" English, manual arts, and menial labor.[6]

This "banking method"[7] sought to prepare socially productive citizens by depositing "American" knowledge into students of Mexican descent.[8] In addition, this schooling approach relied on conservative notions of "appropriate" behavior and management, which emphasized sorting children into levels of cognitive and physical development.[9] For example, educators relied on IQ testing and other standardized tests offered only in English. Without an appropriate Spanish-language exam, schools regularly mislabeled Chicana/o students Educable Mentally Retarded (EMR) and misplaced them in special education classes.[10] As noted in chapter 2, genetic and cultural deficit traditions informed these schooling practices.

In the second half of the 20th century and now into the 21st century, these cultural deficit and behaviorist traditions still shape Chicana/o secondary schooling experiences. While racial segregation has decreased for African American students (although not as significantly as anticipated), it continues to increase for Chicanas/os, especially in urban high schools.[11] Within these segregated schools, Chicana/o students continue to be "tracked" into courses of study that tend to follow a remedial or vocational trajectory.[12] On "regular," vocational, or terminal English-as-a-Second-Language (ESL) curricular tracks, schools underprepare and discourage Chicana/o students from pursuing a higher education.[13] These students rarely gain access to courses that would provide the minimal requirements to enroll in a 4-year college.[14]

For Chicanas/os, access to college-preparatory courses of study remains limited. For example, high school magnet programs—designed to attract students to enroll by offering numerous academically rigorous enrichment opportunities, well-trained teachers, and extensive resources—consistently enroll White students at higher rates than Chicanas/os. This disproportionate underrepresentation in magnet programs occurs both between and within schools. In other words, magnet programs deny access to Chicana/o students by (1) locating magnet schools in districts outside of Chicana/o communities or (2) creating magnet schools in already established comprehensive high schools and restricting enrollment to students from schools/districts outside of Chicana/o communities. Likewise, honors and Advanced Placement (AP) courses disproportionately under-enroll Chicana/o students.[15] AP refers to rigorous academic coursework that allows students to earn an extra 1.0 point on top of each semester grade and college credits for passing AP exams. The few honors and AP courses available in low-income, urban schools contrast the large numbers offered in more affluent schools.[16] Research confirms that the school-within-a-school phenomenon that limits access to magnet programs also occurs with AP courses.[17] In other words, even when Chicanas/os comprise the numerical majority of students at a particular school, they remain significantly underrepresented in honors and AP courses.[18]

Comprehensive programs for English Language Learners (ELLs) at the high school level are virtually nonexistent.[19] Although Federal legislation ensures students have a right to instructional support in their primary language, anti-bilingual education initiatives at the State level have further restricted access to such support.[20] Increasing students' skills in academic English and building on their primary language skills cannot happen without trained and motivated teachers. Certainly, thousands of very well trained and inspirational teachers do genuinely care about students and work to help them succeed. Yet disproportionately, districts place the least trained teachers in schools and classrooms with high percentages of ELLs.[21] Otherwise creative and motivated teachers may find themselves without support in overcrowded classrooms where curriculum is often prepackaged and considered "teacher-proof." These teachers tend to seek transfers out of poor Chicana/o schools, or "burnout" and stop teaching altogether. Given the high teacher turnover rate in predominately Chicana/o high schools, many classrooms feature long-term substitute teachers year-round.[22]

Though research shows the importance of race/ethnic and gender role models and mentors for the development of future professionals, Chicanas/os remain underrepresented in the ranks of high school teachers.[23] For example, in California, while Students of Color comprise the majority of students in public schools, almost 75% of their teachers are White.[24] Furthermore, schools provide Chicana/o students very limited access to guidance counselors. Counselors at the high school level tend to bear such large caseloads they cannot individually interact with each student who needs advice. Even counselors with good intentions may resort to focusing only on students who have already fulfilled the minimum college entrance requisites. For example, Miguel Cejas'[25] research shows that college counselors severely restrict their interactions with "regular track," obstensibly non-college-bound students. These students (who comprise the majority of the school population) tend to receive discouraging advice about pursuing college when they do gain access to speak with the counseling staff.

Negative societal views of Chicanas/os, seen often through racialized media lenses, subtly justify the maintenance of low expectations for Chicana/o students. Secondary school curricula and textbooks reinforce this societal curriculum of racial stereotypes.[26] High school textbooks often ignore the multiple contributions Chicana/o communities make to the United States and the world.[27]

In addition to the metal detectors and daunting fences around most urban schools, Chicana/o students often find a regular police presence on campus. Furthermore, the U.S. military consistently conduct recruitment activities on Chicana/o high school campuses. Though the military has a long history of targeting working-class communities and Communities of Color for recruitment, the No Child Left Behind Act of 2001 (NCLB) now *requires* that high schools give military recruiters access to students' records. Students and community activists challenging this practice in low-income urban schools have found that schools do not regularly inform parents they can "opt out" of the NCLB military request and keep their child's records confidential.[28]

Schools rarely take affirmative steps to engage Chicana/o parents as partners in the educational process. As a result, high school administrators, faculty, counselors, and standardized test scores carry significant weight in shaping Chicana/o educational trajectories. For example, placement on a college-bound curriculum track usually requires teacher and counselor recommendations as well as high scores on standardized tests. Likewise, high school exit exams increasingly prevent students from earning their high school diploma and further discourage their higher education pursuits.[29] Researchers such as Paula García[30] assert that high-stakes assessments provide statistically unreliable, inappropriate measures of student knowledge. In addition, Angela Valenzuela's[31] ethnographic work in Texas reveals that for ELLs and low-income Students of Color, these tests function as especially alienating barriers to education.[32] While 25 states implement or consider similar high-stakes tests, critics point out that high school exit exams penalize students for the failures of the public schools.[33]

Because high schools usually function in ways that "subtract" cultural knowledge and diminish aspirations,[34] Chicana/o students tend to rely on their peers and social networks to navigate through this level of the pipeline.[35] Positive and encouraging messages about pursing higher education usually come from Chicana/o parents, though their guidance may be limited by a lack of experience in the U.S. educational system. Still, studies show that when compared to other working class families, Chicana/o parents maintain higher educational aspirations for their children than do White parents.[36] This parent support fosters students' academic achievements and challenges Chicana/o adolescents to view their bilingual Mexican heritage as a source of motivation and strength.[37] For example, Valeria Talavera-Bustillos'[38] research shows that as Chicana students make their way through the college choice process, these young women rely on the inspiration and cultural affirmation their parents' support provides. Research documenting racial and gender discrimination experienced by both Chicanas and Chicanos—including verbal and nonverbal racial and gender insults, lack of access to information, and minimal guidance—demonstrates that students' efforts in pursuit of higher education can be understood as acts of resistance against racialized inequality. Indeed, the multiple layers of racism Chicanas/os experience in pursuit of academic and career options may function to trigger their resistance and strengthen their drive to "prove" they can succeed.[39]

Though high schools historically discriminate against Chicanas/os and restrict their educational mobility, Chicana/o communities respond, resist, and develop ways to survive and succeed in spite of the system. Researchers provide examples of the many ways that Chicanas/os engage in transformative forms of resistance against schooling inequalities.[40] Extending on this legacy across the United States, today's Chicana/o high school students advocate for equal educational opportunities in multiple ways, including class-action lawsuits and political campaigns to defeat unjust state propositions.[41] Students resist inequality by creating films and organizing protests and vigils to raise public awareness about the dismal quality of their schools and the impoverishment of their communities. Furthermore, they stand against all forms of violence, including police brutality and war. As we move into the 21st century, Chicana/o high school students work to link the struggle for educational equity at the local school level with social justice beyond the classroom.[42]

This chapter's counterstory analyzes social science scholarship, descriptive statistics collected at the school district and State levels, and judicial records to examine Chicana/o high school experiences within a historical context. Set in a composite Los Angeles high school—Bandini High[43]—this counterstory takes a case-study approach to investigate patterns of racial segregation and curricular tracking in California, which also evidence themselves in major cities across the United States. Claudia Vasquez, a Chicana civil rights attorney and professor at Bayside Law School, serves as the narrator for this counterstory.[44] Listening to the experiences of teachers and students at Bandini High, Claudia documents some historical and contemporary realities of Chicanas/os in high school. We begin the counterstory as Claudia arrives at Bandini High and prepares for a focus group discussion with teachers.

THE TEACHERS' LOUNGE

I checked in with the principal's office and a secretary walked me down the hallway. A small group of "off-track" teachers had signed up in advance for this focus group dialogue and I anxiously wanted to meet them. I thanked the secretary as I entered the small room that doubled as a faculty lounge and lunchroom. I saw a refrigerator, microwave, and toaster on a side counter, near a big sink with a sign over it reading, "Your mother doesn't live here so please clean up after yourself." I sat down on the edge of a small couch and put my papers on a lopsided coffee table. Since I'd arrived a few minutes early, I took a moment to re-read over the names of the participants before they joined me: Ms. Darlene White, a veteran biology teacher nearing retirement; Mr. Gilbert Villalpando, a social studies teacher also nearing retirement; Ms. Elaine Knight, a mid-career Spanish teacher; Ms. Belinda Gutierrez, a second-year Government and Economics teacher; and Mr. Antonio "Tony" Delgado, a school counselor of 4 years.

I wandered down the hall, looking for a women's bathroom, and returned to the lounge and introduced myself to each of the participants as they arrived. I looked over my research protocol and the teachers talked among themselves before we started the early afternoon session.

"Can you believe this?" Elaine asked incredulously, "The President wants to cut Upward Bound! How much more straight out can they be about not supporting poor people?" She paused to sip her diet soda and continued reading the newspaper as she shook her head in disgust.

Tony also shook his head as he spread some peanut butter onto his celery stick and sarcastically remarked. "I can believe it. But I can't believe this weird diet my doctor has me on will lower my cholesterol." Without missing a beat, Elaine responded, "Well, you better go easy on the peanut butter. It has 110 calories and 3 carbs per tablespoon." Darlene looked up from her fruit salad and added, "They've been working against poor people since way back. And it's no coincidence that most poor people in the United States are also People of Color. They won't cut that program without a fight though. I can tell you that. It took a fight for us to get Upward Bound and all those TRIO programs that originated from the 1960s civil rights legislation. And it'll be a fight for them to take it from us."

Belinda walked into the lounge as Darlene finished her sentence. "Are we talking about our favorite compassionate conservative trying to cut one of the few opportunities Black and Chicana/o students have to go to college?" Elaine nodded and held up the article she was reading, pointing to the title, "*Is Upward Bound Headed for a Fall? Participants defend the college prep program that President Bush is seeking to eliminate.*"[45] Belinda placed a small plate of what looked like lasagna into the microwave and continued, "I was part of Upward Bound when I was in high school. The mentoring, tutoring, and the summer program were crucial to me being academically prepared for college and successful once I got there."

Darlene remarked, "Well, it's probably before your time, but I remember when it was approved, back in 1964." Gilbert, who had been struggling trying to get a soda from the vending machine, added, "No, Darlene, I'm with you. I remember. And a few years later they added Talent Search, then the Student Support Services component and legislators continued to build on those three successful programs.[46] I was more involved in the Migrant

Education program back then, which came out of the 1965 Elementary and Secondary Education Act. But all of those programs were part of trying to create a better society."

Darlene closed her eyes and said, "Yes, I remember our hopes for the 'Great Society.' My cousin Alice was at the University of Michigan when President Johnson gave that speech in 1964. Johnson spoke of a vision for U.S. society as a place of social and community responsibility, and he worked to make sure that vision turned into social policies."[47] And 40 years after Johnson's legislative 'War on Poverty,' we seem to have much more of a war against the poor instead of a war on poverty," remarked Elaine.

Darlene shook her head as she said, "I usually try to talk about this with my students during Black History Month." She paused and sarcastically remarked, "Of course they schedule Black History for February—the shortest month of the year." She continued on a more frustrated note, "It's hard for students to really get a handle on what school was like before *Brown v. Board of Education*.[48] I tell them, schools and communities were racially segregated."

Belinda remarked, "And look at us here at Bandini High. These students have grown up attending racially segregated schools. So they're probably wondering, what's the difference?" She added, "And I agree with you about Black History Month. I haven't been here long, but I see it's pretty ridiculous to try and create lesson plans for 'Hispanic' Heritage Month, because it starts mid-September, when most of us are focused on beginning of the school year issues. What's the deal with scheduling half of one month and half of another month?"

Darlene agreed, "You're right. Our communities are marginalized in different ways, but marginalized nonetheless. I guess I should be grateful that we got bumped up from 'Negro History Week' that started back in the 1920s,[49] but you know, the curriculum we're given to talk about Dr. King or whoever is usually so watered-down anyway…"

Darlene faded off for a moment and began flipping through a scrapbook filled with what looked like a combination of newspaper clippings, school flyers, and pictures. She remarked, "Maybe students have a hard time relating to the historical realities of *de jure* segregation and the aftermath of desegregation because most of the pictures and films from that period are pretty much black and white. But we experienced racism in vivid color. Although there are some really big differences between the 1950s and today, it's the continuity of racism, in various forms, that's difficult to think about, let alone teach given the constraints often put on us in the classroom."

Listening to Teachers' Oral Histories of Bandini High

"Well, let's go ahead and get started," I said. "I understand that our time today will be relatively short because there is a student event later this afternoon. We'll get a good start, I'm sure. I've met each of you briefly. Again, I'm Claudia Vasquez, and I'm a civil rights attorney and a professor at Bayside Law School in northern California. I am here today to facilitate and audiotape a discussion about the history of Bandini High." I took about 10 minutes to introduce myself more formally to the group, noting that I grew up in San Juan Capistrano and attended public schools in southern California, graduated with my B.A. from UC–Oceanview, earned my J.D. from UC–Berkeley's Boalt Law School, and practiced Civil Rights law for a few years on the East Coast. I mentioned that I recently worked on a few legal cases launched against the University of California and the State of California for disparate treatment of Students of Color and poor students.[50]

I said, "Each of these cases represent class action suits filed on behalf of students, and I'm working with a few groups to add more voices to this dialogue. Today, you are part of a concerted effort to listen more carefully to the voices of teachers committed to equity in education." I assured the group of my interest in *listening* to their histories and experiences. Although each of them had received a written confirmation of their participation in the focus group weeks ago via email, their facial expressions affirmed the importance of this personal contact. I pointed to Darlene's scrapbook and commented that I hoped each of them had brought some materials that would help jog their memories as we worked together to document their experiences through Bandini High's history. Seeing some of them bring out notepads and photos, it dawned on me that I needed to set up the scanner to digitally capture their archival materials.

As I collected their consent forms, set up the audiotape recorder, and plugged in the scanner, I reiterated that as a researcher, I collect school histories from numerous perspectives, including faculty, staff, students, and parents. I thanked the group in advance for their permission to share their stories, and reiterated that in the write-up, I would use pseudonyms and take other precautions to maintain their confidence. "In addition," I reminded them, "you will each receive in-service credits, and hopefully you can provide me with some insights once I get a draft of their stories written up." I remarked, "Hopefully, you're feeling confident you're in the right place and that your stories will serve the greater good."

So as the teachers and counselor gathered in a circle on assorted couches and chairs, they agreed to have each person share her or his story for about 15 minutes each and then we would save most of the discussion for the end of the session. Darlene started us off.

Darlene's Story

"I started teaching here at Bandini in 1965, if you can believe that! I'm retiring this June, so I'm glad to be a part of this study before I leave. This place has changed so much. The community used to be predominately White, and the school was too. In fact, I am the first Black teacher they ever hired. A desegregation lawsuit was filed against the district a few years prior, and I had just moved into the area with my children because my husband Robert's medical unit had been called up. I couldn't live on the base while Robert was in Vietnam. It was too much for me to handle. Maybe it was good timing because they needed a biology teacher, and maybe my light skin helped me seem less threatening, but when one of the men on the faculty hiring committee read on my resume that I had earned my degree and credential at his alma mater, he asked if I could start right away. Most Black teachers at that time were assigned to the schools with the highest Black enrollments. I enrolled my kids at the elementary school down the block and they were also among the few Blacks in that school."

"My younger sister, Shirley, was still in high school then, and she had come to live with me when our parents passed. Darlene held up what appeared to be a high school senior portrait of her sister and passed it around to the rest of the group as she explained, "I tried to enroll Shirley at Bandini, but was told the school had already reached "capacity." Instead, I had to enroll her at a predominately Black school and she was bussed for a few periods of the day to a White school on the Westside. It was actually a community-based, voluntary bussing program where the school board sent kids from the Southside of the city to the Westside.[51] The district eventually expanded this type of bussing for integration as part of the *Crawford v. Board of Education of the City of Los Angeles*[52] court mandate to desegregate Los Angeles schools over a decade after the Supreme Court's *Brown v. Board* decision."

Darlene slowly turned some of the pages of her scrapbook, and I asked, "Were White students also bussed to predominately Black or Mexican schools?" Darlene and Gilbert laughed out loud.

Darlene continued, "The White parents would never have allowed that. I remember that poor Shirley came home crying most days because there were angry White parents who waited for the busses to arrive to those Westside schools. And these White folks would shout racial epithets and picket with threatening signs as the Black youngsters got off the bus and entered the school. It broke my heart, but I had to be tough with Shirley and tell her to walk off that bus each day with her head held high. The White parents called themselves "Bus Stop," and that situation was on the verge of turning into a violent confrontation. Like later in Boston, where White folks violently opposed desegregation busing. When was that? I think it must've been in the mid-1970s?"[53]

Gilbert nodded in agreement as he furrowed his eyebrows. Darlene remarked, "Here in Los Angeles, probably after seeing the response from Whites, the court moved from mandated busing to voluntary busing. And then the court eventually gave up in 1981 or so, finding they had achieved as much desegregation as they could. From 1963–1982 under *Crawford*, the district went from about 60% White to less than 25% White.[54] Now I'd say that's pretty dramatic White flight. All that White flight caused racial 'minorities' to become the racial 'majority' in the district!"

I probed, "Would you say that there was some sort of 'tipping point'[55] where the numbers of Students of Color became 'too much' for Whites?"

Darlene replied, "I'd say so. Here at Bandini, we probably reached a 'tipping point' right around the time I arrived." She chuckled to herself and said, "Maybe I added to the tipping point, because I did notice more and more Whites leaving the school each year. We had enrolled about 60% Whites, 25% Blacks, and 15% Mexicans. And I think the Watts Rebellion in 1965 scared a lot of White people. Civil rights struggles were happening at various levels, from the courts to the classroom, and for White people it probably seemed like change was happening overnight. They preferred *real* 'deliberate speed.'[56] For Folks of Color, the change couldn't come fast enough. But that was a scary time for Black folks too, because we knew change wouldn't come without a price. Like when my Bob came home on furlough and we weren't served at the diner there on 4th Street. Too many Folks of Color paid dearly from violent White reactions—and from too many Whites' inaction. But we kept that train rolling toward change."

As Darlene paused and the group took in all that had been said, I asked, "What was the reaction to those changes here?"

Darlene sighed and explained, "White educators and administrators started really getting mad, because within a relatively short time, their student population had totally changed. They had been comfortable teaching in a predominately White school, but by the late 1970s, Bandini was about 40% Black, 35% Mexican, and 25% White. And since then, it has become increasingly more Mexican than Black. I think in the mid-1990s we were still about 50/50, but since then, I think we've become more like 60% Mexican, 10% Central American, 25% Black, and 5% White and Asian. And our numbers are actually high for the district in terms of Blacks. Across the district, Blacks are now about 12% while Latinas/os are almost 75%. Many districts started magnet programs to attract White students back to the public schools,[57] but the numbers of White students never went back to those pre-1965 levels."

Belinda commented, "I remember graduating high school in the mid-1990s as news stories kept mentioning that in the State of California, Whites had officially become the 'minority' in the K–12 public schools. Of course, the news never gave all the background to that trend." Darlene nodded and said, "Oh yes, Whites continued to leave as the public schools became more 'colorful,' so Whites are now about 35% of K–12 public schools in California and less than 40% of California's public high school population."

I remarked, "So it sounds like the shifts happening within the district here revealed a larger pattern of White flight that eventually occurred across the state. I'm sure you may know that this pattern evidenced itself in different forms across the country, but some states are just now beginning to see the drastic demographic change California has experienced. From what you describe, Darlene, it seems like Los Angeles gave up on school desegregation just a few years before the *Diaz v. San Jose Unified School District* complaint in northern California successfully initiated voluntary, court-monitored, desegregation efforts to remedy the racial imbalance in Northside and Southside schools. Up there, the district limited Mexican students to the downtown, Northside schools while enrolling Whites in the suburban, Southside schools."[58]

Darlene agreed, "Yes, and in places like Boston, the dynamics featured Blacks versus Whites; in San Jose it sounds like a Mexican versus White phenomenon. Here, the issue played out among sizable Black, Mexican, and White populations. Well, in the beginning anyway."

Belinda added, "I'm still pretty new to Bandini, and I'm not sure what kind of insights I can add to this history specifically, but I'm thinking back to one of my college political science classes, *Chicana/o, Latina/o Politics*, and I remember reading about multiple socioeconomic reasons for some of those demographic shifts.[59] In addition to the racist resistance to integration, deindustrialization hit communities pretty hard in the early 1970s and 1980s. Shutting down and moving the steel, tire, and automobile factories to other countries almost wiped out many union towns throughout Los Angeles.[60] People had to seek other employment and even move out of the neighborhood to provide for their families. And reindustrializing the gutted economy meant replacing higher-wage, skilled, union jobs with low-wage, service sector jobs.[61] But also, the Immigration Act of 1965 lifted those racially exclusionary statues that previously restricted Asian and Latin American immigration in favor of northern European immigrants.[62] This led to a major increase in the numbers of Japanese and Chinese immigrants after 1965, and large-scale immigration of Pilipinos, Cambodians, Vietnamese, and Koreans. Throughout the late 1960s and 1970s, but especially in the 1980s, immigration from Mexico, Guatemala, and El Salvador increased substantially. So at the same time folks moved out, immigrants and others moved in. The population of Los Angeles grew tremendously in the 1980s."[63]

Darlene and Gilbert nodded with each point Belinda made. Gilbert added, "It's hard for our students to see, but a place like Boyle Heights, now almost 100% Latina/o, was home to a predominately Jewish community back in the 1950s. I used to go to a Jewish deli right there…" Gilbert sat reminiscing with a smile that almost made my stomach growl. I probably should have eaten a bigger breakfast since I skipped lunch.

Darlene explained, "And when White folks left, they took economic resources with them. The family-owned markets, restaurants, and other small businesses left and Black folks had to then go outside the community to buy what they used to get here. And with very little representation on the city council or other political positions,[64] we had multiple folks who didn't live in our community opening up liquor stores and small convenience shops. Now, I can buy alcohol or a lottery ticket on almost any corner near Bandini, but I can't find a decent piece of fresh fruit in those little markets."[65]

I asked, "How did the disinvestment in the community affect Bandini High?" Darlene replied, "Conditions at Bandini worsened as these demographic shifts occurred. The era of social responsibility and emphasis on the 'Great Society' seemed to leave just like those union jobs. Instead of searching for academic talent, or ensuring these Black and Mexican students were socially and academically 'upward bound,' inner-city schools seemed to begin to renege responsibility and blame the students for not placing enough value on education.[66] I can't even tell you how many times teachers complained that parents wouldn't come to any parent–teacher conferences. They reminisced about the 'good old days' when parents were supposedly much more 'involved' in their students' education. I actually stopped coming to the teacher's lounge for a long time and ate lunch in my classroom so I could avoid their comments."

Gilbert nodded, acknowledging Darlene's experience. He said, "And those were predominately White teachers who didn't even consider that the parents who they accused of 'not caring' about their child's education lived at least 25 miles away from Bandini and often didn't have transportation of their own."

Darlene responded, "Oh, I don't blame those parents at all for not wanting to take time after work, or take the day off work and lose a day's pay, to travel on a city bus for an hour and meet with a condescending teacher who often makes stereotypical and insulting racial remarks. Many of those teachers requested transfers out of Bandini. They wanted to regain some of those 'good old days' by transferring to Westside, predominately White schools. And the administration wasn't too helpful in providing ongoing training for teachers who stayed here. That might have helped teachers reflect on their own racially prejudiced views and begin to build on the cultural knowledge students bring to Bandini High from their communities."

Darlene showed us some school newsletter updates spanning over quite a few years. Realizing that I hadn't been able to record, take notes, listen, and scan at the same time, I asked Darlene and the rest of the group if I could scan their materials at the end of the session. The others agreed that would be fine and Darlene said, "Sure. My husband used to call me a 'pack rat,' so I tried to organize it better, but I threw a lot of stuff away. I'll be sure to tell my Robert that you wanted to use some of this for historical purposes. He'll get a big kick out of that."

I asked, "So how did the administration at Bandini respond to these numbers?" Darlene smiled broadly and shook her head and replied, "Well, though they had refused to allow their numbers to increase beyond 'capacity' when Whites were the majority, we were told to 'make do' with overcrowding as Students of Color became the majority at the school. And because of the ongoing racial discrimination in housing, the real estate tax base for schools diminished in urban communities, which further decreased options for Bandini students."[67]

Pointing to a series of newspaper headline clippings, Darlene explained, "The 1971 *Serrano v. Priest*[68] lawsuit attempted to level state funding allocated to California schools, arguing that Equal Protection under the U.S. Constitution's 14th Amendment required the state to equalize funding to all school districts. But in 1973, the Supreme Court's ruling in the *San Antonio v. Rodriguez*[69] case pretty much ended other hopes for class-action lawsuits about school finance and educational equality. In a close 5 to 4 decision, the Justices ruled that education was not a 'right' nor was 'poverty' a justifiable way to group a class of people as deserving protection under the 14th Amendment. In 1976, the California court followed-up with another *Serrano v. Priest*[70] decision, requiring that all districts equalize their per pupil spending within $100 of one another. But in 1978, Proposition 13 minimized any major impact the *Serrano* case may have had in California, because voters decided to restrict homeowners' tax liability, which of course limited the tax base many districts had relied on."[71] Belinda looked quite interested with Darlene's description of the legal cases, leaning over to look at her scrapbook clippings.

Darlene handed Belinda the scrapbook to browse through as she noted, "But these lawsuits didn't deal with *intra*district funding inequalities. And most importantly, this legislation didn't address the fact that under a series of Republican governors, California shifted its financial priorities away from education. So support for public education decreased in multiple ways at the same time that the state population—and the school-age population in particular—increased dramatically. But White folks didn't want financial responsibility for schools they had left."

I probed, "So it sounds like by the time Ron Rodriguez sued Los Angeles Unified[72] to make the funding equal *within* the district, there was less funding to go around anyway."

Darlene agreed, "And *Rodriguez v. LAUSD* was an important legal complaint. It revealed funding inequity within districts. It exposed the structural inequity within LAUSD, which created predominately Black and Chicana/o, poor, underfunded, underresourced, and overcrowded schools with low test scores and high dropout rates at the same time it generously supported Westside middle-class, predominately White schools with high test scores and low dropout rates. The main district administrative offices received an equal amount of per pupil funds from the state in comparison to other districts. But they turned around and allocated those funds within the district unequally. They relied on the categorical funds—money allocated from the federal government for desegregation, school lunch programs, bilingual education, and funds targeted for poor students. Those categorical funds were supposed to *supplement* basic resources. And few folks realized that extra funding for integration would disappear once the courts released districts from federal or state desegregation mandates."[73]

I asked Darlene, "What effects have you seen within the district and at Bandini?" She explained, "Black and Chicana/o communities in the East and South highest poverty indexed schools, ended up with the least number of qualified, credentialed teachers or counselors. They also suffered with the most substitute teachers and the most overcrowding in the oldest crumbling buildings and facilities. With less support and more students, Bandini began to really see schooling conditions deteriorate. We had asbestos, old textbooks, rarely functioning restroom facilities in our school buildings, and sports fields with no grass. Yet the district held us responsible for serving more students than ever. My class size went from 20 to 45! I felt so sad the first semester I had nothing for the students to dissect in biology lab. I paid for a lot of things out of pocket, and I still do! I know a lot of teachers who pay for all kind of supplies out of their pockets to give students the tools they need and to get them excited about learning. And I won't even go into teacher salaries!" Everyone in the lounge moaned.

Darlene conceded, "Eventually, as they had done with other public facilities, White folks who hadn't left the public schools already began to privatize from within the public system. Some schools within the district began creating parent–community foundations that raised money for their school, to replace the sparse state funding and limited tax revenues. Poorer communities in the district did not have access to such multimillion-dollar fund sources. As you all know, when we finally went to a year-round schedule to minimize the problems with overcrowding, the school assigned students to calendar 'tracks.'"

Gilbert's Story

Gilbert agreed, and remarked, "But curricular tracking had started much earlier. That was one of the main reasons why Bandini students walked out in March 1968, in support of the East Los Angeles students. Remember?" Darlene nodded emphatically, and Gilbert continued, "The physical racial segregation in schools was really not the crux of the problem. It was the lack of *quality* education in those racially segregated schools, no? Chicana/o students, like Black students, were racially segregated into separate schools. Although the courts have gone back and forth on whether Mexicans are racially Indian or White, history shows that White communities worked out various plans so that we wouldn't be educated with their kids.[74] School boards claimed Mexicans didn't have proper hygiene, we couldn't speak English, and we weren't culturally American.[75] Racist ideas informed those excuses. In subtle and very overt ways, folks asserted that Mexicans are biologically incapable of learning abstract thought and culturally unable to prioritize education or plan for tomorrow.[76] So since we supposedly didn't value education and couldn't grasp intellectual ideas, Whites did us a 'favor' by preparing us for manual labor and domestic service jobs in segregated schools."[77]

Gilbert motioned to some of his notes and continued, "In 1946, the lawsuit led by Mexican families in Westminster, California, challenged the segregation of their children into 'Mexican schools.' The Ninth Circuit Court of Appeals upheld the *Mendez v. Westminster*[78] decision, and the California Governor had to repeal all those legislative codes that had previously mandated separate schools by race.[79] As I recall, that same governor served as the Supreme Court Justice on the *Brown* case." "Chief Justice Warren," interjected Darlene. "Yes," said Gilbert, "That's a very interesting history there."[80]

I nodded and waited for Gilbert to continue. He finished off the last of his soda and explained, "Here in our district, the school board bent to White community pressure. Following the already segregated housing patterns, they manipulated attendance zones to maintain racial segregation well after *Mendez*, *Brown*, and as Darlene mentioned, *Crawford*. And it's true, White people were scared of desegregation. And Chicanas/os were scared too, but for different reasons. Our experiences were different than Blacks during and after *de jure* segregation. I think both Black and Chicana/o communities hesitantly supported integration because we knew it meant having to send our kids to White schools. We wanted equal education, and we wanted quality schools in our communities. Black communities had developed a small but strong professional class that included Black teachers and principals. Although they attended schools under very poor conditions, Black students and their parents cultivated 'communal bonds' with these all-Black schools. And desegregation broke those bonds in many ways.[81] After 1964, districts closed a lot of Black schools and displaced students, teachers, and principals. Districts began bussing Black students to different schools, but Black teachers and principals experienced great difficulty finding employment.[82] Darlene interjected, "And then maintaining a job as the only Black teacher? We'd need a whole session just to talk about the racism Black teachers faced and continue to face from White students and faculty colleagues!"[83]

Gilbert nodded and continued, "And the focus remained on integration as opposed to equity, so districts bussed Black students, like your sister Shirley, into racially hostile schools, where they had to endure teachers and students who believed Blacks were inferior to Whites. And unfortunately, long after integration, Black students continue to feel the brunt of those White supremacist assumptions."

I asked Gilbert, "What were some of the experiences of Mexican American public school teachers during desegregation?" Gilbert smiled and responded, "*Pues*, Mexican Americans really didn't have a professional class. *Digo*, don't get me wrong, we did have many 'teachers' in our communities—from parents who taught Spanish to their kids, to activists who organized unions and asserted workers' rights, to newspapers and radio shows that raised community awareness and nurtured cultural identity through music—but these community teachers rarely gained access to formal schooling themselves. So before and after the *Mendez* and *Brown* cases, whether housed in converted barns or in overcrowded urban schools, Mexican Americans dealt with White teachers, White principals, and a curriculum that emphasized English, a labor-intensive vocation, and Americanization. Mexican American parents didn't necessarily want their kids to have to travel on a bus so far from home anymore than Black parents did, but both groups of parents held onto the same hope. They wanted their children to gain the opportunities that come with quality education. They wanted their children to benefit from an education equal to the White students. When Mexican Americans attended racially integrated schools, we were most often resegregated into classes for English-learners even if we already spoke English. I think if anyone really asked Mexican American or Black parents, the answer would have been just as clear then as it is now. The goal was never just to sit next to White students; the goal was to have the same resources and opportunities as White students."[84]

I remarked, "Sounds like you're arguing that folks wanted to emphasize 'quality, not quantity.' And, with desegregation, you saw that counting numbers of Students of Color became more important than assessing the quality of the education offered to the students." Gilbert nodded.

"How did that emphasis impact Chicana/o students?" I asked. "Schools limited options for Chicana/o students both before and after desegregation," Gilbert replied. "Schools took very talented youngsters, and more often than not, crushed their dreams of becoming anything other than a military statistic, a mechanic, or a homemaker. Structurally, Bandini prepared most Chicana/o students for vocational careers. Of course, there's nothing inherently wrong with training for a vocational career, but Mexican American parents worked in those labor-intensive jobs usually hoping their children would have other opportunities. And Bandini minimized those opportunities for Chicana/o students."

Gilbert continued, "I was the first Chicano hired here on staff at Bandini, but I doubled as a baseball coach and driver's education teacher while I finished some coursework over at UC-Oceanview. I graduated as one of the first Chicano Studies majors from UCOV. The principal started me off subbing for social studies classes and eventually offered me my own classes. Maybe they finally read my resume and saw my undergrad degree in History and Chicano Studies along with my credential and a master's degree..."

I probed, "When did you start at Bandini?" Gilbert thought for a moment and said, "I started coaching in the fall of 1967 and the student walkouts were in the spring of that school year. Of course the police investigated all the Chicano staff they could find in the district because they couldn't believe students had planned and executed this large-scale organized protest without adult intervention. Whether or not anyone chose to believe in the organizational capabilities of students, over the course of a few weeks that spring of 1968, over 10,000 students walked out of Los Angeles schools."

Belinda interjected, "I saw a film with some of that footage in one of my Chicano Studies courses in college." Gilbert smiled and nodded, saying, "Yes, Chicana walkout leaders networked, organized, and developed consciousness around the structural problems students identified in the school system.[85] Chicano walkout leaders usually acted as the spokesperson, articulating students' demands to decrease the dropout—or as they put it—the pushout rate for Chicanas/os, which was well over 50%. Students demanded bilingual/bicultural teachers to replace racist and undertrained teachers and administrators. They demanded updated and sufficient textbooks and school facilities. They also demanded that Chicana/o history and culture be part of the high school curriculum. And they demanded an end to the standardized tests and tracking system that underprepared and ultimately denied Chicanas/os access to college."

Gilbert sighed and said, "Hard to believe that was almost 40 years ago. I remember when students walked out of my driver's ed class. Bandini had already reached that 'tipping point' you mentioned earlier, so the Black student population was probably close to 35% by this time. So this young Black student, Audre, asked if she could make an announcement while I was taking roll. Her friend passed out leaflets to students while Audre reiterated to them what was about to happen. The leaflets outlined Bandini students' demands and included a solidarity statement about the actions that had occurred at the other schools in recent weeks. It also provided a short description of how to respond to police or other authorities should the need arise during the nonviolent protest. After her announcement, Audre turned to me and said,

> I'm sorry, Mr. V. We mean no disrespect, but this school is pushing us out so we'll have to cook and clean for White folks. Well, as Malcolm X said, 'Cotton pickin' don't move me.' We're trying to assert our right to an education and we're willing to do it 'by any means necessary.'[86]

And with that Malcolm X–inspired comment, most of the class silently left their desks and joined their colleagues heading for a rally in front of the school and to a local community center for a teach-in."

After a slight pause, Gilbert added, "Since I couldn't hold class without any students, I decided to go see what was happening at the rally. The principal at the time saw me there and pulled me aside. I remember he said something like, 'Our students could never have planned this. They love Bandini High. Maybe those Mexicans from the Eastside infiltrated our students.' And at that point, I saw Darlene, who was also observing the rally. She smiled real big and pointed to student signs that read 'Schools Yes, War No,' and 'Bandini High Demands Equal Education.' Annoyed at my silence after his comments, the principal warned me, 'It's such a beautiful day, Vasquez, I hope you don't ruin it by making me fire you.' I remember my heart pounding loudly and tears welling up in my eyes. I turned to the principal and said, 'It's a beautiful day to be a Chicano.'[87] Hoping my wife Bernadette—who was a few weeks away from giving birth to our second child—would understand, I joined the students' march off campus, and Darlene and I offered our support for the teach-in."

Gilbert stood up and turned away from the group, resetting the coffee machine to make a fresh pot. I noticed he quickly wiped his eyes as we all sat in reflection for a few moments. Darlene sighed with a smile and distant look in her eyes.

Elaine's Story

Elaine broke the silence and teased, "So that's why you two have such a reputation!" We all laughed. Darlene explained, "Yes, they were going to transfer Gilbert to another school, but students really advocated for him. The principal transferred out not too long afterward."

"And you Elaine?" I asked. "Oh, I started here in 1978," she replied. "The same year that the *Bakke*[88] case ended affirmative action as a program of goals and timetables to desegregate higher education. Both Darlene and Gilbert's stories really help put this article about the potential elimination of Upward Bound into context for me. There's a continuity to these attacks that I'm beginning to see now." "And a continuity of resistance to the attacks," reminded Belinda. "Yes," said Elaine, "that's becoming much more clear."

Elaine continued, "In contrast to those White teachers who couldn't get their transfer petitions approved to get out of here fast enough, I chose to be here at Bandini because I wanted to make a difference. In the mid-1970s, I was part of another program that had originated out of the 'Great Society'—Teacher Corps. At first, I think I definitely came from a more naive perspective. I saw my social and cultural background as the standard and wanted to help culturally and socially 'disadvantaged' students aspire to more, and achieve more. But I learned a lot from my Teacher Corps colleagues and from reading Paulo Freire's work.[89] I learned to listen more to my students and their parents. I realized they had very high aspirations and they didn't need another arrogant John Wayne–like teacher, coming in to be a hero on a white horse."

"So students and parents confronted you?" I asked. "Well, not in an aggressive way," replied Elaine. "But it was more like they consistently called me out on my assumptions. A few times it did take me off guard though. Fortunately, I still kept in contact with my Teacher Corps colleagues, and they don't pull any punches, so they also helped me. Over time, I began questioning my own White privilege and assumptions about my role as a White teacher in a predominately Mexican and Black school. Take for example my habit of calling students 'smart' for scoring well on a standardized test. That showed my assumption about whether those tests could appropriately measure students' intelligence or capability. But more layered issues took longer for me to recognize. Some of my students would invite me to community events and I picked up a few books that also pushed my thinking. It's hard to see that as a White woman, I benefit from racism in countless ways, from not being accused of stealing at the mall to receiving pleasant service at a restaurant. But it's painful to recognize that I receive institutionalized racial privileges and preferences as a result of a violent legacy of oppression against communities made up of individuals like my students."[90]

"Can you talk a little more about institutionalized racial preferences and privileges?" I asked. Elaine thought for a moment and replied, "To start with, I benefited more from civil rights legislation than most Students of Color. The Affirmative Action program that helped me get admitted to a university was originally intended to remedy the racism that denied and still denies access to Students of Color. Some say that White society only allowed civil rights gains to the extent that they would benefit.[91] And, in terms of the Cold War coinciding with a lot of civil rights legislation, that makes sense. Whites needed to maintain the perception that the U.S. practiced the freedom and pluralistic democracy they preached internationally."[92]

Pausing to look at some of the pictures she had brought, Elaine showed the group a few photos of herself with a feathered hairdo like Farrah Fawcett from the mid-1970s. She explained, "I learned Spanish as a second language, so that's another huge privilege right there. When I first arrived here at Bandini High, I focused on teaching students Spanish with cultural references to Spain. That's what I learned in grad school. I had studied a semester abroad in Madrid! So my training prepared me to teach students Spanish as a *foreign* language. And though they already spoke Spanish, many students totally disengaged from my class."

Elaine bit her bottom lip and hesitantly said, "I remember my first year, I complained to Gilbert that 'Mexicans just don't care about education.' Gilbert nodded. Elaine continued, "I fell right into that whole stereotypical reaction that the students aren't performing well academically, so that must mean they don't really prioritize school or value education. And as I ranted about this, I realized Gilbert looked quite annoyed. So I said, 'But not you, Gilbert, you're different.'" Gilbert nodded with his eyebrows raised with a look that again showed he remembered that insulting remark.[93]

Elaine shook her head and winced, acknowledging her colleagues' patience. She looked down at some of her notes and recalled, "Within a few years, the administration asked me to chair the English-as-a-Second-Language (ESL) Department. They wanted to make sure Bandini complied with the 1974 *Lau v. Nichols* Supreme Court decision.[94] The Court allowed states and districts to decide which form of language support to provide students. In practice, this meant 'bilingual programs' tended to be a bit disjointed depending on how districts interpreted language support. And most programs targeted the elementary school levels. You remember? Those early- or late-exit programs that provided actual instruction in a students' primary language up until the second or even sixth grade, for example. But the programs almost always emphasized transitioning students into English, as opposed to maintaining their Spanish or Chinese, or other language."

Gilbert added, "And those programs provided very little support for teacher training." Tony, who had been listening intently but had not spoken yet, interjected, "I read that the original language of what became the Title VII Bilingual Education Act of 1968 emphasized the importance of maintaining students' primary language, and seeking Puerto Rican and Mexican teachers as role models and language, culture experts."[95] Elaine responded, "Yes, that would have complemented some of the affirmative action programs nicely. But legislators pretty much negotiated that goal away before approving the final version. And as Title VII was amended and amended, other goals were also watered down, like the idea that primary language maintenance should go hand-in-hand with learning English. In practice, too few programs emphasized true bilingual education, where students were immersed in their primary language and English with a goal of literacy and fluency in two languages. And I guess those few programs, though successful, weren't enough to convince universities to really recruit and train more Mexican and Puerto Rican teachers."

Elaine continued, "As the Chair of the ESL Department, I tried my best. Some of our dedicated teachers spent their weekends translating English textbooks chapter-by-chapter and typing up new texts to create more challenging and age-appropriate substantive material. But that was too much of a burden put on just a few teachers. So many of our students had not been well served at the earlier grade levels, and they were often placed in classes with a first-year teacher who had no language training.[96] Like for example, a college graduate who spoke Spanish, but majored in Sociology. Our ESL approach identified students as limited, deficient, and lacking. And that added to the assumptions already held by many teachers about Mexican Americans being culturally and socially disadvantaged. In observing a lot of classes to prepare for a Title VII compliance visit, I saw so clearly that language and accent really matters in teacher–student interactions.[97] Most teachers held really low expectations for students who had 'Mexican' accents.[98] And on the 'regular' track, teachers called on Chicana/o students who spoke 'with an accent' less than they called on students who spoke academic English 'without an accent.'"

I remarked, "Sounds like you're identifying multiple layers to the racism Darlene and Gilbert talked about." Elaine nodded, adding, "And my students internalized a lot of that racism from early on in their schooling. Many did not speak Spanish or were unwilling to speak Spanish by the time they reached high school. Which made it all the more ironic that they could not graduate from Bandini without learning a 'foreign' language. I stopped being surprised that a lot of students wanted to learn French or

German in high school. Those languages carried less negative racial stigma. Many people still perceive a European accent as the epitome of high-class sophistication."

I noted, "And you had probably learned Spanish with a Castilian accent!" Elaine shook her head and said, "Oh yes, I emphasized Spain, and added to the perception that being Mexican was low-class. This didn't hit me right away, obviously, but thankfully, the combination of my students and colleagues giving me feedback helped me move toward being more critically conscious of my pedagogy. I looked back to my training in Teacher Corps and realized my curriculum added to the problem of seeing students as 'limited' and treating them remedially. Instead of using a Freirean approach, I ignored students as a very big resource in my classroom. I taught Spanish grammar in the context of Spain, when my students had multiple local contexts, rich in history and cultural diversity that they could draw on. They had so much cultural knowledge, as you mentioned too, Darlene. So I began to rework my curriculum entirely. I eventually threw out my 'banking approach,' which had me trying to deposit language into students' supposedly empty heads,[99] and I began dealing with students' linguistic realities and strengths. I found that they really did have a lot of language skills. And from their own family histories, they began to write essays and then entire research projects with important insights about Chicana/o, Mexican, and Central American history. They became researchers and I worked to facilitate the process of re-discovering their academic talents." Tony's eyebrow raised at the mention of the word *re-discovering*. Elaine noted this and conceded with a smile, "I didn't say my journey was over in questioning my own privileges and biases, but I've come a long way. I'm still working on it."

Tony's Story

Tony remarked, "I'm just giving you a hard time, Elaine. Your willingness to learn from your students is so unique. Most teacher training programs emphasize cultural difference and more of that deficit approach you mentioned.[100] It seems like being part of the Teacher Corps program gave you a good start in connecting teaching to that larger struggle for justice and equity." Elaine nodded, making a face as if she were considering what led her to become more critical. Tony continued, "Most teachers here at Bandini have a difficult time being self-critical and are not really willing to acknowledge how this place is structured to 'school' instead of 'educate.' As Ray Gwyn Smith asks, 'Who is to say that robbing a people of its language is less violent than war?'[101] It's really ironic that society and schools shame the language out of students in elementary school only to require 'foreign' language courses in high school and college. I'm just feeling really grateful right about now for being here with all of you. This has been a really great history lesson. I only wish we had more time before the student *encuentro* starts."

I agreed and asked Tony, "Can you tell us a little about your experiences?" "Sure," he replied. "I was a pretty shy student here at Bandini, and I stopped going to classes after the 10th grade really, so I didn't get a chance to know most teachers back in the day. I'm very happy to be here now as a counselor. It's been a really long road for me and in many ways my path connects to the history you've each described. At the end of my freshman year, I went to ask the counselor how to get on the college preparatory track. Of course I didn't tell the counselor that I had a crush on a White girl named Donna, who was on that track." Tony paused as he saw the rest of us shake our heads with smiles at his side story. He added, "Don't you remember that *La Bamba*[102] came out and it was suddenly cool for a Chicano to get with a White girl because of Richie Valens' story?[103] I used to sing the song to her, 'I had a girl and Donna was her name, since she met me, I'll never be the same...Oh Donna, Oh Donna...'" Tony dramatically paused and then recalled, "My singing impressed her, anyway." We laughed and waited for him to get back to his story.

Tony took a moment, perhaps reminiscing about his youth and the 1980s, before continuing. He explained, "The counselor told me, 'Tony, you're just not college material. I think you should sign up for a school-to-work vocational training program.' And I didn't know what I wanted to do when I was 14 years old. That sounded good to me. So I didn't have any academic electives, or actually any classes that could have counted for college. I took basic English and math, which I later found out were remedial-level courses that didn't accrue credits toward college. That seems so wrong to me now—that some students can go to high school for 4 years and not even be close to meeting the basic requirements for college. Back then, I thought it was cool to have so many courses in wood shop, metal shop, and PE. But the freedom I thought I had at the time ended up really limiting my options. By my sophomore year, I spent most of the day working off campus, as part of the vocational program. I remember my junior year, I had substitute teachers for English for the whole year. I wanted to do something with hip-hop, which had been breaking, or should I say break dancing, into the mainstream. I would spend hours breakin' and poppin' everyday. We even moved the chairs out of the way in class and held contests. The substitutes didn't care."

Tony had brought a yearbook from his freshman year and pointed himself out to the group. He explained, "I don't think most of my teachers cared about the students at all.[104] I didn't want to be in the vocational program, so I tried to get back into the regular high school track, but there was 'no room.' I thought that sounded pretty strange, but I didn't know who I could ask. I remember one substitute teacher in particular was annoyed when students complained about an assignment that we had already done the week before, but she made us repeat it. We usually had to copy pages from the textbook by hand. Something brainless like that. What they really wanted us to do was to sit quietly for the 50-minute period. They emphasized behavior instead of learning. Anyway, the substitute teacher said, 'I don't care if you don't do this assignment. You don't have to be here at all. Within a few years, most of you will either be pregnant, in prison, or dead because you're in a gang.' And I remember being so angry. She wasn't the first racist teacher I had and I know not all teachers are racist, but it felt useless to keep going. If the teachers didn't care that students weren't learning anything and the counselor thought I wasn't 'college material,' I figured I could help my family out a lot more if I just worked."

"So you stopped attending altogether?" I asked. Tony nodded his head affirmatively and explained, "I worked with my uncle laying sheet metal for a few years. But I hurt my back in a break dancing competition, which put me out of work for a bit. And about that time, I ran into some friends from my freshman year at Bandini. They were going to a local community college and encouraged me to go too. I mostly went because I had a crush on one of the girls I knew from back then. One of the *women* I should say. A Chicana this time." Elaine and Darlene rolled their eyes with a smile. Gilbert said, "Whatever gets you there." Tony smiled sheepishly.

Belinda interjected, "Your story sounds a lot like my older brother Mando, except that part about chasing girls, and he never got to see a counselor. He went one time to the college center and signed in, took some pamphlets, and they never called him for an appointment. They didn't really take notice of him probably because he wasn't on the 'college-bound' track, but he had a decent grade point average. And he did really well in math and science too. But since the college center shares space with the military recruiters, those recruitment officers started calling our house every week, telling Mando and my parents that the military could help pay for college. And so, Mando ended up going into the Marines straight out of high school. He was part of the 1989 U.S. invasion of Panama, and he didn't re-enlist. He saw a psychologist for years afterward because he showed signs of post-traumatic stress disorder. The mainstream media distorted the story so we didn't realize until much later the horrific extent of what he participated in and witnessed. U.S. troops killed thousands of Panamanian civilians…"[105] Belinda drifted off for a moment.

She continued, "Like I said, if I didn't have Upward Bound, I would have probably gone into the military too. I was very lucky to have been connected up with that program. My brother's experience actually sparked my interest to learn more about politics in college. It's like the military has always targeted our communities, working-class and poor communities." Gilbert added, "During the Vietnam war, East Los Angeles alone experienced unbearably high numbers of casualties, because Chicanas/os were drafted in disproportionate numbers to serve in Vietnam."[106]

Belinda remarked, "My brother had such high aspirations in junior high and high school. I remember he called himself 'the mad scientist' and he conducted all kinds of cool experiments and built weird contraptions out of scraps of metal and wood in the backyard. Of course my mother was always afraid he would burn the house down. My parents would usually say, 'That's great *mijo*—what is it?' They had very high hopes for all of us, but they didn't know how to make sure the school was helping us 'be all we could be.' The recruiters told us Mando could get training to become a mechanical engineer or something, but instead he learned how to be a sniper—which isn't very useful outside of the military. Now he works laying carpet. I love my brother and I'm very proud of him. But I sometimes wonder whether things would have worked out differently if the counselor had called him to talk about college."

Belinda paused, looking at each person in the room empathetically, and added, "And I know it's hard on counselors because there are too many students. And it's difficult for teachers because of the barrage of standards and state mandates, 'teacher-proof curriculum,' and constantly changing assessments, and now with the high-stakes testing.... I mean, who has time to really ask, 'What are we really doing here and why don't we listen to the students, the folks we're actually supposed to be serving?'" Belinda stood up to look out the window facing the quad, and said, "Speaking of which, we'd better get over there to the gym for the students' meeting."

A Student Encuentro

A few minutes later, I joined the teachers in chairs just outside of a talking circle students had set up at one end of the gym. About 40 students, mostly Latina/o and African American, engaged in individual conversations or waited quietly for the meeting to begin. A dark-skinned, thin student with black hair slicked back into a ponytail introduced herself as América and said, "*Bienvenidos*, welcome to this *encuentro*. As you can see from the sign here, we're meeting after school to start a dialogue among 'Students Who Care.'[107] We've invited a few teachers to join us here today—to *support* us here today I should say. And both MEChA and BSU officers and some members are also here today. The *Mechistas* are wearing BSU shirts and BSU folks are wearing MEChA shirts. This is one way of showing we support each other."

Lynette, a very petite girl with medium brown skin and red hair woven into her black braids sat next to América. Lynette explained, "As the President of the Black Student Union, I've been working with América in talking to a few other schools in the district, and we're setting up a website so we can have all kinds of students talking about what's happening in their schools."

América continued, "Yes, and today we're hoping to get your input to explain what's happening at Bandini so we can upload this dialogue. Then, other students can comment on issues happening at their school. And I'd like to start us off by saying that Bandini is falling apart. Literally, most of us have been hit in the head by falling ceiling tiles. It's a basic lack of respect to have us in classes that don't even have enough desks or books. I see some students just ditching when they don't have a place to sit in their class. Carmen almost passed out the other day after running the mile in PE because we couldn't find water fountains that work. The bathrooms are either locked shut, or if they're open, there's no toilet paper or soap, and there are no doors on the stalls.[108] Students start losing respect for the school, so there's tagging everywhere in the bathroom. There's even tags on the toilet seats! Maybe someone should bring the art classes back."

América sat down and a student who others called Nick stood to speak, "This place looks like a prison. How are we supposed to feel good about going to a school with big fences, gates, and police everywhere?" Nick had dark brown skin with a combed-out Afro hairstyle. He was one of the BSU students wearing a MEChA shirt. He continued, "As if we don't have enough tensions between Blacks and Latinas/os on campus as it is. Bars on the windows, metal detectors, random backpack searches, and no one is remembering that almost every single one of those horrible shootings happened when White boys brought guns to school. We're not the enemy here. We're just trying to get an education." Many of the students clapped as Nick sat down and slumped back into his chair.

"The news said those White boys who shot up their school were crazy and needed counseling," said a student named Monica. Monica had medium brown skin and short, wavy brown hair. She wore a soccer jersey that had the flag of El Salvador on the sleeve. She asked, "Instead of giving us counseling, we get more police? What, we don't deserve counseling? Not even college counseling? There's only one college counselor for 5,000 students? That's ridiculous."

Aaron, one of the *Mechistas* wearing a BSU shirt, spoke next. Aaron had dark brown skin, short, curly black hair, glasses, and the beginnings of a moustache. He said, "We get harassed everywhere we go. I was carrying the tripod the other day for yearbook class and the campus police stopped me and asked for my student ID. I had to wait there while they asked me questions and I missed the beginning of the event I was supposed to be taking pictures at. They told me I look like a gangster who might be carrying a weapon. Like Nick says, we're seen like criminals instead of students. And Bandini is like two schools in one. One school with students who take AP and college prep, and one school with students who are in the regular, voc, or ESL classes. Mr. Delgado was just telling me about a program up in Oakland that has students taking metal shop but they're learning to be engineers—*all* their classes are college prep."

Lynette asked, "I know it might not sound related, but did you know your parents can sign a waiver so the school doesn't release your information to the military? I'm trying to go to the college center to get information about college, but first I have to sign in with the recruiters? For me, it's related to the college prep issue because why doesn't the school automatically release our information to colleges and universities?"

América motioned to a student who had been taking notes. I leaned over to Tony and he said the student's name was Roberto, but everyone called him Junior. Junior had very short black hair, medium brown skin, and was a pretty large kid. Standing up, he must have been over six feet and he was built real big like my cousin Memo, who we affectionately called *El Chiquilin*.[109] In a surprisingly quiet voice, Junior remarked, "Most of the community won't be able to be on the Internet, so we'll probably plan community meetings after we hook up with some other schools. So far, it sounds like these are the main complaints: broken water fountains, falling ceiling tiles, bathrooms closed and no toilet paper or soap, lack of access to college prep/AP classes, too much military and police, not enough college counseling." As I strained to hear this quiet recap, I wondered to myself whether young Men of Color like my cousin Memo or like this student Junior might feel pressure to develop a persona of a gentle giant in order for people not to feel intimidated by them.

Lynette thanked Junior and said, "It's like Bandini is stuck somewhere in the past, when they built this place to fit 1,200 students—who were pretty much White. And maybe that was in the 1950s or something. But they're still acting the same. All this has changed and there are 5,000 students now. Maybe they're waiting for those old days to come back, but it seems like they're really disappointed they got stuck with us. I think if we had more classes that helped us learn about ourselves and our histories instead of just 'the White guy did this, and the White guy did that' kind of history we get now—that would be a good start. Then we can learn about each other too. My older brother told me that he saw a film about Afro-Mexicans at that Magic Johnson film festival a little ways back." A few students giggled, looking at Nick's hair, so Lynette clarified, smiling and shaking her head, "No, not that kind of Afros, I mean Black Mexicans, they were mixed." She paused and then remarked, "I just think schools could help us deal with our reality more. Black and brown folks live right next to each other. And our histories are connected. Like we learned from that guest speaker in Mr. Villalpando's class, Black students walked out of their messed-up high school back in the 1950s and that led to the whole country changing the law so we don't have to go to separate bathrooms and schools.[110] And then Mexican students walked out of their high schools here in L.A. in the 1960s because things weren't getting better."[111] Gilbert winced slightly, trying to hide his pleasure at these comments and looking around quickly to see if any administrators were in earshot. I smiled, wondering how teachers muster the daily courage to go beyond the textbook and challenge students to make critical, real-world connections with history.

Another student added, "Mr. V. said that Bandini students also walked out in the 1960s." Lynette nodded and said, "Yeah, so let's walk out!" She smiled at Mr. V. "Nah, I'm just kidding—at least for now," she teased. In a more serious tone, Lynette concluded, "Anyway, this *encuentro* with MEChA and BSU is going to start happening once a month, and we're going to invite other schools too. There's a Pilipino student group in Long Beach who we're meeting with next week and we're going to ask Bandini alumni to help us find connections with community college student groups. And of course we'll need all of you to be part of this. I guess I'm saying that we need to understand each other more. We need to know where we're coming from so we can work together to change this thing up. Otherwise, we're just competing over little crumbs anyway." Students nodded and a few nudged each other as Lynette made this last point. I had read in the paper a few years back that Bandini had a 'race riot' between Black and Latina/o students. I was quite impressed that these students had made such apparent strides in coalition building. I made a mental note to ask later about how these efforts were initially mediated.

Aaron said, "Among Latinas/os we also have issues we need to deal with. On the ESL tracks, we sometimes have students who just got here from Mexico or Central America and they don't speak Spanish or English. They speak Mixteca, or Nahuatl, or Zapotec. And they're usually from places in the country instead of the city. So here we are thinking that we're better than these students just because we were born here or we speak English or whatever. But they're probably smarter than us. They have to learn two new languages, Spanish and English. I think we need to first have more classes here that teach us about culture, immigration, history, or whatever so we don't treat students on the ESL tracks like aliens or wetbacks."

Gilbert looked ready to interject into the dialogue when he heard the derogatory language, but he waited as a student named Maya spoke. Maya had medium brown skin and straight brown hair that barely reached her ears. Her lip quivered but her voice stayed calm as she spoke. She said, "You know, *I* am one of *those* students who was called wetback when I first got here. And I think I know what you're trying to say, Aaron, but let's first question the whole idea that a person, a human being, can be illegal or a wetback. So, all of you are only a green piece of paper away from being an alien? We shouldn't treat anyone like that. If we are supposed to be all united and be 'Students Who Care,' then we should start by caring about each other. We need to have a goal for all of us, not just for one group to be on top and then everyone else gets treated like *chusma*."[112] Other students nodded along with Maya's comments.

The students sat quietly, reflecting on all that had been said. After a few moments of silence, Chepe, a light-skinned student with straight black hair, a round face, and dark eyebrows asked, "Can you add racist teachers to that list? Most Bandini teachers don't expect us to even pass their class. Like they've seen too many of those movies. We're not those Hollywood *Dangerous Minds, 187, The Substitute* kind of students.[113] I don't even think there *is* that kind of student. Bandini is pretty much the barrio, the ghetto, whatever, and you never see students threatening the teachers and dancing on the chairs in class. So where did they get those images from? You know what? I'm not like that. My dad is not like that. My brothers aren't like that. My cousins aren't like that. You know, it's a lie... And it's not fair that... every major film shows just the bad side of Mexicans.[114] And then on the news, the TV only talks about bad things coming out of Bandini High. How am I supposed to do good in my classes when my teachers treat me like I'm a drug dealer? I have a car because I've been saving my money from working since I was 11! Not because I sell drugs."

Nick teased, "But you do have a nice car, though." Chepe rolled his eyes and smiled, sitting back in his chair and saying, "I know, it's pretty cool, but you know what I'm saying." "For sure," Nick nodded emphatically.

Monica remarked, "There's just too many of us in a small space. We should put that on the list. There's too many students for one school, even on the year-round tracks. And if we add up what Lynette and Chepe said, it's like we need to look at the ways the school expects us to fail and actually prepares us to fail. I'm not in AP, but doesn't that mean I should have *more* instead of less? More teachers who know what they're doing, better books, and actual animals to dissect in science class instead of just a worksheet to read about it? Why do they give all the extra stuff, the good teachers and everything to the students who are probably already going to college? What about the rest of us?"

América added, "Exactly! I'm one of like four Latinas/os and Blacks in the AP classes. And the only reason is because my older sister, Alejandra, goes to UC-Oceanview. She helps me sign up for my classes and she made the teacher accept me into the AP class last year. She told me I need to get higher than a 4.0 GPA if I want to go to a university straight from Bandini. A lot of students at other schools take like 18 AP classes and pass so many AP exams they start college as a sophomore already![115] I feel lucky to have the chance to be in AP classes. I'm lucky to have a sister in college who can guide me on what to do to get there. But so many other students are smarter than me. They're gifted and talented, but they just aren't lucky, so they don't get the chance to go on."

Maya responded, "Education shouldn't depend on luck." Many students shook their heads. Lynette added, "And we want to go to college without having to risk our lives going to the military first." Students nodded their heads.

The basketball team walked into the gym from the locker room and started warming up for practice. Seeing that the meeting would have to end, América stood up and said, "Well, we didn't have a chance to talk about the stupid exam that seniors have to pass to graduate, so make sure we have your info and we'll plan another *encuentro* soon." Some students stood and stretched, picking up their backpacks to leave. América got Lynette's attention and they started clapping their hands together slowly. The MEChA and BSU students caught on right away and joined in the clap. Soon, all the students and the teachers were clapping in unison. "*Que viva los estudiantes!*" Gilbert yelled. "*Que viva!*" we all yelled back.

And the Train Keeps Movin': Claudia's Reflections of Bandini High

Watching the beautiful stars in the night sky on the train ride home, I thought about Bandini High. I would have to follow up with the teachers and figure out how we could continue our dialogue. Even though I stayed for a few hours after the student *encuentro*, I didn't quite finish scanning all their documents and photos. And since this was such a short trip, I hadn't had a chance to connect with my colleague Leticia Garcia at UC-Oceanview.[116]

The day's discussions flew by so fast! I didn't get to share with the teachers that I had clerked with Justice Thurgood Marshall for a few years after law school. Marshall was the only Justice to dissent the majority opinion when the *Crawford* case was argued before the Supreme Court in 1982. He was frustrated that California voters had approved Proposition 1 in 1979, which forbade State courts from mandating bussing or any desegregation plan. Eight of the nine Justices found that Proposition 1 didn't violate students' Fourteenth Amendment right to equal protection, and therefore the State court could not mandate the Los Angeles school board to bus students. Justice Marshall's dissent pointed out that Proposition 1 rewarded the very school boards that maintained segregated schools with the right to decide what form of remedy they would enact.[117] Justice Marshall and I discussed the frustrating reality that the majority of California voters were White, and according to the school districts' and State records, most of them no longer enrolled their kids in public schools. Even so, his colleagues on the Court insisted that Proposition 1 was race-neutral.[118]

I ordered a cup of tea from the service cart attendant and sat back down to go over my notes. Taking small sips of the very hot herbal tea, I read through my scribbles and marveled at the way history came to life through the experiences of the teachers and students at Bandini High. Even though I went to high school in suburban Orange County, I heard so much of my own experiences in their stories.

Toward the end of the students' discussion, the idea of talent and luck really struck me. The notion that schools regularly label White students as having talent and merit, but Students of Color feel lucky when granted the opportunity to attend a university. And students expressed that many teachers, staff, and administrators seemed disappointed to be "stuck" with them. Bandini would never again be the predominately White, middle-class neighborhood it once was. One out of every two Chicana/o youth under the age of 18 lives in poverty.[119] The connection between race and class hits right there at Bandini High everyday. But instead of being beaten down by the layers of racism, the teachers and students I met and listened to today seemed to be drawing strength from their experiences and histories.

I jotted down a few notes so I would remember some of the multilayered concerns expressed by students and teachers:

- Emphasis on military instead of college: more military than college recruiters
- Heavy police presence: students feel school is a prison, and they're treated like criminals
- Overcrowding: very high student–teacher ratio, no toilet paper, no water fountains
- Low teacher expectations, teacher turnover rate high, substitutes all year long
- Counselors discouraging students' dreams instead of nurturing aspirations
- Textbooks: not enough for each student, culturally biased, outdated
- Standardized tests: holding students accountable for failures of system, they don't consider schooling conditions, lack of trained teachers, we give them the worst and then blame them for not performing well
- Tracking: ESL/sheltered, vocational, college prep, and AP, like a caste system?

I then thought about the numerous lawsuits we had discussed in the teachers' lounge. Chicana/o parents initiated many of those cases. From *Alvarez v. Lemon Grove* and *Mendez v. Westminster* to *Serrano v. Priest, Rodriguez v. LAUSD*, and *Diaz v. SJUSD*, and so many others. It amazes me that there is still an assumption that Chicana/o parents "just don't care" about their children's education. And legal remedies are only one form of resistance against inequality. I wrote:

- AP courses develop students' academic talents so they can continue to advance.

I paused again, trying to recall the authors' names from a study showing that White parents threatened to pull their children out of a public high school that granted Chicana/o and Black students access to AP and honors programs.[120] AP means students can earn higher GPAs and college credits, which of course means they are more likely to be granted admission to a 4-year university straight from high school. And that preferential treatment for White and Asian American students comes at the expense of Chicana/o and Black students. Forty years after civil rights legislation, access to quality education remains elusive.

I had recently worked on two cases focused on the link between AP and university access. In the *Daniels v. State of California*[121] case, four high school Students of Color from the predominately African American—increasingly Latina/o—California community of Inglewood sued the State for denying equal access to AP courses across school districts. These students emphasized that the responsibility for making sure students are college bound resides with those sending institutions—local school districts—and ultimately with the State. A consent decree was reached before the trial, and the State promised an "AP Challenge Grant Program" to support high schools in building stronger AP programs.[122] I couldn't help but feel a little cynical, though, thinking about the governor's recently proposed cuts to education in the State budget. I wonder how the AP Challenge Grant money will fare in this "budget crisis" and whether students in the many school districts across California have seen a difference in their high schools' AP programs. Inglewood is adjacent to Lennox, a predominately Mexican and Salvadoran neighborhood near the Los Angeles airport. I thought back to Lynette's remarks about the close proximity of Black and Latina/o communities and the tenuous relationships between them. Her comments reveal wisdom beyond her years.

In the *Castañeda v. University of California Regents*[123] case, African American, Latina/o, and Pilipino students argued that the receiving institutions—universities—perpetuate racial inequality by rewarding extra grade points and college credits for AP, knowing not all students have AP access. *Castañeda* also went to consent decree, and UC-Berkeley agreed to document and make publicly available their admissions data, broken down by racial subgroups.[124] I felt quite disappointed with this consent decree because the defendants will seemingly continue with the same admissions policies and procedures that privilege Whites through AP. I still wonder whether the outcome would be any different had *Castañeda* gone to trial. But then again, it has become much more difficult to show "disparate impact" because of Supreme Court rulings insisting individuals and groups who claim discrimination must show that the discriminator *intended* to hurt them.[125]

And neither *Castañeda* nor *Daniels* addressed the racialized school-within-a-school aspect of AP. As the students iterated today, even predominately Black and Chicana/o schools like Bandini often restrict AP course access to Whites and Asian American students.[126] I sighed, thinking that sometimes legal remedies don't feel like remedies at all. Racism keeps changing forms, and it seems change through the law occurs at a much slower pace—with much more "*deliberate* speed."

Of course, AP is just one window into all the educational inequalities Chicanas/os face. And that's why TRIO programs—which take those affirmative steps to ensure students are "upward bound"—continue to be necessary. Taking down a few more notes, I wrote:

- What if we focused on *affirmative development*? What does it mean to affirm and develop the academic talents of Chicana/o and Black high school students with the intent of preparing them for college?[127]

Then, I scribbled a reminder to myself to send an email to Letty and ask her about some of her articles referencing the effective schools[128] and accelerated schools[129] literature. Letty and I took different paths since college, but we both ended up in academia, still committed to civil rights. I felt a deep pang in my stomach, thinking about all those Chicana/o students the system failed—students whose talents were not affirmed or developed.

Finishing up my *te de manzanillo*, I found a small travel blanket in my bag to drape over my legs. I gazed out at the full moon reflecting off the dark water[130] and felt both depressed and hopeful. Schooling still has the power to oppress and marginalize along the "color-line" that W.E.B. DuBois wrote about over a century ago.[131] Can education—rooted in a sense of community responsibility and with a goal of racial and social justice—transform society? Looking at public schools today, clearly U.S. society knows how to reproduce racial inequality through the school system. The steady sound of the train moving down the tracks began to lull me to sleep. Still, I reminded myself, Chicana/o communities have responded and resisted this pattern of structural inequality in various forms. Education also has the potential to emancipate and empower ... As I dozed off, I began to dream of having a conversation with Letty about whether the revolution in education would be televised.[132]

NOTES

1. Bandini is a composite comprehensive high school in Los Angeles, California.
2. For population growth trends, see Chapa & Valencia, 1993; For segregation and desegregation trends in public schools, see Orfield & Monfort, 1992; For segregation and desegregation trends emphasizing Chicanas/os in particular, see Donato, Menchaca, & Valencia, 1991; Valencia, Menchaca, & Donato, 2002; For current school conditions, see for example report by Californians for Justice, 2003.
3. *Williams, et al. v. State of California*, 2000. Case No. 312236, Superior Court of the State of California for the County of San Francisco. Settlement, August 2004. The 2004 *Williams v. State of California* settlement is one example of legislative efforts to ensure minimal standards in public education. Plaintiffs requested well-maintained school facilities that can meet the capacity of the number of students, trained teachers, and sufficient numbers of updated textbooks. See Oakes & Lipton, 2004
4. See Carter, 1972; Carter & Segura, 1979; Arias, 1986
5. See González, 1990; Menchaca, 1995; Moreno, 1999
6. Historian George Sanchez (1997) explains, "In the schools, socialization in American values and language skills were even more emphatically combined with a goal of social stability.... At the secondary level, citizenship classes were integrated into vocational training for laundries, restaurants, garages, household work, and agriculture (p. 105).
7. Paul Freire (1973) identifies and critiques this banking method.
8. This experience is not necessarily unique to Mexicans; rather, public schools have historically prepared Black, Puerto Rican, Native American, and low-income students to take direction without question, memorize without critical analysis, and focus on remedial, manual, labor-focused curriculum rather than a college-bound curriculum. Indeed, the traditional curriculum prepares Students of Color and working class Whites to serve upper and middle class interests (Anyon, 1980; Bowles & Gintis, 1976; McLaren, 1994). Students of Color are most often prepared to fill the ranks of the working class through curriculum that minimizes their intellectual growth and maximizes opportunities to teach menial labor skills.
9. Frederick Taylor (1911) outlined this "scientific management" approach. Inspired by the productivity of the industrial revolution, scholars theorized that the functionality of the industrial assembly line should transfer to the curriculum—to the schoolhouse. This meant developing school curriculum that could "produce top-of-the-line" students (Bobbitt, 1918, 1924; Bloom, 1966, 1969). See also the Tyler Rationale (Tyler, 1949).
10. See Valencia & Aburto, 1991; See also Rueda, Artiles, Salazar, & Higareda, 2002; Valdés & Figueroa, 1994.
11. Valencia, Menchaca, & Donato, 2002.
12. Jeannie Oakes (1986) describes: "Poor and minority youngsters (principally black and Hispanic) are disproportionately placed in tracks for low-ability or non-college bound students ... minority students are consistently underrepresented in programs for the gifted and talented ... blacks and Hispanics [are] more frequently enrolled in programs that train students for the lowest-level occupations (e.g., building maintenance, commercial sewing, and institutional care)" (p. 14).
13. Haycock & Navarro, 1988; Oakes, 1985, 1990; Valencia, 1991, 2002

14. For example, to be minimally eligible for admission as a freshman to a University of California (UC) campus, high school students must take a college preparatory curriculum called the "a–g" requirements. These requirements include 2 years of history, 4 years of English, 3 years of math, 2 years of laboratory science, 2 years of foreign language, 2 years of college preparatory electives, and 1 year of a performing or fine arts elective. Not all high schools in California offer the "a–g" requirements, and within schools that do offer these courses, many students are tracked away from these classes. Only 23% of Latinas/os who graduate from public high schools in California have completed the minimal requirements to enroll in a 4-year state college. California Congressman Richard Alarcon's Senate Bill 383 has attempted to make the "a–g" requirements the "de facto" preparatory framework that all students take, but vocational education advocates have repeatedly lobbied against this bill. Successful implementation of such a bill would require structural changes at earlier levels of the pipeline so that students would be academically prepared to engage in a rigorous college preparatory program of study in high school. On June 14, 2005, after extensive student and community organizing, and with the support of School Board President Jose Huizar, the Los Angeles Unified School District School Board voted 6–1 to approve a curriculum plan mandating that all students complete the "a–g" requirements to graduate high school (Hayasaki, 2005). In Oakland, California, activists and educators have mobilized to ensure vocational education programs and college preparatory programs are not mutually exclusive. This approach aims to teach vocational skills while preparing students to study those vocations in college. Instead of preparing students to work as menial laborers after high school, this approach assists students to continue on to college and pursue careers in engineering, architecture, and science.
15. Pachon & de la Garza, 1996
16. See Pachon & Tokofksy, 2000
17. Solórzano Ornelas, 2002
18. Solórzano & Ornelas, 2004
19. See Hispanic Policy Development Project, 1984; Lucas, Henze, & Donato, 1990
20. See Proposition 227 in California; Proposition 203 in Arizona.
21. See, for example, tables from California Department of Education, http://data1.cde.ca.gov/ dataquest. See also Harris, 2002
22. Californians for Justice, 2003; Harris, 2002
23. Darling-Hammond, 1988; Haycock & Navarro, 1988; Los Angeles County Office of Education, 1994; Malcom, 1990; Tomas Rivera Center, 1993
24. Statewide for the 2003–04 school year, students enrolled in California public schools were 32.5% White, 46% Latina/o, 8.1% African American, 2.5% Pilipino, 8% Asian American, 0.6% Pacific Asian Islander, and 0.8% Native American. During the same 2003–04 school year, California teachers were 73.5% White, 14.2% Latina/o, 4.7% African American, 1.2% Pilipino, 4.5% Asian American, 0.2% Pacific Asian Islander, and 0.6% Native American. Most California counties had 80–90% White teachers. Exceptions to this pattern included Imperial County, where teachers were 48.2% Latina/o, 47.5% White, 1.1% African American, 0.5% Pilipino, 0.9%, Asian American, 0.1% Pacific Asian Islander, and 0.6% Native American; and Los Angeles County, where teachers were 57% White, 33% Latina/o, 9.8% African American, 1.7% Pilipino, 7.3% Asian American, 0.3% Pacific Asian Islander, and 0.6% Native American. See http://data1 .cde. ca.gov/dataquest/
25. Ceja, 2001
26. Cortés, 2000; Council on Interracial Books for Children, 1977
27. See Garcia, J., 1980; Salvucci, 1991
28. For specifics about the NCLB, see "Guide: the No Child Left Behind Act's Military Recruitment Provision & Opt-Out Practice" from Josh Sonnenfeld of the Santa Cruz-based Resource Center for Nonviolence http://www.rcnv.org/counterrecruit/optout/ (Retrieved June 20, 2005). As a result of the NCLB, students, parents, and other activists have organized to inform communities about military recruitment in public schools. See for example, Cave, 2005; Hakeem, 2005; Paton, 2005; Weill-Greenberg, 2005.

29. See Valencia & Bernal, 2000
30. For further discussion of standardized exam policies for English language learners to graduate high school in Arizona, Texas, New Mexico, and California, see Garcia, P., 2003.
31. For discussion of Texas' high school exit exam, see Valenzuela, 2000.
32. See García, P. A. & Gopal, 2003
33. See Californians for Justice Education Fund, 2003; Helfand, 2002
34. See Valenzuela, 1999
35. See Stanton Salazar, 2001
36. See Espinosa, Fernández, & Dornbusch, 1977; See also Solórzano, 1992
37. Still, students who are showing academic potential and persistence receive very little direction in terms of how to pursue their academic goals. For example, research shows that Chicanas excelling in high school science courses received minimal guidance about how to pursue a science career or how college was linked to their science goals. See O'Halloran, 1995
38. See Talavera-Bustillos, 1998
39. For more on "triggers" of resistance in pursuit of higher education, see Talavera-Bustillos, 1998; for more on the concept of "prove them wrong," see Yosso, 2000
40. Delgado Bernal, 1997; Solórzano & Delgado Bernal, 2001
41. For example, Youth Organizing Communities (YOC) is a network of youth organizers from Los Angeles, Oakland, San Diego, and San Francisco who fight for "schools not jails," educational and environmental justice, more youth programs, ethnic studies classes, and social change (http://www.SchoolsNotJails.com). In addition, see *Questions for Answers* (Social Justice in Education Project, prd., 2004), created by high school students in Tucson, Arizona. See also Project YANO. Since its founding in 1984, the nonprofit organization Project on Youth and Non-Military Opportunities has sought to educate school officials about the need to give students a more balanced view on the military, urging schools to make students and their families more aware of how to protect their privacy by using their right to opt out if student information is going to be released to military recruiters (http://www.projectyano.org/). See also Twin Cities based student group: Youth Against War and Racism (http://www.yawr.org/cr.htm).
42. Even though student resistance that takes on a transformative form is rarely deemed "newsworthy," a sampling of recent news headlines confirms this pattern of student organizing. "Students Protest in Walkout at Fremont," (Smith, 1999); "High School Students Organize 'Union' to Work for Change," (Schwartz, 2000); "South LA Pupils Demand More College Prep Classes," (Helfand, 2000); "High School Students Protest Poor Facilities, Programs in Compton," (Mathews, 2000); "Pupils Press Demands for Prep Classes," (Helfand, 2001); "*Exigen escuelas para el este de LA*" (Durán, 2003); "Schools see an awakening of student activism," (Hayasaki, 2003). See also "School Progress in Eastside Too Slow," (Vasquez, 2004). In this protest, students, parents, and community activists held a press conference displaying a banner that read "*Escuelas Si, Guerra No!*" and demanded that the school district move faster to construct new high schools to relieve the overcrowding of Roosevelt and Garfield High—two of the multiple East Los Angeles high schools where students walked out in protest of poor conditions in 1968. More and more, students articulate these struggles as multiracial and multicultural movements.
43. I named this composite Los Angeles school Arcadia Bandini High School, in honor of the historical figure by the same name. Bandini (1827–1912), a Mexican philanthropist from California, donated expansive parcels of land for schools, hospitals, cemeteries, parks, and other public facilities throughout Los Angeles and surrounding cities. Further discussion of her history and philanthropy extends beyond the scope of this chapter.
44. Claudia is a composite character who also appears in Solórzano & Yosso, 2000, 2002a. Bayside Law School refers to a composite school of law in northern California.
45. Alvarez, 2005
46. Upward Bound originated from the Economic Opportunity Act of 1964 and the Johnson administration's War on Poverty and Talent Search came out of Title IV of the Higher Education Act of 1965. The TRIO programs have since become Upward Bound, Talent Search, Student Support Services, Educational Opportunity Centers, the Ronald E. McNair Postbaccalaureate

Achievement Program, the TRIO Dissemination Partnership Program, the Training Program for Federal TRIO Programs Staff, and Upward Bound Math/Science. For more information and history on TRIO programs, see http://www.ed.gov/about/offices/list/ope/trio/index.html.

47. For example, Civil Rights Act, 1964; Voting Rights Act, 1965; Fair Housing Act, 1968.

48. *Brown v. Board of Education of Topeka*, 347 U.S. 483 (1954).

49. Carter G. Woodson founded Negro History Week in 1926 and because Frederick Douglas and president Lincoln share a February birthday, February was chosen in the late 1960s for the implementation of Afro-American History Month, also known as Black History Month.

50. *Daniels v. State of California*, 1999; *Castañeda v. Regents of the University of California*, 1999; *Williams v. State of California*, 2000.

51. For example, see John Caughey's (1973) discussion of community-based "Transport a Child," and "Parents for Better Educational Exchange," as well as the school board's APEX program, pp. 28–34; See also Rogers, 2004a

52. *Crawford v. Board of Education of the City of Los Angeles* was filed in 1963 and first went to court in 1968. See Cal. 3d 280, 302, 551 P. 2d 28, 42 (1976) (*Crawford I*). In response to the court's finding that Los Angeles schools were indeed racially segregated, the school board created magnet schools, "voluntary" busing plans, and developed cluster schools to encourage voluntary desegregation. See Carlos Haro's 1977 monograph on concerns over *Crawford* in relation to Los Angeles' Chicana/o communities. In 1979, voters in the State of California passed Proposition 1, a ballot initiative forbidding state courts from *mandating* school districts to transport or assign students for desegregation purposes. It did not preclude school districts from taking affirmative steps to desegregate, but it ensured those steps would be voluntary unless the federal courts deemed otherwise. In reviewing *Crawford* in 1982, the U.S. Supreme Court voted 8 to 1 that California's Proposition 1 did not violate the Fourteenth Amendment, and therefore, school districts maintained the right to determine which type of desegregation they would implement (458 U.S. 527 (1982) (*Crawford II*).

53. See *Boston Herald* photo by Stanley Forman. Photo republished by *The College Board Review* (2004) with the caption: "The face of northern racism, 22 years after *Brown v. Board*. An anti-busing demonstrator turning the American flag into a lance, joins an attack by other whites on an African American lawyer outside Boston City Hall in 1976" (p. 46).

54. Argued before the U.S. Supreme Court in March 1982, and when the Court rendered its decision on *Crawford* that June, the majority opinion cited this demographic change: "In 1968 when the case went to trial, the District was 53.6% white, 22.6% black, 20% Hispanic, and 3.8% Asian and other. By October 1980 the demographic composition had altered radically: 23.7% white, 23.3% black, 45.3% Hispanic, and 7.7% Asian and other" 458 U.S. 527, 530. The lower court had also noted this trend, adding that "The number of white pupils in grades K–3 had fallen to 16.1%" 113 Cal. App. 3d 633, 642 (1980). White flight began well before the *Crawford* case made it to court (Rogers, 2004b).

55. See Bell, 1986

56. *Brown v. Board of Education*, 349 U.S. 294 (1955). (Brown II). In his draft of the ruling striking down segregation, Chief Justice Warren initially wrote "Decrees in conformity with this decree shall be prepared and issued forthwith by the lower courts," but after conferencing with the other Justices, he changed the text to read "all deliberate speed" (349 U.S. 294, 299).

57. For example, the *Los Angeles Times* quotes Long Beach Unified School District Superintendent Carl Cohen confirming that magnet programs aim to attract and serve White students. The article contends, "School officials also launched two magnet programs for gifted and academically talented students that are widely credited as instrumental in [Long Beach] Poly's turnaround....The magnet programs, [Superintendent] Cohen said, 'were clearly designed to bring in white youngsters from other parts of the city'" (Shuit, 1998, p. A1).

58. *Diaz et al. v. San Jose Unified School District* was originally filed in 1971 on behalf of "Spanish-surnamed" students who resided predominantly in the northern downtown parts of the city and attended segregated schools. At the trial in 1974, the District in this case argued that they were indeed racially imbalanced, but had no control over demographic and residential patterns,

which were racially segregated. See *Diaz v. San Jose Unified School District*, 412 F. Supp. 310, 334 (N.D. Cal. 1976). White flight in San Jose occurred at a slower pace than in Los Angeles public schools. As San Jose's population grew, new schools were built in the South to accommodate predominately White suburban students, while the number of portable classrooms increased on the Northside. The plaintiffs repeatedly appealed using the language of *Crawford*. In 1983, the Ninth Circuit judges decided that the District was not *intentionally* maintaining segregate schools and the state could not *mandate* the form of desegregation. See 633 F. Supp. 808; 1985 U.S. Dist. Instead of following the outlined "controlled choice" plan of the plaintiffs, in March 1986, San Jose Unified implemented a combination of voluntary student assignment programs, including magnet, enrichment, and programs of "excellence" to desegregate the district. This voluntary desegregation plan was affirmed by the court in 1988, see *Diaz v. San Jose Unified School District* 861 F.2d 591; 1988 U.S. App.

59. See, for example, the course reader "Race, Class and Power in Latina/o Communities" from Political Science m147A on file with Raymond Rocco, Associate Professor, UCLA.
60. See Nicolaides, 2002
61. See Soja, 1989, 1987; Villanueva, Erdman, & Howlett, 2000; Zentgraf, 1989
62. This act also granted exceptions for political refugees and family members of U.S. citizens.
63. Moore & Vigil, 1993; Sassen, 1992
64. Lopez-Garza, 1992; Valle & Torres, 1994
65. See similar commentary on availability of basic necessities and quality of life issues connected to schooling in Tucson, AZ in film by Cholla High School students, *Questions for Answers* (Social Justice in Education Project, 2004).
66. Pamela Bettis (1994, 1996) speaks to some of the effects of deindustrialization on urban, working-class high school students.
67. See Shapiro, 2004
68. *Serrano v. Priest*, 487 P.2d 1241 (Cal. 1971).
69. *San Antonio Independent School District v. Rodriguez*, 411 U.S. 1 (1973).
70. *Serrano v. Priest*, 557 P.2d 929 (Cal. 1976).
71. Indeed, there is strong evidence indicating that voters in California voted for Proposition 13 hoping to circumvent perceived effects of *Serrano v. Priest*. See Fischel, 1989, 1996, 2004; See also Silva & Sonstelie, 1995. Furthermore, James E. Ryan (1999) cites two studies (Reed, 1998; Tedin, 1994) from Texas and New York suggesting that White voters in these states supported tax reform–based on their beliefs that Blacks were privileged by the current system and that Whites would benefit from tax reform. See Reed, 1998; Tedin, 1994
72. *Rodriguez v. Los Angeles Unified School District* C611 358. (1986). The consent decree (1992) asserted that starting in the academic year 1992–93 and with a target date of no later than the 1997–98 school year, LAUSD would: (1) Equalize of basic norm resources, (2) equalize of access to experienced teachers, (3) build new schools to alleviate overcrowding, (4) reorganize large schools into more educationally sound structures, and (5) bring decision making to the local level.
73. See Ryan, 1999; Wells & Crain, 1997
74. See Haney Lopez, 1994; Montoya, 2001; Perea, 2004
75. See *Álvarez v. Lemon Grove School District*. (1931). Superior Court of the State of California, County of San Diego, petition for Writ of Mandate, No. 66625; Espinosa, 1986; González, 1990, 1999; See also Menchaca, 1995
76. For example, Edward Banfield (1970) believed lower-class students should be "schooled" in a vocation because culturally they could not appreciate or benefit from a comprehensive, liberal arts "education." Cecilia Heller (1996) asserted that Mexican Americans maintained cultural values that hindered their social mobility.
77. Sanchez, 1997
78. *Mendez v. Westminster*, 64 F. Supp. 544 (S.D. Cal. 1946). The ninth Circuit court upheld the district court opinion. In *Mendez v. Westminster*, 161 F. 2d 744 (9th Cir. 1947).
79. See Education Codes 8003-8004. California Statutes and Ammendments to the Codes: Division 4, Chapter 1, Article 1, Public Schools. Section 8003 "Schools for Indian children, and children

of Chinese, Japanese, or Mongolian parentage: Establishment. The governing board of any school district may establish separate schools for Indian children, excepting children of Indians who are wards of the United States Government and children of all other Indians who are descendants of the original American Indians of the United States, and for children of Chinese, Japanese, or Mongolian parentage." (Repealed by Statutes and Amendments to the Codes 1947, chapter 737, p. 1792). See also Section 8004 "Same: Admission of children into other schools. When separate schools are established for Indian children or children of Chinese, Japanese, or Mongolian parentage, the Indian children or children of Chinese, Japanese, or Mongolian parentage shall not be admitted to any other school." (Repealed by Statutes and Amendments to the Codes 1947, chapter 737, p. 1792).

80. See for example, Aguirre, 2004; Valencia, 2005; Wollenberg, 1976, 2004
81. See Morris, 1999
82. See for example effects on teachers in Florida schools (Abney, 1974).
83. See Smith, 2004
84. See Love, 2004; Perea, 2004
85. Delgado Bernal, 1998
86. See X, Malcolm, 1992
87. Sal Castro interview. See Racho, 1996
88. *Bakke v. Regents of University of California*, 438 U.S. 265 (1978). For further discussion of this case, see Solórzano & Yosso, 2002a.
89. Freire, 1970, 1973
90. See Leonardo, 2004; McIntosh, 1989
91. The "interest convergence" theory, posited by Derrick Bell (1980, 1987), asserts that civil rights gains are usually granted because White society benefits socially, economically, or politically.
92. Mary Dudziak's (1988, 2000) historical analysis of the Cold War era confirms Bell's "interest-convergence" theory.
93. For more on racial microaggressions, see Solórzano, 1998
94. *Lau v. Nichols*, 94 S.Ct. 786 (1974) confirmed the rights of English language learners set out by the 1968 Bilingual Education Act. The Justices in the *Lau v. Nichols* case found that Chinese students in San Francisco were being discriminated against because the school district did not support their primary language.
95. Lyons, 1990
96. Ortiz, 1977
97. See Laosa, 1977
98. Bailey & Galvan, 1977
99. Freire, 1973
100. Persell, 1977
101. Quoted in Anzaldúa, 1987, p. 53. Anzaldúa cites Smith's unpublished book *Moorland is Cold Country*. Originally from Wales, Smith worked as an artist in Los Angeles, in the late 1960s and since then has continued painting and exhibiting from her studio in the Santa Cruz mountains. This is likely where Smith met Anzaldúa, who resided in Santa Cruz for much of her professional career and up until her death in May 2004. In 2004, Smith created a painting also titled, "Moorland is Cold Country." See http://www.raygwyn.com/
102. See Columbia Pictures' *La Bamba*, written and directed by Luis Valdez (Hackford & Borden, prds., 1987).
103. *La Bamba* portrays the biography of Mexican American rock-and-roll legend Richie Valens (Valenzuela). According to the film, the song "Oh Donna" was written about Valens' high school sweetheart, a young White woman whose parents disapproved of their daughter dating a Mexican American.
104. Angela Valenzuela's (1999) ethnographic study of Chicana/o high school students in Texas demonstrates that the sense that teachers and administrators "don't care" about students resonates in contemporary school settings. She finds that high school structures, practices, and discourses "subtract" from Chicana/o students' cultural identity and academic aspirations, and eventually

push them out of the system altogether. See also Marcos Pizarro's (2005) ethnographic account of Chicana/o students in urban East Los Angeles and rural Washington state high schools.

105. The documentary film *The Panama Deception* reveals some of the U.S.-led assault while also addressing the mainstream news media's complicity with the military (see Empowerment Project, prd., 1992). *The Panama Deception* won the Academy Award for Best Documentary Film in 1993.

106. For a first-hand account of Chicanos in Vietnam, see Trujillo, 1990

107. BSU (Black Student Union) and MEChA (*Movimiento Estudiantil Chicana/o de Aztlan*) refer to actual student groups often organized on high school and college campuses. Students Who Care represents the many student-initiated coalitions in these same settings. See also the community-initiated coalition addressing ongoing racial inequality in Rockford, Illinois public schools, People Who Care (Chapman, 2005; *People Who Care v. Rockford Board of Education*, 2001).

108. For further discussion of the health hazards posed by unsanitary bathroom conditions in schools enrolling predominately low-income Students of Color, see Californians for Justice Education Fund, 2003.

109. The little one.

110. High school student Barbara Johns organized a student strike against Moton High School in Farmville, Virginia, and led 450 students to a walkout on April 23, 1951, to demand a new, updated, and quality school. Thurgood Marshall persuaded attorneys from the NAACP to meet with the students and broaden their demand for a new school to instead insist that the court eliminate segregated schools in Virginia. The students' actions led to the *Davis v. the School Board of Prince Edward County* lawsuit, one of the five suits brought before the Supreme Court in *Brown v. Board of Education* in 1954.

111. See Delgado Bernal, 1997; Racho, 1996

112. Lowlifes.

113. These Hollywood films portray Latina/o and Black students as unintelligent, prone to violence, and in need of a teacher or administrator to save them (Mandel, dir., 1996; Reynolds, dir., 1997; Simpson & Bruckheimer, prds., 1995). See analysis of these and other urban-high-school genre films by Robert Bulman (2002). See also Yosso, 2000, 2002a

114. Chepe's remarks draw directly from interview data compiled in Yosso, 2000. See also Yosso, 2002a

115. This represents the average number of AP courses taken by UCLA freshman admitted in the 1997–98 school year.

116. See Solórzano & Yosso, 2002a.

117. "California's Proposition 1 works an unconstitutional reallocation of state power by depriving California courts of the ability to grant meaningful relief to those seeking to vindicate the State's guarantee against de facto segregation in the public schools" Justice Marshall's dissent in *Crawford v. Board of Education of the City of Los Angeles*, 458 U.S. 527, 547.

118. Justice Marshall's dissent points out that the *Crawford II* ruling contradicted previous rulings conceding that racial minorities experienced a "special burden" in trying to challenge state initiatives like Proposition 1, which carried specific "racial overtones." He believed Proposition 1 was racial "beyond reasonable dispute" and instead of helping the victims of segregation remedy their situation, the Court was violating the Fourteenth Amendment rights of California's schoolchildren.

119. See U.S. Bureau of the Census, 2000

120. See Wells & Serna, 1996

121. *Daniels et al. v. The State of California et al.* Superior Court of the State of California, Los Angeles. Superior Court, Case No. BC 214156, Plaintiff complaint, 1999. In this case the plaintiffs argued that they did not receive equal and adequate access to AP courses because their high school had too few AP courses available and offered very little encouragement or support to enroll in AP or take AP exams. This lack of access at the high school level meant plaintiffs could not compete fairly for university admissions. *Daniels* reveals that across California, a college preparatory, AP curriculum is more often available in predominately White and middle-class school districts than in urban or rural districts, where the population is predominately Students of Color.

122. *Daniels et al. v. The State of California et al.* Los Angeles Superior Court, Case No. BC 214156. Consent decree, 2003.

123. *Castañeda et al. v. Regents of the University of California et al.* United States District Court Northern District of California, Case No. C99-0525SI, Plaintiff complaint, 1999. High school students argued that UC Regents and UC-Berkeley violate the civil rights of Students of Color with admissions policies and procedures that privilege AP credits without acknowledging unequal access to AP. Plaintiffs contend that while UC-Berkeley's policy appears to be race-neutral, it has a disparate impact on African American, Latina/o, and Pilipino students, who are disproportionately denied admission. The policy emphasizes (1) AP enrollment, which means it looks highly on students who enroll in AP courses, as available at their high school. It also places importance on (2) weighted grade point average (GPA). Since students earn an extra grade point for each semester enrolled in an AP course, AP grades are "weighted" and students can thus earn more than a 4.0 GPA. In addition, the policy accepts passing scores on (3) AP exams for university credits. The *Castañeda* case asserted that given these layers of AP privilege in UC-Berkeley's admissions policy, highly qualified Students of Color cannot compete fairly for admission.

124. *Castañeda et al. v. Regents of the University of California et al.* Northern District of California Case No. C99-0525SI. Consent decree, 2003.

125. Eric Yamamoto and coauthors from the Racial Justice Center analyze legal cases up through the year 2000 that reduce the possibility for individuals to seek legal action to remedy institutionalized forms of discrimination that has a "disparate effect" on groups (Yamamoto, Serrano, Fenton, Gifford, Forman, Hoshijo, & Kim, 2000/2001).

126. See Ornelas & Solórzano, 2004.

127. Alexander Astin (1990) and Daniel Solórzano (1992, 1996) examine the need for a talent development approach in college and university settings. The concept of affirmative development generates from educational researcher Grace Carroll and her work with high schools and African American communities in Oakland, California.

128. See Brookover, 1985; Edmonds, 1979, 1984, 1986; Irvine, 1988; Solórzano & Solórzano, 1995

129. See Levin, 1986, 1987a, 1987b, 1989

130. See DuBois, 1920/2003

131. See DuBois, 1903/1994

132. See Scott-Heron, 1971. "The Revolution Will Not Be Televised." In *Pieces of Me* [Album]. This is also the name of an album released in 1974 where this spoken word/song is the lead track.

4

CHICANA/O UNDERGRADUATE
"STAGES OF PASSAGE"

Campus Racial Climate at Midwestern University[1]

INTRODUCTION

Out of every racial or ethnic group in the United States, Chicanas/os complete the fewest number of bachelor's degrees. The inequality of elementary and secondary school conditions—lack of access to quality facilities, teachers, and counselors; minimal access to college preparatory and enrichment curriculum; overreliance on biased standardized tests; and dismissive treatment of Chicana/o cultural strengths—contribute to these dismal statistics. This chapter begins to show how postsecondary education perpetuates many of these institutionalized inequalities.

Only 26 of every 100 Chicana/o elementary school students continue on to college. Chicanas/os most often begin their college career in a community college rather than a 4-year college or university.[2] Community colleges traditionally charge very low enrollment fees and maintain an open admissions policy, accepting all those who apply. With little access to appropriate high school counseling, courses that provide the minimum requirements to a 4-year college or university, or financial support, the community college often becomes the most viable option for Chicanas/os to pursue their education after high school. For example, of the 26 Chicanas/os who continue on to college after high school, 17 begin at a community college. Nationally, 70% of Chicanas/os who enroll in community colleges aspire to transfer to a 4-year college or university. However, less than 10% of these students reach their goals of transferring and earning a bachelor's degree.[3]

The same conditions that limit the opportunities for Chicanas/os at the primary and secondary levels of the educational pipeline persist as barriers to their success at the postsecondary level. For example, poor counseling, overcrowding, and limited financial resources contribute to the low transfer rates of Chicanas/os from community colleges to 4-year colleges and universities.[4] Often, upon arriving at the community college, students learn that they have been academically underprepared by their high schools and therefore must enroll in remedial coursework. These students may find only limited information about which courses "count" as units toward transfer. Overcrowding in community colleges, especially in urban areas, usually means limited access to courses, counselors, professors, library materials, and other support services. To fulfill necessary transfer requirements in this setting, students may need to wait until space opens up in impacted courses. In addition to these often unavoidable delays in their academic progress, Chicana/o students tend to receive misinformation about financial aid options and even when qualified for this assistance, most students still need to work full time while attending community college. For Chicana mothers, lack of access to quality childcare can also severely limit academic success.

Informed by cultural deficit beliefs about Chicanas/os, many community college administrators and counselors tend to encourage Chicanas/os toward vocationally oriented 2-year terminal degree programs (e.g., service technicians, medical assistants). So, even though Chicanas/os most often enter the community college with goals of transferring, low counselor and faculty expectations play a role in "cooling out" these dreams.[5] Rather than recognize the institutional responsibility to transfer Chicanas/os, many community colleges take the same position as their primary and secondary school counterparts and blame the students' culture, claiming Chicanas/os do not place enough "value" on higher education. Indeed, increasing access for Chicanas/os to postsecondary education requires that community colleges work to "develop an effective institutional transfer culture" that builds on the strengths and aspirations of Chicana/o communities.[6]

Of the 17 Chicanas/os who started their college education at the 2-year community college, only one will transfer to a 4-year college or university. At the 4-year college or university, the struggle continues for the one transfer student and nine Chicanas/os who started directly after high school. The success of Chicanas/os in U.S. historically White universities depends on their access to financial aid, counselors with high expectations, and quality retention programs. Again at the university level, Chicana/o students may feel underprepared and overwhelmed by the requirements of their new courses. They often must develop a whole new set of study skills and strategies to excel academically. Although these students have overcome seemingly insurmountable structures of inequality, they experience extreme levels of pressure to "prove" their intelligence and merit. While Chicanas/os meet and often exceed the requirements for college entrance, many students and faculty assume they arrived with "special admission" status and do not really "deserve" to attend a selective university.

Indeed, Chicanas/os experience much higher levels of stress compared to White undergraduate students. As they struggle to survive and succeed at the university, Chicana/o students express concerns about (1) student loan debt and employment to offset loans, (2) academic work and socioacademic adjustment, and (3) contributing financial support to their families.[7] For example, Chicana/o students may feel anxious about how they will pay for their books, uncomfortable as the only Chicana/o in their science classes, or even feel guilty for "making it" to college when their family and most of their community never received such an opportunity. However, Daniel Muñoz finds that these students "are often unaware of the sources of their anxiety, unhappiness, or guilt or of the effects that these can have on academic performance."[8] Because most Chicana/o parents cannot afford to financially support their child's college aspirations, many Chicana/o students take on more than one job, and some work full time while balancing a full course load. This leaves little time to speak with professors in office hours or ask an academic counselor for guidance, let alone participate in academic enrichment opportunities, tutoring or research programs. In addition, as students seek out mentors or role models to help guide their college journey, they rarely have opportunities to interact with Chicana/o faculty, who nationally make up approximately 1% of the professoriate.[9]

This chapter focuses on Chicana/o college experiences, and the processes of navigating through what researchers call a negative campus racial climate.[10] A negative campus racial climate refers to a social and academic environment that exhibits and cultivates racial and gender discrimination against People of Color. Within such a climate, People of Color often experience racialized verbal or nonverbal insults[11] (microaggressions) in academic and social settings. Through these racialized and gendered insults, students, professors, or staff question Chicana/o students' academic merits and their very presence on a university campus. Enduring racial microaggressions in an already isolating context may cause Chicana/o students to feel disregarded, alone, and frustrated. Eventually, these microaggressions can also lead to a diminished sense of confidence.

To excel at the university then, a Chicana/o undergraduate must succeed academically, and survive a hostile social climate where racial and gender stereotypes threaten to diminish their potential. Claude Steele and Joshua Aronson's research explains that in high stress standardized testing situations (e.g., SAT, GRE), societal stereotypes about race, gender, and intelligence become more salient for Students of Color, and pose a "stereotype threat."[12] Specifically, this research shows that Students of Color believe their test performance will reinforce racial and gender stereotypes presupposing for example that Blacks lack intelligence or women lack capacity for mathematics. Internalizing these racial and gender stereotypes causes Students of Color to doubt their ability to succeed. Steele and Aronson find that in testing situations where students believe their intelligence or aptitude will be measured, the "stereotype threat" becomes a reality. The tests usually prompt students to indicate their race and gender as part of their identifying information. These prompts, as well as other visual and verbal incidents occurring before an exam (e.g., seeing a Chicano gardener, talking about an African American sports figure, seeing a Chicana with children) may serve to remind students of the stereotypes associated with being a woman or a Person of Color in the United States. As a result, students underperform on the exam.[13]

When subtle and overt incidents of racial and gender discrimination occur daily, this phenomenon of "stereotype threat" extends beyond a testing situation and becomes an environmental threat. For example, in a negative campus racial climate, Chicanas/os tend to feel extreme pressure to serve as the spokesperson and representative for all Latinas/os. If a Chicana/o succeeds academically, she/he may be perceived as an exception to racial and gender stereotypes. However, when a Chicana/o does not excel, she/he may indeed feel her/his actions have confirmed racial and gender stereotypes. In this context, failure does not reflect on an individual Chicana/o, but instead becomes representative of all Chicanas/os. A negative campus racial climate thus injures Students of Color, who may eventually change majors (often away from math, science, or engineering), extend their time-to-degree, leave school, earn a low grade point average, and/or end up with a diminished self-concept.

Still, just as they critique inequalities at the K–12 levels, Chicana/o students resist racism and sexism through higher education.[14] Chicana/o college students also give back to their communities by sharing their struggles and successes with young Chicana/o students.[15] To share some of these experiences, this chapter's counterstory draws primarily on three sources of empirical data, including: (1) Focus group and survey data investigating campus racial climate at four universities in 2000 (University of Michigan, Michigan State, Harvard, and UC-Berkeley);[16] (2) Focus group data addressing navigation experiences of UCLA Chicana/o undergraduates in 1999;[17] and (3) Individual interview and survey data examining influences of racialized and gendered media portrayals on Chicana/o students attending a Los Angeles community college in 1998–99.[18]

This data offers insights into the experiences of those navigating through the dismal statistical reality that out of every 100 Chicana/o elementary school students, only seven will graduate with a bachelor's degree. A

Chicana undergraduate student majoring in Chicana/o Studies, Esmeralda Martinez, narrates the counterstory in this chapter. Esmeralda attends a large research university in a Midwest United States city (Midwestern University, MU). We follow along with Esmeralda on a rainy Tuesday, halfway through the spring semester of her junior year. We meet up with her in a Chicana/o Studies class lecture/discussion. Later, we reflect with Esmeralda as she prepares an essay draft in connection with this class.

9:20 AM—CLASS LECTURE: RECONSIDERING "THE MASTER PLAN" FOR HIGHER EDUCATION

My stomach growled and the student next to me giggled, but I'm glad I decided against stopping for coffee and a breakfast snack. The heavy rains last night and this morning delayed the train, and I didn't want to miss any part of the lecture. I plan out my schedule so I can take at least one of the few Chicana/o Studies courses offered each semester. This particular class ended up giving me an extra dose of much-needed oxygen during an especially suffocating year. I chewed my gum rapidly and read through the lecture outline passed around by the class TA, Soledad.

Professor Tamayo explained, "The California Master plan for Higher Education created a three-tier system in 1970. Designed by Clark Kerr, this plan aimed to increase access and opportunity to higher education. The community college tier provides students maximum access—even for those pushed out at an earlier point of the pipeline. The next tier includes the state colleges, or teaching institutions, and they also prepare most of the state's K–12 teachers. Then we arrive at the UC-university tier, which emphasizes research and produces doctorates. A very well-thought-out plan, right? A lot of people think so. That's why our state legislators have discussed implementing an updated version of the California Master Plan here."

Professor Tamayo paused to confirm with Soledad that everyone had received an outline. She then continued the lecture. "When we look at per pupil dollars, though, we find community colleges systematically underfunded and state colleges receiving far less per pupil dollars than the UC-universities.

"Because the K–12 system chronically underprepares Students of Color and tracks them away from college preparatory courses of study, only 21% of Latinas/os who graduate from a public high school in California have completed the minimum entrance requirements to enter a state college or university.[19] So students graduating from underfunded K–12 schools must now navigate through another poorly funded system—the community college—while students who attended well-funded K–12 schools with various college-prep enrichment resources usually enroll directly into another well-funded school-system, the UC."[20]

"Nationally, the largest increase in Chicana/o college enrollment has occurred at the community college level. But very few Chicanas/os who enter community college with a goal of transferring to a 4-year college or university meet that goal. What happens to Chicanas/os with high aspirations, goals of transferring to universities, and plans for continuing on in higher education? Burton Clark[21] believed community colleges may serve a 'cooling out' function. So instead of the institutions taking responsibility for fulfilling their transfer function, they 'cool out' the dreams Chicanas/os expressed about pursuing their education.[22] Some of us remain concerned that the community colleges have not fulfilled their primary role as transfer institutions during the 30 years of California's Master Plan.[23] What measures should be implemented to ensure the transfer function works here?"

"California's Master Plan does not account for the legacy of discrimination still affecting Chicanas/os. Would our legislators account for it here? When Professor Claudia Vasquez came to speak with us a few weeks ago, she reminded us that in 1968, Affirmative Action originally sought to remedy some of the racial discrimination that denied college access to People of Color. The policy asked colleges and universities to take 'affirmative action' to enroll more racial 'minorities,' more students from historically underrepresented groups. And slowly but surely, colleges and universities did set up goals and timetables to basically desegregate their campuses. But the 1978 *Bakke v. UC Regents* case ended the goals and timetables universities had begun to implement. And in its place, a limited form of affirmative action continued, which allowed a student's race to be considered as *one* factor in university admissions. And the purpose of using race after 1978 became limited to helping colleges bring a diverse student body to their campuses. After 1978, Affirmative Action programs eliminated the goal of remedying racial discrimination. Twenty years later, in 1998, Californians passed Proposition 209, ending the already restricted use of affirmative action so that colleges *could not* consider race even as a plus factor to diversify their campuses. A few years later in the 2003 *Grutter v. Bollinger*[24] University of Michigan Law School case, the Supreme Court ruled as they had in 1978 with the *Bakke* decision—affirming that university admissions practices *can* use race as one factor to diversify campuses. And to be consistent with that ruling, some California legislators are now challenging Proposition 209 and working to reinstate affirmative action as a way to consider race to diversify campuses."[25] Remember, the goal of remedying racial discrimination isn't the goal of today's institutions practicing affirmative action. Why would they want to admit they racially discriminate in the first place? While they're in denial, they also might not want to mention that White women have benefited more than any other group from affirmative action or that other forms of racial preferences benefiting Whites have yet to be eliminated."

"Even though you may be accused as a Student of Color on this campus of being underqualified, the truth is, none of you came in under affirmative action. Affirmative action never meant admitting unqualified students, it meant holding the institution responsible for the ways it historically discriminated against qualified students—and questioning what unqualified and qualified means when the K–12 playing field is not equal. So we need affirmative action at the K–12 level too."

"So this provides you a little more context to what you've been reading. Are universities taking affirmative steps to remedy the racialized barriers to education or are they also engaged in 'cooling out' the aspirations of Chicana/o students?"

9:50 AM—BRIEF CLASS DISCUSSION: INTRODUCING STAGES OF PASSAGE

"Esmeralda! What do you think of this idea?" I had been writing notes furiously and wasn't aware that I had become part of the lecture. I looked up from my notebook with a worried expression and asked, "Can you repeat the question?" Realizing my hyper-focus on writing down every word left me unable to listen well, Professor Tamayo pointed to a quote she had projected on the overhead screen and repeated herself. "Within the context of the Master Plan for Higher Education, we're trying to understand some of the experiences of Chicanas/os navigating through the university. So thinking about your own experiences in relation to the readings, what do you think of this idea?"

Looking at the quote on the screen, I read to myself:

Vincent Tinto's[26] Stages of Passage model argues that students engage in three processes early on in college: separation, transition, and incorporation. Separation refers to disassociating from your pre-college community (i.e., family and friends). Transition takes place during and after separation, when students let go of their old norms and behaviors and instead acquire new college norms and behaviors. Incorporation refers to the process of integrating yourself into various college communities.

After an awkward pause, I cleared my throat and said, "I think it's really interesting, but it doesn't go with my experiences and not really with anyone who I know. The readings we've had don't seem to support this idea." "Can you explain further?" the professor asked.

"I can try," I said and continued, "first of all, it emphasizes assimilation. That we all assimilate, leave our family in the *barrio* and get a new language, new clothes, new attitude, or whatever, and then we forget where we come from. It also seems too neat and clean, because I don't see where it takes into consideration all the struggles we go through trying to get through college."

Professor Tamayo probed the class, "OK, so what do the rest of you think about what Esmeralda is saying?" Gustavo, a tall Chicano with wavy black hair, dark brown skin, and glasses, raised his hand. When called on, he leaned back in his chair and said, "I think we do get a new language when we come to the university. I can't go home and just expect my parents to engage in a discussion about epistemology or pedagogy. As far as new clothes, my financial aid got cut last semester, so, I don't know about that." The class chuckled as Gustavo continued, "And some people in here, I'm not going to mention any names, but some people do think they're too good. They think they're too good to go back and eat at the little taco stand they used to." I rolled my eyes and noticed students shifting a lot in their chairs.

Michelle, a tall, light-skinned Chicana with light brown hair always perfectly combed into a ponytail or braid, quickly jumped into the discussion. She sat a few seats away from me and spoke loudly so all could hear her sarcastic remark, "*No te hagas*[27] Gustavo, you know we saw you yesterday eating a fancy 'wrap,' which is really a *burrito* at twice the price." The class laughed again, and this time the professor rolled her eyes and announced, "OK then, you're making me hungry with all this talk about food. Let's pick up this discussion after a 15-minute break."

10:00 AM—COFFEE BREAK AND PHENOTYPE REFLECTIONS

The rain stopped for the moment at least, so I headed straight to the little campus coffee and snack shack. As I waited in the long line of hungry students, I smiled thinking about Michelle's witty comeback for Gustavo. Michelle was from a very rural town near the Mexico–U.S. border and she was the whitest and tallest Mexican girl I had ever met. She had green eyes, very light skin, and sandy blonde hair. Looking at her, you might think she was White, but as soon as she spoke, she clarified that right away. She code-switched from Spanish to English constantly.[28] Those of us who knew her were all pretty used to it, but some people really tripped out on her. Some people would even get offended. I sometimes wondered whether Michelle felt that she had to "prove" her *Mexicanidad* through language. I remember one time as a group of us ate lunch, she said that sometimes she wished she had dark skin. Those of us with darker skin laughed and asked her why. Her response really surprised me. She said that she received many layers of privilege for being light-skinned.[29] Most people assumed she was White. People in her family nicknamed her "*Güerita*," which could mean light-skinned girl or White girl.[30] And although she liked receiving positive attention, she always felt it was unfair that her brother, who was darker-skinned, seemed to receive a lot of negative attention. She said after being ridiculed by their cousins, her brother tried to scrub the "dirt" off of his face and hands, realizing after scraping up his face that he wasn't dirty, he was brown. And what really bothered Michelle was when White students would make racist comments about Mexicans in her presence. When she told them she was Mexican, they would be surprised and say, "Oh, well, when I was talking about those Mexicans, I didn't mean you."[31]

That brief conversation with Michelle actually sparked my interest in phenotype.[32] That next semester, I took an independent studies course in Chicana/o Studies to learn more about phenotype in Chicana/o history. With guidance from Professor Tamayo, I analyzed how Chicanas/os internalize racism. Professor Tamayo encouraged me to start out with readings that explain the difference between racism and prejudice. I began to understand that People of Color can be racially prejudiced against each other, but racism is a system of prejudice plus power. People of Color have never had the power to set up institutions and social structures that systematically discriminate against entire communities. And of course Whites are not all individually racists, but they experience multiple privileges based on the legacy of racism.[33]

When people don't know Chicana/o history, they might not even realize that the southwestern U.S. used to be northern Mexico, and indigenous people lived there for centuries before the European arrival.[34] The Europeans instituted a system of racism and forced indigenous Mexicans to learn Spanish.[35] When the United States instigated war against Mexico and then annexed half of Mexico, communities who lived in northern Mexico suddenly became foreigners on their own land.[36] As the t-shirts for our campus MEChA read: "We didn't cross the border, the border crossed us!" And of course Mexicans resisted the U.S. invasion just as they resisted the Spanish conquest. They resisted by maintaining indigenous languages, religious practices, and cultural traditions in spite of centuries of oppression. By the late 19th and early 20th Centuries, Americanization schools functioned to perpetuate the European system of racism, attempting to force Mexican students to learn English and assimilate to "American" ways.[37] Historically, teachers corporally punished Chicana/o students for speaking Spanish. With negative images of Chicanas/os in the media and textbooks that stereotype or ignore Chicanas/os altogether, it's no wonder that

Chicana/o students tend to internalize ideas that dark skin is not attractive, speaking Spanish is not "normal," and that anything Mexican is inferior.[38]

In the context of these legacies of racism and resistance, Chicana/o parents, just like other parents, want the best for their children. For many Chicana/o parents, this has meant taking whatever measures necessary to prepare their children for a society that values English over Spanish. Based perhaps on their own schooling experiences—enduring teachers who could not pronounce their name, being slapped for speaking Spanish, suffering embarrassment for speaking with an "accent," or being unable to defend themselves in English—Chicana/o parents may refrain from teaching their children Spanish altogether as a coping mechanism or a way of survival.

Ironically, here at the university, Chicana/o students tend to internalize the hierarchies of racism and sometimes resurrect discriminatory behaviors against each other. As they learn about this history of struggle, they reflect on slavery, colonization, and globilization and gain a new appreciation for their culture, language, and history. Yet they may pass negative judgment on their peers who do not speak Spanish. Sometimes, in our student organizations, Chicana/o students try to "out-Chicano" each other, much like some cultural nationalists of the 1960s and 1970s. These students often make arguments that essentialize what it means to be a Chicana/o. So in their view, if you have dark skin and speak Spanish, you are considered *very Chicano*. If you are from East Los Angeles or if your parents are farmworkers, then you are also seen as *very Chicano*. But if you have dark skin and do not speak Spanish, you might be considered *less Chicano*—someone who does not identify with being Mexican or someone who is "too good" to speak Spanish. You might even be called a "coconut"—brown on the outside, White on the inside.

From what I read that semester and since, I don't think research has fully addressed the long-term consequences of internalized racism on Chicana/o communities.[39] Here at MU, I know that a growing number of student groups on campus consider themselves apolitical and they function as social groups. Underlying tensions sometimes boil over between these newly formed Latina/o fraternities and sororities[40] and the more historically established, overtly political groups who originated out of the 1960s' Chicana/o student movements.[41] I wonder if this is in part because of the perception that the political groups may not welcome a broad range of what it means to be Chicana/o. On the other hand, I also wonder whether it is even possible to be apolitical. Doesn't that mean you just watch from the sidelines and you don't take a position? I feel like my whole purpose here is to challenge the status quo, so, being part of an organization that is centrally focused on social justice affirms my Chicana identity.

Learning about how I have internalized racism is an ongoing process for me.[42] And it's always painful to see how some of my peers who haven't worked through their internalized racism lash out against other students. Maybe Michelle's light skin calls her identity into question for some students. All I know is that she likes to make sure it's clear—she might be light on the outside, but she's brown on the inside—she's Chicana *y que!*[43]

Michelle probably feels comfortable to code-switch in Professor Tamayo's class because we're mostly all Chicanas/os in there and the professor breaks down the hierarchical, "I'm the great professor you're the lowly student," vibe of most other classes. I wondered at the beginning of the semester if the professor spoke Spanish or not, but almost immediately, I realized that she was bilingual, and I began to really respect how she handled Michelle's code-switching.[44] Without being condescending to either Michelle or the students who did not understand Spanish, the professor would do a tag-team-like English translation of the Spanish words, almost like an echo. Sometimes, she couldn't think of the word in English, so she would ask a student to help her. Other times, she would laugh along with the class at the way a Spanish word translated humorously into English.

10:18 AM—BACK TO CLASS: ASSIMILATION VERSUS ACCULTURATION

A student in line nudged me and the cashier raised her voice, saying, "Next!" Realizing I had become totally engrossed in my own thoughts and the line had taken too long, I quickly paid for my snack and coffee. I grabbed five French vanilla creamers and put them in my jacket pocket so I could stir them in later. Jumping over large puddles and trying not to burn myself with the coffee, I rushed back to the classroom and listened in on the discussion already underway.

I heard Michelle saying, "Of course we get a new language, but that doesn't mean we forget Spanish, or our hometown slang, *o lo que sea.*[45] I went to a barbque at my cousins' last week. I haven't seen them for a while, and they told me, *'ya te olvidaste de los pobres.'*[46] But I know they just like to tease me. They know I don't think I'm better just because I'm over here in college. Actually, they're way smarter than me. Always have been. They just didn't get the opportunities that I did." Michelle noticed the professor raising her eyebrow, waiting for her to bring us back to the subject at hand, so she cleared her throat and continued, "*Pues*, I agree with what Esme said before the break. We might acculturate to our new situation, but we don't necessarily assimilate."[47]

Michelle explained that she saw acculturation as a process of adding what you have to the new situation, whereas assimilation meant giving up some of who you are to conform to the new situation. Professor Tamayo offered that maybe there was a range within each of these terms, so that acculturation might look different for some people and in certain situations. She also asked the class to think about whether there is a range of what it means to assimilate, and who determines what is acculturation and what is assimilation. I really liked this discussion, but it made me uncomfortable because the professor's questions reminded me of the complexity of it all. I would probably be thinking about these issues for a long time.

Libertad, a petite, dark-skinned Chicana with very short hair recently dyed purple, wondered out loud, "Maybe these stages aren't Chicana/o stages, maybe they're White stages or something." Professor Tamayo probed, "Can you expand?" Libertad smiled and continued, "Sure. We've been discussing this whole semester about how the system wasn't designed with Chicanas/os in mind. You know, Martha Menchaca,[48] Gilbert Gonzalez,[49] Richard Valencia,[50] Sylvia Hurtado,[51] and so many others have explained that the system has actually been structured to racially segregate, linguistically marginalize, push out, and discriminate against Chicanas/os. So I'm thinking that the stages Tinto writes about are based on the experiences of White students. Like using them as the standard and then trying to generalize to everyone else's experiences."

As Libertad spoke, I re-focused on taking detailed notes. Libertad double-majored in History and Chicana/o Studies. I think her parents are professors or political activists or both, but when Libertad speaks, she seems so confident and well read. I hadn't really thought about White privilege embedded in research, and it reminded me of the cultural deficit theories we discussed earlier in the semester. Researchers continually created models trying to understand educational inequality but their models usually center on the experiences of White middle-class students as the "norm," so Students of Color and working-class students end up de-centered and considered "abnormal" by default.

I looked up from my notebook when Professor Tamayo said, "OK, let's get into discussion groups and address the article on campus racial climate." She asked us to think about what Chicana/o students' stages of passage might look like. Professor Tamayo assured us that she and Soledad would be walking around to each group if we had any questions.

10:30 AM—BREAKING INTO SMALL GROUPS AND "WHATNOT"

The room looked a little chaotic for a minute as students picked up their backpacks and moved to another desk or pulled their desks together in their small discussion groups. My group included five students—Lupe, Sammy,

Michelle, Gustavo, and me. Gustavo started out right away, explaining, "I know I was joking around earlier, but I do think that we tend to separate ourselves a little like Tinto's model says. Some of us moved very far from our communities to attend MU and it's only natural, but that's not the whole story. We do bring our community with us to help us through this place. To help us deal with the campus racial climate. I think that White students don't really separate themselves either, though. They still have their parents' money, their vocabulary from the yacht club, and whatnot."

I laughed and added, "And whatnot? Sounds like you've been hanging out at the yacht club! I mean, you know that not all White students own yachts, right? Some White students might also be working class, just like some of us. But I think I see where you're headed, Gustavo. Overall, White students can go through this separation, transition, and incorporation process without the repercussions we have. They may have a head start already because the college climate is pretty much built for them.[52] But with Chicanas/os, the stakes change. We don't have the middle-class income or vocabulary to fall back on." I used my fingers to indicate quotation marks emphasizing certain words and continued, "We have to 'become White' to succeed. It's like saying to 'separate from your Mexican traditions, transition onto a White campus, and incorporate yourself into middle-class America!'" Gustavo nodded in agreement, "Right, supposedly to succeed in college you must melt into the pot."

Lupe, my roommate and best friend, interrupted and helped keep our conversation on track. Everyone said Lupe and I looked like twins—short, medium brown skin, straight black hair, and "smarty" glasses. She remarked, "I think we should discuss what the campus racial climate is like here, then we can see how Chicanas/os are navigating through the climate. Whether or not they are melting into the pot or not."

Sammy added jokingly, "you mean or whatnot." Lupe didn't laugh. I guess she and I weren't so identical in terms of our sense of humor. Lupe transferred to MU and double majored in Global Studies and Political Science. Sammy transferred in the same year as Lupe and he majored in History. Sammy looked pretty athletic, with spiky hair, medium brown skin, and a well-groomed mustache. He opened up his notebook when Lupe's stern look reminded us that we needed to get down to business.

SMALL GROUP DISCUSSION CONTINUES—FOCUSING ON CAMPUS RACIAL CLIMATE

Sammy continued, "OK, well, starting with what the article says, campus racial climate is 'the overall racial environment of the college campus... When a campus racial climate is positive, it includes at least four elements:

(1) the inclusion of Students, Faculty, and Administrators of Color; (2) a curriculum that reflects the historical and contemporary experiences of People of Color; (3) programs to support the recruitment, retention, and graduation of Students of Color; and (4) a college/university mission that reinforces the colleges' commitment to pluralism.'"[53]

We each scanned through our highlighted sections of the article to remind ourselves of some of the examples the authors gave. The study examined campus racial climate at four predominately White universities and focused on African American students' experiences. I said, "Check out this footnote here on that same page. It says that the authors define pluralism and racial diversity as synonymous.[54] They say pluralism at a university would feature underrepresented racial and ethnic groups (1) *present* on campus and (2) viewed as *equals* on campus." Sammy added, "Yeah, the environment here? It's hostile to Students of Color. Let's say there's 50 people in a class and then there's one Student of Color. It's very hard for minorities to succeed in that position because it's hard to relate to people." Michelle added, "Yes, as a math major, *estoy sola!*[55] It's harder if you're the only person there. It's hard for other people to relate to you based on your differences. And I don't mean to sound like I'm essentializing or that it's us versus them, but sometimes it feels like there's almost no common ground. You're alone in how you look, how you speak, how you act, and even what you like to do when you're not in class." I interjected, "Yeah, like go home, blast some *cumbia* music real loud, and dance like Selena?!"

Lupe shook her head with a smirk, acknowledging my joke while continuing the momentum of the discussion. She said, "And that's just the students, but there's barely any minority or women faculty, and that makes it worse. At the College of Engineering, I always had a hard time going up to the professors or even the teaching assistants. The couple times that I did, the professor gave me a 'get out of my face' answer." Sammy exclaimed, "Yes! On the first day of my history senior seminar class, I asked the professor to clarify one of the writing assignments listed on the syllabus. Instead of explaining briefly, she pulled the syllabus out of my hand and read that section to me!"

Lupe commented, "There's a lot of ignorance on campus and other students don't necessarily realize it. Their concept of racism is very different. They don't realize minor things can be considered racism. A friend of mine introduced me to a group of students. You know, we were doing introductions. And everyone kind of stated their name. And she introduced me, saying, 'This is Lupe, she's Mexican.' You know, I'm not saying that I'm not proud, but it's just not necessarily how I introduce myself. Every time I meet people you know, 'Hi, I'm Lupe, I'm Mexican.' I know she didn't do it on purpose, but it's just this layer of ignorance here that I've noticed."

Gustavo added, "I've just experienced some of the joking, the stereotypes, you know. People might make a Taco Bell joke, Chihuahua jokes. One guy, I swear, now whenever he sees me, he blurts out in a crazy high voice, 'ay caramba!'"

Sammy commented, "I'll be walking down the block and someone will cross the street just to avoid me. That mostly happened to me my first year because I lived on campus. Girls grabbed their purses and guys grabbed their backpacks."

Sammy's comment surprised me because I thought he had such a kind face. His moustache reminded me of my *tio*[56] Memo. I shook my head in disgust thinking about all this as I said, "It's almost automatic or something. They don't realize they're being offensive. Like when I was a freshman and my dorm roommate asked me where I learned English because she couldn't believe that I speak without what she called a 'Mexican' accent. And when I get offended they don't understand why." Michelle added, "I'm a female and I'm a minority. It kind of feels like it's a double-edged sword, like I have twice the reason not to be here. Some students find it very easy to point that out to me. But supposedly *yo soy la delicada*."[57] Lupe said, "Another thing that adds to this is when some fraternities and sororities on this campus are so obviously racist against People of Color and the university doesn't really take action against them. Like last semester when that fraternity had a theme party called, 'The Border.'" The rest of us nodded our heads as Lupe continued, "They had White guys 'dressed' like undocumented immigrants and they had to pass through hazing activities before getting a 'green card' to enter the party. And just like many universities across the nation, even when fraternities carry on that legacy of racism, they continue to be funded, almost like nothing."[58]

We all paused for a moment, each in our own thoughts. I searched through the article for something I thought sounded familiar. "The authors say that some of what we're describing can be considered 'microaggressions.'" I read a quote I had highlighted from the text: "The authors explain that microaggressions are '(1) subtle verbal and nonverbal insults directed at People of Color, often automatically or unconsciously; (2) layered insults, based on one's race, gender, class, sexuality, language, immigration status, phenotype, accent, or surname; and (3) cumulative insults, which cause unnecessary stress to People of Color while privileging Whites.'[59] And they argue that a negative campus racial climate features these ongoing, cumulative, subtle, and obvious racial incidents." Gustavo adjusted his glasses and added, "I highlighted that section too! I think we definitely have a negative campus racial climate going on here."

Walking by our group, the teaching assistant, Soledad, overheard this last comment. She asked our group rhetorically, "So how do Chicanas/os respond to the White privilege and uneven educational playing field of a negative campus racial climate?" We all paused and thought about that question as Soledad went to assist a group trying to get her attention from the corner of the room. With her light skin and dark brown straight hair, I wondered if Soledad had experienced some of the same issues of pheno-type privilege as Michelle. This was the first time Soledad worked as a TA in one of my classes, but I had met her last year, while volunteering in the *Sí Se Puede* tutoring program. Students worked with the janitors' union to develop a tutoring program as one form of support for the mostly Spanish-speaking Latina/o immigrant service workers on campus. Teaching these janitors to read and write in English felt very humbling, but also very re-warding. One of the janitors Soledad worked with—Don "Teo"—recently wrote a poem in English about how the tutoring center made him feel less invisible.[60] Soledad told him she felt the same way.

Sammy realized none of us had been taking notes and volunteered to write up our discussion points if we would remind him what we had talked about so far. We noted that we had only briefly addressed the stages of pas-sage, and had focused more on trying to find personalized examples of how we experienced the campus racial climate. So far, we had identified feelings of isolation and incidents of racial discrimination, or verbal and nonverbal insults that the authors called microaggressions.

Lupe noted, "And Soledad's question about how do we respond re-minded me of the authors' remarks that microaggressions maintain White privilege and cause us unnecessary stress." Michelle agreed, "Yes, stress! Do I respond to each insult? How do I respond?" I added, "Do I explain each time why I am offended by their comments?" Lupe remarked, "And what about how do we relieve that stress? What kind of toll does it take on our bodies, our minds, our spirits? There's a big burden in being 'the only one' because depending on how we respond to a microaggression, we are seen as 'representing' all Chicanas/os. So if we get angry, then we confirm for that person that Chicanas/os are hot-tempered. If we don't respond, we might confirm their assumption that we're passive or submissive. And if we do re-spond or if we don't, we're still thinking about it hours later. We can't sleep, thinking, 'oh, I should've said this,' 'why didn't I say that?' or 'next time I'm going to do this or that.'" Michelle again added, "And if we do respond, people are usually shocked like if we're just being oversensitive. So we still might be stressed out later, questioning ourselves, like 'did I overreact?' 'am I crazy and oversensitive like they said?' or 'what should I have said dif-ferent?' And because I have light skin, I probably don't even get as many microaggressions directed at me as Chicanas/os with darker skin, like my brother!" Lupe nodded and sighed, "*Verdad!*[61] It's exhausting carrying all that with us all the time.[62] Maybe after so many insults, over time, we might start thinking bad about ourselves. Like 'maybe they're right, maybe this isn't the place for me.'" Sammy closed his eyes while dramatically whispering as if in a horror movie, "The stigma!" We laughed at his attempted comic relief.

I shared with the group about my friend Alma, the only Latina in the Art School. She won a very prestigious art scholarship because of her excellent grades and artistic talent, but when the other students talked about friends who didn't get into the university, she felt that they constantly looked at her like, 'What are you doing here?' One of her classmates actually accused her to her face of receiving the award simply because she was a minority. "Like she can't get anything based on her intelligence and talent?" I asked incredulously.

Michelle explained that she actually started out in physics, but changed majors because of the difficulties she faced in a field dominated by men and alienating to her as a woman and as a Chicana. Similarly, Lupe noted that she transferred to MU as an engineering major, and changed to social sciences after multiple negative experiences. She said, "It sounds like we responded to various forms of ongoing discrimination and layers of White privilege and male privilege. And to balance out the hostility, we looked for academic spaces that seem more welcoming for Students of Color. Chicanas/os tend to be stigmatized as unqualified and never quite good enough. I wonder how long we carry that feeling with us or if that's one of the long-term effects of a negative campus racial climate." Gustavo reminded, "And some folks who end up changing majors as a result of too many microaggressions and racial hostility probably end up graduating later than planned." Libertad added, "Or, they might double major or pick up a minor in Chicana/o Studies or Black Studies or maybe Women's Studies to try and balance out the negative climate. And even within their more traditional major, they might still try to take electives in Chicana/o Studies. Remember Maggie? She took that one-unit Mexican music class eight times! She said it was like her oxygen." I thought to myself how this class was oxygen for me.

Michelle began to contextualize her earlier point, "*Pues, no me prepararon muy bien en la high school, no tenía chansa de hablar con una consejera.*[63] One college counselor for 5,000 students, *por favor, y las clases de 'Advanced Placement' siempre están llenas.*[64] It's just been unequal for a lot of us *desde el principio.*[65] I don't think most White students understand that we have to deal with that. And even with all that, we still fight our way through. In high school, I earned a 4.0 GPA and scored 1330 on the SAT. I was an athlete, I held a leadership position in student government, and volunteered in my community. And yet other students made me feel like I was a special admit." Gustavo shook his head and chuckled as he said, "My roommate

Ethan *is* actually a special admit student, but I doubt anyone would ever ask him that. His dad went here and so the university made an exception based on 'legacy status.' That's like affirmative action for White people."

"A lot of people make assumptions about our capabilities and whether we deserve to be here, but we're supposed to assume every White student deserves to be here, just because they're White. And they want to ignore that we have gone through very different circumstances to get here. Our educational opportunities, when we had them, usually came through struggle," said Lupe. I nodded in agreement, remembering Lupe had shared with me in confidence that she graduated valedictorian from her high school but had to attend a community college because she was undocumented and could not afford to pay the 'non-resident' tuition fees at a 4-year public university.[66]

Sammy added, "I played on the soccer team the first year I transferred here, and we had one Mexican and one Black player, *digo*[67] one African American player. And it was 27 of us and they always made jokes—racial jokes—and I just sort of got used to it. I knew they were joking but I also knew they did it on purpose. They knew my name, but they called me Paco. And I didn't say anything, because there was one of me and 25 of them and coaches and everything. This year, I decided not to even try out because—well, I don't enjoy playing soccer in that environment."

Professor Tamayo tapped Sammy on the shoulder as he was jotting down notes in outline form, "We're going to have to wrap this discussion up and get ready to share your group's main points with the larger class." She gave our group an encouraging smile and made her way across the room to check in on the other groups.

11:00 AM—CLASS DISCUSSION OF HOSTILE CAMPUS RACIAL CLIMATE

Breaking out of the small group discussion, we moved our desks again to face the front of the room and participate in the larger class discussion. Professor Tamayo began by asking each group to go over the main points of our discussion. I started to worry because our group didn't complete the whole assignment, but listening to the other group reports, I realized we weren't the only ones. The professor reassured us that she knew there was a lot to cover and we would continue this discussion, but she wanted to make sure we touched bases before today's class ended. She asked us to write a critical reflection paper about the class discussion for the next week. Soledad offered to read drafts of our write-up if we could get them to her by her Thursday office hours.

In the larger discussion, I learned that Libertad's group had discussed the lack of Chicana/o professors and lack of Chicana/o topics in the curriculum. This group commented that out of the 52 full-time faculty members in the Math Department, there are no Women of Color, no Black males, and only two Latinos. They also mentioned that out of the 68 full-time faculty members in the Department of History, there are only seven Faculty of Color: two Black women, one Chicano, two Latinos, and two Black male faculty. Zero Chicana, Latina, or Native American faculty work in the History Department.[68] Libertad summed up, "It's really hard to find any Professors of Color outside the Ethnic Studies programs." Professor Tamayo explained that other "selective" institutions hire even fewer Faculty of Color than MU. At this comment, many students shook their heads in frustration, perhaps trying to imagine an even more isolating place. Another student, Marisol, explained, "I don't think I had a Chicana or Latina professor until, well, until this class and of course, this is cross-listed with Chicana/o Studies." Marisol continued, "I want people to see who I am, and that's kind of like what I look for in professors. You don't have to be Latino—I just need you to understand. As long as professors can teach me and really empathize. We need more of those kind of professors."

Casandra, another student from that group, said, "Every time I go to office hours, I prep for like a whole week about what I'm gonna say, to make sure I have good questions, make sure I know something. I don't want them to think that I don't belong here. And, I feel that sometimes I have to work twice as hard just to be considered average, just to prove I belong here. There's a lot of proving around here." I put a star next to my note about this comment so I could get back to this idea later.

Another group spoke about the isolation we had briefly talked about in our group. A woman named Berta explained, "We don't feel there are enough Students of Color here at MU. Chicanas/os used to be almost 10% and now, we're down to less than 7%. I think the number of Blacks admitted has gone down even more dramatically. And that's problematic. Shouldn't those numbers be going up? Maybe if there were more of us, the administration would start to change. Maybe they would feel obligated to be more welcoming or something. With more of us, we could at least have more of a sense of community among the students." A guy named Hector said, "In the English Department, I'm the only Mexican. I took a Milton class. There are two Latinos. One lady and myself, and one African American. Where are we? Sometimes, I do feel a little left out." Another guy, Moises, stated, "I took biology in the spring and I was the only Latino there. There were no African Americans. Everyone was White and a couple of Asians. It's a little frustrating that I don't see more People of Color in the sciences." I made a note that this reflected our group discussion where Michelle and Lupe both switched majors away from physical science/engineering largely because of this alienation.

The final group didn't get to finish their report, but they had focused on how Chicanas/os responded to all the sources of discrimination. They mentioned that they had compiled a list from memory of the student-initiated organizations on campus and the institutional types of support for Students of Color. Professor Tamayo seemed quite interested, but the sounds of zippers and paper shuffling interrupted the discussion as some students began packing up their books. The professor glanced at her watch and conceded, "We'll continue this discussion next time. Keep up with your readings and in your reflection papers, be sure to describe the campus racial climate, its effects, and students' responses. This will help you conceptualize what the 'stages of passage' look like for Chicanas/os." She paused, and then exclaimed, "And don't forget! The film *Shattering the Silences*[69] is playing tomorrow night at 7:00 PM in The Lounge. As you go on to graduate school and beyond, I want you to go with your eyes open."

Sammy and I had a history study group to prepare for a Friday midterm exam, so we gathered our notebooks, backpacks, and umbrellas and headed across campus.

9:30 PM: ESMERALDA'S REFLECTIONS

Hours later, after my history study group ended and I caught the night van back to my apartment, I began thinking again about campus racial climate. The concept of microaggressions really spoke to our everyday experiences of racism. I sighed, remembering that Michelle also resorted to starting her own math study group with Chicana/o and African American students in the class when they had been excluded from other students' study sessions. And then I thought about all that drives Chicanas/os collectively to persist even in the midst of experiencing a negative campus racial climate.

I went to grab a snack from the fridge, and saw that Lupe had left me a note that my mom called earlier and that the *Chicanas Adelante* group meeting had been rescheduled to a different room tomorrow. Ah! I panicked for a second, remembering that I had to bring the list of Westside middle schools to that meeting so we could plan out the expansion of our after-school mentoring/tutoring program. I found the list on my desk and put it in my book bag before I forgot.

Realizing the late hour, I knew I'd have to call my mom back tomorrow. I missed my family so much it hurt sometimes. I definitely learned a lot about how to navigate through this place by watching my parents' struggle, which is weird, because they themselves never made it past middle school. They didn't have the opportunities that their work has now given me. My first year at MU, I wanted to leave, my mom told me, "OK, fine, you're tired, come home and clean bathrooms like me. That's what you want to do? You pick. You can either go to school or you can come back and vacuum rooms at the hotel with me." My dad also tells me that he wants me to succeed so I don't have to work as hard as them. He shows me his hands and says he never wants my hands to be rough and weathered like his. I always tease him that some of his fingers are crooked, and we laugh that he can't give good directions because he points in one direction and one of his fingers points in the opposite direction. I guess that's part of what happens when you work in construction and you have poor or no health insurance. Tinto's "stages of passage" model would assume that I wouldn't draw on the lessons I've learned from my family to get through this place. But actually, I couldn't sustain myself here if I didn't have the support of my family, emotionally, spiritually, culturally, in so many ways.[70]

11:45 PM—ESMERALDA'S ESSAY DRAFT: ANALYZING CHICANA/O NAVIGATION

I took a moment to change into sweats and my fuzzy slippers to warm up my cold feet. I spent the next 2 hours looking for quotes and trying to tie all the discussion topics together so I could start to develop a draft by Thursday. I knew I wouldn't have much time to write tomorrow, and I wanted to at least get my thoughts out so I could ask for Soledad's feedback. I started by making a list of the main issues I saw in my notes from class. I read to myself:

- Chicanas/os experience numerous instances of racial microaggressions both on and off campus. These often subtle and automatic insults are layered with racism, sexism, and other forms of oppression. As they accumulate, microaggressions cause unnecessary stress to People of Color while privileging Whites (negative campus racial climate).
- Chicanas/os and their perspectives are often excluded and undervalued in their departments and classroom curriculum and discussions (feeling frustrated and isolated).
- Chicanas/os feel they have to repeatedly "prove" that they are qualified to be at the university (assumption that we are all "special admits," but what about legacy admits and other forms of affirmative action for Whites?)
- Numbers of other Students and Faculty of Color are going down instead of up (we need more so we can better challenge the negative campus racial climate).

I flipped through an old course reader to find an epigraph by Gloria Anzaldúa:

> *I am visible—see this Indian face—yet I am invisible. I both blind them with this beak nose and I am their blind spot. But I exist, we exist. They'd like to think I have melted in the pot, but I haven't, we haven't.*[71]

What a powerful quote, I marveled. Though she wasn't referring to higher education, Anzaldúa's words offer a nice challenge to the assimilationist tendencies of Tinto's "stages of passage," while also giving a glimpse of how some Chicanas/os might feel in the midst of a negative campus racial climate. I sketched out how I pictured Tinto's model (figure 4.1) and stared at it for while.

Looking at my notes, I remembered the multiple comments in class today where students admitted feeling isolated and alienated. Students shared so many stories of racial and gender discrimination! It's more like we experience the university initially as a stage of culture shock. We see our family and communities as a resource to combat the isolation, alienation, and discrimination we experience at the university. Responding to the culture shock through "separation" wouldn't really be positive or helpful. Actually, separation would take us away from our resources and strengths.

Most of the Students of Color I know at the university end up building a sense of community to ease the culture shock. The class discussion today reminded me that all of us face racial microaggressions daily, both in academic and social spaces. And we rarely have a class space to talk about the racial hostility so prevalent on and around campus. I drew a circle to represent this first stage of navigation for Chicanas/os at predominately White universities (figure 4.2).

Instead of separating from our communities to help ease some of the pain from such a hostile climate, we often create new communities—counterspaces—on and around campus. Our counterspaces are academic and social and sometimes both at the same time. I began to jot down a few more notes as I thought about the study group earlier tonight. Study groups and student-organized academic study halls on campus function like academic counterspaces. They can foster our learning at the university and nurture a supportive environment where our experiences are validated and viewed as important knowledge.

Figure 4.1. Tinto's Stages of Passage

Figure 4.2. Culture Shock

Faculty co-create some of these counterspaces with students in classes like Professor Tamayo's. But with so few Faculty of Color and few faculty willing to co-create these academic counterspaces, Chicana/o students may find it difficult to develop academic networks of support. The campus retention center proved to be a crucial academic counterspace for me. I receive free tutoring and counseling at the center. Along with other Students of Color, first-generation college students, and low-income students, I learn study strategies and note-taking skills.[72] The tutors read drafts of my papers for me, and they don't make me feel ignorant. And now as part of the tutoring program with the janitors, I try to offer that same level of dedication and support to others.

Some counterspaces exist within more social settings on campus through student organizations. The academic peer groups I've developed seem to merge with my social peer groups. Social counterspaces allow room, outside the classroom confines, for students to vent frustrations and to get to know people who share many of their experiences.

I paused for a while, wondering whether the counterspaces we create on campus always provide safe spaces for Chicanas/os. Reflecting on Michelle's experiences and some of the students in the class who don't speak Spanish, I know that a lot of diversity exists within our Chicana/o community here on campus. And because of internalized racism, questions about authenticity continue to surface. What does it mean to be a "Chicana/o"? And how can we support diverse experiences of being Chicana/o?

Last year, in the *Chicanas Adelante* group, we went through a painful process of trying to make our organization a safe space for queer Chicanas.[73] That meant working to recognize the ways we have internalized patriarchy and admitting that we often exhibit heterosexist behavior. I thought about Anzaldúa's insight that knowledge is painful because it changes us.[74] Once we realized we did not provide a safe space for all Chicanas, we couldn't continue to marginalize queer voices and experiences. A few women expressed concerns that in our efforts to empower queer Chicanas that we might marginalize straight Chicanas. Sometimes, in the midst of these debates, it seemed like being a lesbian Chicana meant being more radical, challenging patriarchy with everything you have and everything you are. But this also sounded a little bit like trying to "out-Chicana" each other, like the essentialist arguments of what it means to be a Chicano, but with a gendered, sexuality twist. One woman shared that she lived in fear for many years because she was an undocumented immigrant. She cried as she spoke, explaining that she didn't want to participate in a group that perpetuated fearful silence.

I wondered if we could nurture a safe space for all Chicanas, or if we would always end up marginalizing some experiences. Even though it wasn't always comfortable, I liked that we were struggling through these issues instead of just sweeping them under the rug. That experience was critical to my thinking about what type of community I wanted to build at the university. It also reminded me to listen more to my parents' *consejos*,[75] like my dad's favorite *dicho* from Benito Juarez, *"el respeto al derecho ajeno es la paz."*[76] And my mom often quoted biblical proverbs[77] as she encouraged me to engage with others using kind words, *"como la miel Esme, dulce pero tambien saludable."*[78]

For Chicana/o students, Tinto's "Transition Stage" seems to represent a space between the two worlds of home and school. In this space, students primarily draw upon home and community resources while we pick and choose certain aspects of the university to help us combat isolation, alienation, and discrimination. As I drew another circle to demonstrate the stage after culture shock, I thought about how seeking out social and academic peer networks helps us build community in the midst of a hostile campus racial climate (figure 4.3).

I've seen that for many of my friends, building community helps support overall efforts to demonstrate or "prove" to those who assumed we'd fail that Chicanas/os can and do succeed.[79] As part of our larger goal to "prove them wrong," we use multiple daily strategies. We take Chicana/o Studies classes to learn our history. We talk and listen to friends and family to receive support. We maintain high self-expectations and we work very hard to make sure our actions show Chicanas/os in a positive light.[80] We're trying to make change happen by achieving educational goals for ourselves and our *familias*. We're refusing to be complacent or to allow ourselves to be perceived as defenseless victims. Even when we commiserate and share our frustrations and pain, we build a community of survivors.

Figure 4.3. Community building

Student-initiated organizations have historically played a large role in community building and in helping Chicanas/os survive both socially and academically. Student-initiated organizations also provide opportunities for Chicana/o students to "give back" to our communities[81] on and off college campuses. Even on weekends, Chicana/o students work and socialize in these counterspaces, reinforcing that history of building community and "giving back."

Chicanas/os negotiate between the world of home and the world of the university, but we negotiate from our unique social location on the margin. I paused, thinking that I really didn't like the word "negotiation" that much. It seems to infer that we have to give up something in order to get something, like a trade-off. It reminded me of the discussion we had in class this morning about acculturation versus assimilation. I wondered to myself what kind of trade-offs I had made. Maybe navigation was a better word? For me, navigation sounds more like we control the direction we're headed in, and we don't necessarily have to give something up. Maybe we just steer around those rough waters if we don't want to negotiate? Hmmm… Listening to the comments made today in class and reflecting again on all our readings, it seems like White students may be leaving their families and communities behind in order to acquire new resources at the university. On the other hand, Chicana/o students continue to draw on our families/communities and utilize the margin as a navigational resource. And we look to build on this foundation so we can develop a community of support at the university.

Before drawing one last circle that I felt could describe the stage after community building, I paused for a moment, realizing that Chicana/o students navigate through Tinto's "Incorporation Stage" just as we navigate through the Separation and Transition stages—on our own terms (figure 4.4).

Chicana/o students incorporate the cultural values of our families/communities into the university and we also utilize university resources to fulfill the needs of our families/communities. Often motivated by a desire to "give back" to our communities, critical navigation between multiple worlds ironically helps "incorporate" Chicana/o students into various university communities and greatly contributes to our academic and social success.[82] Our activities both on and off campus empower us, but sometimes it's hard to

Figure 4.4. Critical Navigation between Multiple Worlds

balance between academic responsibilities as a university student and participation in academic and social counterspaces. We need the counterspaces to help nurture our spirits and share strategies to "prove them wrong." We are working to bring in a new generation of Chicanas/os to the university. But at the same time, we need to make sure we're working to graduate each other. Battling the racial hostility on campus is like a job all by itself.[83]

Chicanas/os develop "critical resistant navigational skills"[84] so we can survive and succeed through the educational pipeline. But for me, as I know for many other Chicanas/os, I need to know there's a "point" to the struggle. We want to know that the experiences, skills, and knowledges we may gain from the university can ultimately benefit our communities.

I typed up some more notes and printed them out. I would have to polish this up tomorrow so I could show Esmeralda a rough draft on Thursday. It made me giggle to myself to think about how I would have to word it for the paper: "Tinto's Stages of Passage offer important insights into how to analyze undergraduate experiences. However, research indicates that this model insufficiently accounts for the navigation experiences of Chicana/o university students. Tinto's approach is limited by its focus on White students. When we shift the research lens to focus on Chicanas/os, we find that instead of the stages of separation, transition, and incorporation, Chicanas/os tend to experience stages of culture shock, community building, and critical navigation between multiple worlds." Wow! Who am I, to challenge this established scholar's research model? My nervous giggle calmed as I sketched out the new model with all three sections (figure 4.5).

It wasn't just me challenging Tinto, I reminded myself. I was listening to the experiences of my peers, analyzing the research about Chicana/o college students across the nation, learning from a history of struggle against racism, and acknowledging ongoing stress related to a negative campus racial climate.

Again, as in class today, I began to realize that I am not alone. This essay represents a collective challenge to research that centers the experiences of White students and marginalizes Chicana/o experiences. My pause caused the screen saver to slowly appear on my computer screen. I smiled and sighed, seeing the picture I uploaded last month of my niece at her first communion. She is one of my biggest supporters. I'm her *tia* who "goes to

Figure 4.5. A Model of Chicana/o Undergraduate "Stages of Passage"

college!" It's hard to be away from her so much, studying or participating in weekend projects with *Chicanas Adelante*. Hopefully, someday she'll understand why her *tia* Esmeralda couldn't visit her very often. I hope my efforts here at the university will mean that she won't have to struggle so hard on her way through the educational pipeline. Although the racial climate on her college campus might still be hostile, at least she can learn from my critical navigation between multiple worlds.

My niece's picture faded to black when I shut down the computer. As I cleaned off my dish and washed up to go to bed, I made myself a mental note to email Soledad and make an appointment to see her during Thurday's office hours. I had planned to take some courses abroad next fall semester and I hoped to graduate next spring, but I wanted to know more about the process of applying to graduate school. I wonder how Soledad experiences and responds to the campus racial climate at the graduate level.

NOTES

1. Midwestern is a composite 4-year college representing a flagship research university, located in an unidentified city in the Midwest region of the United States.
2. Fry, 2004; Rendon, 1992
3. Ornelas & Solórzano, 2004
4. Ornelas, 2002; Vigil Laden, 2000
5. Clark, 1960
6. Ornelas & Solórzano, 2004, p. 244
7. See Muñoz, D. G., 1986. These stresses contrast the White students, whose greatest stresses are personal, such as difficulty in getting a date. White students also reported financial stress in regards to whether their parents would continue contributing financially to their education.
8. Muñoz, D. G., 1986, p. 148
9. For more discussion of Chicana/o undergraduate navigation experiences, see Octavio Villalpando's (2003) counterstory discussing claims that Students of Color "self-segregate" on college campuses. His composite characters argue this may be an effort toward "self-preservation."
10. See Hurtado & Carter, 1997; Solórzano, Ceja, & Yosso, 2000
11. See Pierce, 1970, 1974, 1989, 1995
12. This stereotype research examines the "immediate situational threat that derives from the broad dissemination of negative stereotypes about one's group—the threat of possibly being judged and treated stereotypically, or of possibly self-fulfilling such a stereotype" (Steele & Aronson, 1995, p. 798).
13. See also the 1970 documentary film *Eye of the Storm*, for evidence of diminished academic performance during a one-day experiment with elementary-age White children (Peters, prd., 1970). The teacher (Ms. Jane Elliot) separates the blue-eyed children from the brown-eyed children and on alternative days elevates one group above the others, praising one group and belittling the other. The students who the teacher calls "superior" also begin to ridicule their peers who have a different eye color. The supposedly "inferior" students immediately underperform on their daily academic tasks. The teacher's experiment attempts to show her White students some of the pain of racism that People of Color face everyday. See also the film *A Class Divided*, which follows up with Ms. Elliot's students and reflects on the ongoing need to challenge racism in and beyond our classrooms (Peters, prd., 1985). For transcripts, tapes, teachers' guides, and additional resources, see http://www.pbs.org/wgbh/pages/frontline/shows/divided/

14. Alva, 1991, 1995; Arrellano & Padilla, 1996; Cuádraz & Pierce, 1994; Solórzano & Villalpando, 1998; Solórzano, Villalpando, & Oseguera, 2005
15. Cuádraz, 1997
16. The student dialogue throughout this counterstory draws directly from the Latina/o undergraduate focus groups conducted as part of this larger campus racial climate study (Allen & Solórzano, 2001; Solórzano, Allen, & Carroll, 2002). All personal identifying information has been changed to maintain confidentiality.
17. See Solórzano, 1999
18. See Yosso, 2000
19. The California Postsecondary Education Commission (CPEC) explains, "The freshman admission criteria for the UC and the CSU require applicants to complete college preparatory curricula called the a–g requirements." This percentage of Latina/o students completing these courses in California decreased from 23% in 1998 to 21% in 2003. See CPEC Report 05-05, University Preparedness of Public High School Graduates. p. 2, Display 2: "Percentage of a–g Completions per Ethnicity." March 2005.
20. For example, in one of his last interviews, Kerr again expressed his concern that although he and others had worked in the 1960s to create a system of equal opportunity to education, "the good high schools developed advanced placement classes and the UC began taking advanced placement classes into account in accepting students. The poor school districts had none at all. While we were trying to increase equality of opportunity, there was being built by this new system of advanced placement inequality for those from low income areas" (see Falcone, 2002).
21. See Burton Clark, 1960
22. Ornelas, 2002; Ornelas & Solórzano, 2004
23. Clark Kerr worried too. In his testimony for the Joint Committee to Develop a Master Plan for Education Kindergarten through University on August 24, 1999, Dr. Kerr stated, "I will use the word 'disgrace' three times this afternoon, and one of the areas where I'm going to use the word disgrace is the variation in the number of junior college transfers that go on to upper division work in the CSU or the UC system … the discrepancies in Advanced Placement opportunities among the high schools of the state is just absolutely enormous, and along with the discrepancies in transfer run absolutely contrary to what the Master Plan was all about which was to give young people more equal opportunities. Too often in the State of California, these opportunities for people to advance are being decreased rather than being increased. Keep those opportunities open" (Retrieved August 8, 2005 from, http://www.ucop.edu/acadint/mastplan/kerr082499.htm). See also the University of California History Digital Archives http://sunsite.berkeley.edu/uchistory /archives_exhibits/masterplan
24. *Grutter v. Bollinger*, 539 U.S. 306 (2003)
25. See Assembly Bill No. 1452 submitted February 22, 2005 by California Congressman Nuñez. California Legislature 2005–06 Regular Session.
26. Tinto, 1993
27. Don't pretend.
28. See Garcia, E. E., & Padilla, 1985; Hakuta, 1991
29. Hunter, 2002
30. Moraga, 1983
31. Solórzano, 1998
32. Hunter, Allen, & Telles, 2000
33. See Tatum, 1997
34. Acuña, 1972
35. Cope, 1994
36. Gómez-Quiñones, 1994
37. Sanchez, 1993, 1997
38. See Cota-Robles de Suarez, 1971; Council for Interracial Books for Children, 1977; See also study by David Bergin and Helen Cooks (2002) discussing Mexican American and African American high school students' efforts to achieve academically amidst assumptions that doing

so means "acting White." The researchers found that in contrast to previous studies claiming Black students underperform academically to avoid the label of "acting White," (Fordham, 1988; Fordham & Ogbu, 1986) these Students of Color maintained strong ethnic identities along with their high grades. They also expressed annoyance that anyone would assume their academic success diminishes their ethnic (racial) identity. Likewise, Prudence Carter's (2003) study "found no evidence" of African American students minimizing their academic aspirations to avoid accusations of "acting White" (p. 147). Further research is necessary to increase our understanding of racism's multilayered affects on Students of Color—to understand why some students may want to be *Anything But Mexican* (Acuña, 1996) while some high-achieving Chicana/o students demonstrate "invulnerability" (Alva, 1991, 1995; Arrellano & Padilla, 1996) and maintain strong ties to their language, culture, and community in the face of societal and campus racism.

39. See Arce, Murgia, & Frisbie, 1987; Murgia & Telles, 1990, 1992, 1996; Padilla, 2001; Quintana, 1999
40. See Heidenreich, in press.
41. Garcia, I.,1997; Muñoz, C., 1989
42. Fanon, 1967
43. So what!
44. See Olmedo-Williams, 1981; Valdés-Fallis, 1978
45. Or whatever.
46. You already forgot about us poor folks.
47. See Gordon, 1981; Ong Hing, 1997
48. Menchaca, 1995
49. See González, 1990, 1997
50. Valencia, 2002b
51. Hurtado, Milem, Clayton-Pederson, & Allen, 1999
52. Carbado, 2002; Delgado & Stefancic, 1997; McIntosh, 1989; Leonardo, 2004
53. Solórzano, Ceja, & Yosso, 2000, p. 62
54. Daniel Solórzano, Miguel Ceja, and Tara Yosso (2000) define pluralism and collegiate racial diversity as "manifestations of a situation in which underrepresented racial and ethnic groups are present on the college campus and viewed as equals on the college campus; and where all students are willing to affirm one another's dignity, ready to benefit from each other's experience, and willing to acknowledge one another's contributions to the common welfare of students and faculty on the college campus" (p. 62). See also Julie Lopez Figueroa and Eugene Garcia's (in press) discussion of Latino undergraduate experiences with campus racism and the need for implementation of reflective, responsive, responsible, reasonable, and respectful strategies to embrace diversity.
55. I'm alone.
56. Uncle.
57. I'm the sensitive one.
58. In her chapter "Campus Racism: Tip of the Iceberg," Elizabeth "Betita" Martinez (1998) discusses some of the overt racism these historically White student organizations continue to practice (see pp. 130–141). See also Heidenreich, in press
59. See Smith, Yosso, & Solórzano, in press (Adapted from Pierce, 1969, 1970, 1974, 1980, 1989, 1995)
60. See Freedman, 2005
61. True.
62. Smith & Allen, 2004
63. Well, they didn't really prepare me well in high school, I never had a chance to speak with a counselor.
64. Please! And the Advanced Placement classes were always already full.
65. From the beginning.
66. Recent legislation has begun to address this issue. For example, In California, recently passed Assembly Bill 540 allows undocumented immigrants who graduate from California high schools

after having been enrolled for three years to pay in-state tuition. In Utah, a similar Senate Bill 144 recently passed. Anti-immigrant groups in both states are challenging these bills respectively. U.S. Congress has not yet passed The DREAM Act, which would function as the national version of these state bills. For further discussion of navigation issues for undocumented female Mexican college students, see Rangel, 2001.

67. I mean.
68. For example, see Becerra, 2004; See also http://www.ucop.edu/acadadv/datamgmt/welcome.html (Retrieved September 25, 2004).
69. Nelson & Pellet, (prds.), 1997. For transcripts, teaching guides, and further resources, see http://www.pbs.org/shattering
70. Delgado Bernal, 2002
71. Anzaldúa, 1987, p. 86
72. Sylvia Hurtado and Luis Ponjuan's (2005) recent research on campus climate confirms the importance of academic support programs for Latina/o college students.
73. Revilla, 2003, 2004a, 2004b
74. Anzaldúa (1987) explains, "Knowledge makes me more aware, it makes me more conscious. 'Knowing' is painful because after 'it' happens I can't stay in the same place and be comfortable. I am no longer the same person I was before … *No hay más que cambiar* (pp. 48–49).
75. Advice.
76. Respect for the rights of others is peace.
77. See Proverbs 16:24
78. Like honey, Esmeralda, sweet, but also healthy.
79. This strategy seems to demonstrate itself in three processes: confrontation, motivation, and navigation (see Yosso, 2002a).
80. For more on "prove them wrong" strategies, see Yosso, 2000
81. Muñoz, D. G., 1986
82. See Astin, 1984, 1996
83. For more on "racial battle fatigue," see Smith, 2004
84. Solórzano & Villalpando, 1998

5

"IT'S EXHAUSTING BEING MEXICAN AMERICAN!"

Navigating through Graduate School at the University of the Southwest[1]

INTRODUCTION

The structural inequalities evidenced earlier along the pipeline hinder Chicana/o access to postsecondary education.[2] In terms of the number of doctorates produced over the last 20 years, Chicanas/os remain the most underrepresented population compared to White, African American, Asian American, Native American, and Latina/o women and men.[3] Chicanas/os earned 1% of all the doctorate degrees produced in U.S. universities from 1990–2000.[4]

Outside of some initial works in the 1980s, most research on Chicana/o doctorate production has occurred in the last 10 years.[5] Research up until this time primarily examined the career paths of select samples of Ph.D.s such as Nobel Prize recipients in science,[6] Nobel Prize women in science,[7] sociologists,[8] women psychologists,[9] and professors from the working class.[10] Each of these works identified those factors shaping career paths, but none focused primarily on Scholars of Color and only one study included a single Chicana case.[11] The few studies that did discuss Latina/o underrepresentation in graduate school rarely provided information by specific Latina/o subgroups (i.e., Chicana/o).[12]

Over the last decade, an increasing number of scholars have examined Chicana/o educational and career paths utilizing qualitative research methods and datasets that allow for disaggregation of data by Latina/o subgroup. Each of the studies mentioned below function to fill some of the gaps in our knowledge about Chicana/o graduate school experiences. This research also demonstrates the importance of breaking down the data by racial subgroup and gender.

For example, Patricia Gándara's[13] research focused on 20 Chicana and 30 Chicano Ph.D.s, J.D.s, and M.D.s, and documented their journeys to the doctorate with a special emphasis on family, neighborhood, and K–12 influences. Gándara describes the process Chicanas endure in pursuit of the doctorate being as difficult as "passing through the eye of a needle."[14] Aida Morales[15] and Shirley Achor[16] conducted research with 100 Chicana doctorates in the field of education, and noted that these scholars' mothers—who had acquired very little formal education themselves—strongly supported and influenced their daughters' academic pursuits. Gloria Cuádraz[17] studied 17 Chicana and 23 Chicano former doctoral students at the University of California, Berkeley, and found they developed strategies of "endurance labor" to survive graduate school. In addition, Daniel Solórzano's[18] research centered on the critical life experiences of 22 Chicanas and 44 Chicanos who successfully earned their Ph.D. and received a Ford Foundation Minority Fellowship. Moreover, Luis Urrieta[19] interviewed 24 Chicana/o professors negotiating their "activist" identity within the constraints of academia, and documented their road from undergraduate studies through graduate school and into the professoriate. Other research reflecting on Chicana/o experiences in graduate school includes Eric Margolis and Mary Romero's[20] study of 26 Women of Color graduate students enrolled in sociology Ph.D. programs.

Furthermore, doctoral dissertations over the last decade also address Chicana/o graduate school experiences. For example, Celia Villalpando's[21] research recounts the graduate education pursuits of 35 Chicana, Latina women from working-class backgrounds. She found their drive to persist often generated from family support, cultural pride, and a sense of community responsibility. Scott Heimlich's[22] study describes the socioacademic roads of 12 Mexican Americans in the process of earning their Ph.D. in science at a leading research university. Patricia Ponce[23] documents the life histories of 20 Chicanas/os who earned their Ph.D. before 1965. She addresses their experiences as "pioneers" blazing a path for Chicana/o scholars to follow. Rebeca Burciaga's[24] research examines the personal and professional aspirations of Chicana doctoral students, and explores graduate school as a space/place of *nepantla*[25]—a threshold of multiple realities with immense potential for transformation.

Autobiographical accounts of Chicana/o scholars also add to the scholarship on Chicana/o graduate school experiences. For example, in Raymond Padilla and Rudolfo Chavez's edited volume, *The Leaning Ivory Tower: Latino Professors in American Universities*,[26] 12 Latina and Latino Ph.D.s write about some of their student and faculty experiences in academia. Likewise, in the edited volume, *Telling to Live: Latina Feminist Testimonios*,[27] 18 Latina professors reflect on their lives within and beyond academia. Gloria Cuádraz and Jennifer Pierce's article, "From Scholarship Girls to Scholarship Women: Surviving the Contradictions of Race and Class in Academe,"[28] shares their personal experiences as a Chicana and a White woman both from working-class origins, struggling through graduate school. Similarly, Chicano legal scholar Kevin Johnson's manuscript, *How Did You Get to Be Mexican?: A White/Brown Man's Search for Identity*,[29] recounts his personal and educational journey. Moreover, the autobiographical essays of Chicana/Latina scholars Yolanda Flores-Niemann,[30] Concha Delgado-Gaitan,[31] Martha Montero-Sieburth,[32] Margaret Montoya,[33] Leslie Espinoza,[34] Maria Matute-Bianchi,[35] and Martha Bernal[36] insightfully document their graduate school and academic experiences.[37]

Examining critical transition points along the Chicana/o educational pipeline may provide insights for those concerned with the severe underrepresentation of Chicanas/os earning graduate and doctorate degrees. Research indicates for example, that almost one quarter of Chicanas/os who earned their doctorate from 1990–2000 began their postsecondary education at a community college.[38] This pattern confirms the crucial and under-researched role of the community college transfer function for Chicanas/os pursuing higher education.[39] Since only 7% of Chicanas/os earn their baccalaureate, 93% of Chicanas/os do not have the basic prerequisite for graduate studies. Indeed, the baccalaureate degree represents an important step on the road to the doctorate.[40] Studies of the baccalaureate origins of science doctorates date back to the 1950s and continue to the early 1980s.[41] Solórzano[42] updated this baccalaureate literature through his research on the undergraduate origins of Chicana/o doctorates from 1980–1990. This chapter begins to extend beyond Solórzano's baseline work,[43] with some preliminary analysis of Chicana/o doctorate production from 1990–2000.[44]

Just as the high schools many Chicanas/os attend restrict students' access to information about higer education options and college preparatory courses, universities seldom promote a graduate-school-going culture for Chicanas/os. Because most Chicana/o undergraduates are first-generation college students, they may not know anyone who has attended college, let alone come in contact with a role model who can guide them through the process of applying to graduate school. Such guidance may, for example, reveal that to successfully pursue a Ph.D., undergraduates need to conduct research with faculty and begin to develop their own research interests. This often requires voluntary, time-intensive commitment , which may prove quite difficult for an undergraduate student who works full time to financially bear the cost of college. In addition, Chicanas/os may feel uncomfortable or ambivalent about approaching professors, especially when it seems unclear whether faculty will belittle or encourage Students of Color in their pursuit of graduate school. Furthermore, Chicana/o college students tend to find severely limited access to role models in the form of Chicana/o faculty. While discriminatory hiring practices exacerbate the already low numbers of Chicana/o faculty, the conditions leading up to the doctorate and the doctoral process itself contribute to the dismal number of Chicana/o academics.[45]

Chicana/o undergraduates applying for Ph.D. programs will find that to be considered for admission, they must not only demonstrate a strong academic record, but in addition, their research interests need to match those of the graduate program's faculty. Most often, admissions committees at the graduate school level assess incoming applications for consistent scholastic excellence and high scores on standardized exams (e.g., LSAT, GRE, MCAT). Even though standardized exams such as the Graduate Record Exam (GRE) provide invalid and culturally biased measures of academic potential, graduate programs continue to uses these exams to deny admission to and financial support for Chicanas/os. In addition, committees consider the student's statement of purpose and the strength of letters of recommendation from faculty who address the student's academic record and potential for graduate study. Chicana/o students' enrollment in graduate school depends on the extent that they can garner (1) undergraduate faculty support through research opportunities and recommendation letters; (2) graduate faculty support through a common research interest; and of course (3) financial support.

After surmounting these admissions and enrollment barriers, a Chicana/o student must deal realistically with the fact that she/he may be the only Chicana/o and perhaps the only Person of Color in her/his graduate program. Most graduate programs feature racially segregated, predominately White student and faculty populations. Additionally, graduate school curricula tend to exclude Chicana/o histories and perspectives. Within this isolating context, Chicanas/os regularly experience racial and gender microaggressions,[46] lowered expectations from faculty, and pressure to be the spokesperson for all Chicanas/os or all People of Color.[47] Often, Chicana/o scholars reflect on graduate school as a place where they felt invisible[48]—like outsiders[49] or imposters.[50] Such experiences cause many Chicanas/os to doubt their academic abilities, question the value of their academic contributions, and reconsider their decision to pursue the doctorate.[51]

Research suggests that in response to racial microaggressions and marginality, Chicana/o graduate students engage in strategies to survive and succeed, strategies to "prove wrong" those who assumed they could not or would not achieve the doctorate.[52] For example, Chicana/o students who feel silenced by the curriculum and class discussion may maintain strategic silence in the classroom, and refrain from speaking until a moment when they believe others will acknowledge their remarks.[53] Some students also strategically separate themselves from the racial and gender hostility of graduate school by creating counterspaces of academic and social support.[54] These counterspaces may take the form of a course led by a supportive faculty member, a student-initiated writing group, or a community service organization. Counterspaces in graduate school help Chicanas/os nurture a sense of confidence in their academic abilities and reaffirm the value of their research contributions. As evidenced along the other levels of the pipeline, Chicanas/os actively resist the pervasive racism and sexism that works to marginalize them in graduate school. These Chicanas/os choose to redefine the margins as a place of possibility instead of a place of oppression.[55]

In addition to examining the above outlined social science scholarship along with the autobiographical and biographical reflections of Chicana/o Ph.D.s, the counterstory in this chapter draws on data from (1) The National Research Council's Survey of Earned Doctorates from 1990–2000,[56] and (2) focus groups conducted in 2000 at the University of Michigan Law School.[57] To address this scholarship and data, the counterstory engages two composite characters in dialogue about Chicana/o graduate school experiences—Paula Guevara and Professor Sanchez. Paula is a graduate student studying sociocultural education at a large research university in the southwestern United States (University of the Southwest, USW). Dr. Tomás Sanchez is a senior professor at USW and chairs Paula's dissertation committee.[58] Professor Sanchez and Paula meet in a coffee shop adjacent to the university to discuss their collaborative work in progress. Their story begins here:

TOMÁS CAFÉ CON LECHE?: BEGINNING TO EXAMINE CHICANA/O GRADUATE SCHOOL EXPERIENCES

"Professor Sanchez! Hi, I'm sorry I'm late, I had a little scare with a rattlesnake on my front porch." "Uh oh," replied Sanchez, "He was just looking for shade probably. Are you and your roommate OK?" "Oh yeah," I said, "It just took me a while to convince Eva it was safe to make a run for the car. She sends her *saludos*." I reached out to shake his hand and he stood and gave me a hug across the little round table. Seeing he already had some coffee, I offered to get him a refill and asked, *"Tomás café con leche?"*[59] He smiled and said, "Some nondairy creamers are fine for me, thanks Paula." I then realized my own joke—his name was also Tomás. I'm so used to calling him Professor Sanchez, I don't think I've ever called him by his first name. As I ordered a piece of zucchini bread, an iced decaf carmel coffee, and a refill for Sanchez, I went over in my head some of the main issues I needed to remember to discuss with him. The editors of a new journal focused on Chicanas/os in education invited Sanchez to submit an article and he graciously asked me to co-author with him. With the deadline coming up, we needed a draft soon.

I sat back down at the table and unloaded a small pile of nondairy creamers and a stirrer for Professor Sanchez, who was skimming over headlines from the local newspaper. He began to stir in the creamers and asked me how I was doing. Since we usually began our meetings with social updates before jumping into the academic issues, we spoke for a few minutes about *Las Madres*, a parent group I'd been working with for a few years. I asked him whether he believes in ghosts and shared with him a strange encounter I experienced at a recent *Las Madres* meeting.[60] After listening intently to my recounting the events of that evening, Sanchez calmly said, "I hope we have some of that same spirited inspiration for our work." Then pointing out the window, he asked me, "Is that Gloria Anzaldúa out there?" I gasped, and turned to look out the coffee shop window, quickly realizing Sanchez was teasing me.

We laughed and then his face turned more serious as he said, "Paula, I am so proud of you. I finished reading over the latest draft of your dissertation and it is really, really good." Seeing the broad smile on my face, he cautioned, "I do have some feedback, but you're doing really good work. I like how you're re-conceptualizing parent involvement and community cultural wealth—I've always told you, you're bad!" I laughed out loud, partly to ease my embarrassment and partly because of Sanchez's use of the term "bad." I managed to say, "Thank you, I'm so glad you like it. I know I still have some work to do, but I am starting to feel a little better after addressing some of the concerns you had. You wanted to make sure I really listened to the parents' voices and let them tell their own story. And I never would have been able to do this without your encouragement." I paused and then said, "After so much struggle to get here, it's hard to believe I'm so close to jumping through this last hoop." Sanchez replied, "Yes, almost there."

I took a quick sip of my caramel-covered coffee and asked, "How are things with you?" I broke off a piece of zucchini bread and offered to share with Sanchez. He took a small piece and dipped it in his coffee before eating it. He replied, "Things are good. I just made plane reservations to go visit my niece in California. It's her first quarter at UC-Oceanview, so Melinda and I are going to go hang out for a few days. You know how important that first quarter is, that first year actually, especially for Chicanas/os. She's the first of the nieces and nephews and hopefully not the last. My brother wanted her to stay here, maybe go to USW instead of going out-of-state, but he's very proud and happy for her. They took the train out there last month and he helped her settle into the dorms. Apparently, she has two roommates in her half of a dorm suite that connects to another room, and six people share the bathroom." I nodded knowingly and Sanchez continued, "My brother said she was all excited to be close to both the beach and the city. But he's been an emotional wreck. And for me, of course, it's just been crazy with writing letters of recommendation, chairing a faculty search committee, teaching a new course, and trying to revise and resubmit an article that I'm writing with one of my former students who is now an assistant professor over there at UC-Oceanview. Have you ever met Leticia Garcia?" "I don't think so," I said. He paused briefly, then continued, "Leticia and I are writing an article about whether it's possible to engage in Freirean methodology, to practice critical pedagogy within the constraints of university structures.[61] We actually began working on it at a sociology conference last year." "I'd be very interested in reading that," I remarked. "Maybe you can read over our draft and offer some suggestions?" he offered. I nodded and ate a piece of the zucchini bread.

POSTPONING FAMILIA FOR ACADEMIA?

"Professor Sanchez, I got that job notice you emailed a couple weeks ago and I don't want to disappoint you, but I'm seriously thinking about whether I should apply to work at a Research I institution or not." I started to tear up, so I took a deep breath and a sip of my sweet, cool drink to calm down. I looked down as I continued; "It's just that I'm still feeling so out of place. Sometimes, I feel like I'm suffocating. Outside of USW, I could be working with so many communities. And I feel like I do a lot of talking about social change without having any time or energy to even engage in the activism I used to do." I paused briefly and looked up at him and said, "And I feel like I'm getting old already, and graduate school is just postponing my life."

Professor Sanchez's eyebrow raised, and he smiled slightly, "OK, now that's a lot of concerns to unpack. To start, 'activism' comes in many forms, and you are actively engaged working with *Las Madres*. But I think I also know what you mean about reassessing your role as a scholar-activist or activist-scholar. Many of those who struggled for civil rights over the years will tell you to expect a series of gains and setbacks in the fight for social and racial justice, but we rarely tell each other about the personal and emotional gains and setbacks we experience during those struggles. I often feel the same way about whether I'm 'doing enough.' Hopefully that discomfort keeps us grounded, so we don't start thinking too highly of ourselves—and it also keeps us going."[62] Sanchez paused to drink some coffee before adding, "Let me ask, though, what do you mean by *old*?" I smiled and felt my face get hot, though I knew he was joking.

I continued, "This last weekend, after being a bridesmaid at yet another one of my friend's weddings, I went home and downloaded some articles and came across this report by Mary Ann Mason and Marc Goulden." I pulled my folder out from my bag and flipped through the articles quickly, placing a report on the table next to Professor Sanchez's coffee, titled *Do Babies Matter?: The Effect of Family Formation on the Life Long Careers of Academic Men and Women.*[63]

Looking through the article, he nodded and said, "Yes, a colleague forwarded this to me when it came out and then I just downloaded the second part of the study last week." He pulled his laptop from his bag and turned it on. After searching briefly through his computer desktop files, he said, "Yep, here it is, *Do Babies Matter Part II: Closing the Baby Gap.*"[64] "Oh wow!" I responded, consistently amazed at his ability to stay up-to-date in addition to all his other teaching and research responsibilities. I don't know if I will ever reach that level.

I explained, "Well, as you know then, Mason and Goulden utilize the Survey of Doctorate Recipients (SDR), to investigate 'the theory that the workplace structure does not accommodate families with children,'[65] and they find that for women, yes, babies do matter." I paused and made a face at Sanchez, sarcastically noting, "Thus the answer to the question in the title. But they also find that the timing of babies matters so much so that 'there is a consistent and large gap in achieving tenure for women who have early babies in contrast to men who have early babies.'[66] So women who have babies within 5 years of earning their Ph.D. are 24% less likely to receive tenure in the sciences than men and 20% less likely than men to earn tenure in humanities and social sciences. And the authors compare these women to men who have babies, not just single men working toward tenure. The data indicate that 'Overall, women who attain tenure across disciplines are not likely to have children in the household.'[67] I skimmed through the article searching for a specific quote and added, "But here comes the real kicker. It says that 'Women in science who achieve tenure are twice as likely as men to be single!'[68] And that the gap between the numbers of women versus men who remain single in the social sciences and humanities also looms quite large. I took a deep breath and blurted, "I don't know, Professor. As a Chicana, how can I apply to a Research I school?"

"As a Chicana?" he asked. I continued, "Well, yes, this research confirms that the demands of a Research I institution may mean I have to choose between having a partner and a family or achieving tenure. According to most of my uncles, my cousin Itza and I have been 'old maids' since we reached our mid-20s. Sanchez laughed out loud, "Old maids, huh? Did your cousin also go to graduate school?" "Yes," I replied, realizing that saying 'old maids' out loud did sound pretty funny. "Law school. She's now studying for her bar exams."

Professor Sanchez regained his composure, took a sip of his coffee, and said, "These are the times when I really wish a Chicana scholar could give you some insights. Though I don't think we can get into all the gendered expectations your uncles have for you and your cousin, maybe we can address what the article says about women in the academy." I nodded in agreement and said, "OK, well, Mason and Goulden outline two theories that can account for the disparity in tenure achievement. The first is what they call the 'glass ceiling theory,' which emphasizes gender discrimination." Sanchez looked through the article again, and noted, "Ah, yes, they draw on the phrase 'a thousand paper cuts'[69] to refer to the patterns of subtle and overt gender-based incidents that keep women in subordinated positions to men." "Yes," I said, "And they separate discrimination theory from theoretical models emphasizing structures and systems that perpetuate gender inequality." Sanchez sipped his coffee as he skimmed and noted some of the author's findings, "Conflicts arise when the system requires academics to work 60 hours per week, travel to conferences, and relocate to wherever the jobs are available." He remarked, "Yes, they basically say the tenure track structures don't allow for the flexibility women with families need. So remind me, what do Mason and Goulden suggest?"

I sighed as I flipped through the article, found the recommendations sections, and responded, "They make some very good recommendations about how universities can provide mentoring for graduate students around issues of family/career conflicts," I paused with a smirk, acknowledging our participation in just such a mentoring moment. I went on, "They recommend policies for stopping the clock, taking leaves, discounting the 'résumé gap,' and allowing for ladder-rank faculty to be on a part-time track without penalty for re-entry to full time,"[70] I trailed off.

Seeing that I looked unconvinced about the researchers' suggestions, Sanchez gently asked, "But?" I bit my lower lip, thinking about how to word it, "Well, maybe they have it in the more recent article, but besides the fact that there are no recommendations for me as a single woman finishing her Ph.D., they don't break down the gender numbers by race. So as I went through, I kept asking, 'What about Chicanas?' I think the lack of a racial/gender breakdown restricts the authors' ability to 'see' the connection between structural inequality and discrimination, as opposed to referring to them as two separate theories."

Sanchez scrolled through the article on his laptop and responded, "It looks like in this follow-up article, they don't give suggestions for single women per se, but they urge institutions to incorporate more family-friendly policies that would perhaps encourage some women who weren't sure about the timing of getting married and having children before tenure." I winced as he continued, "They find that 'Only one in three women who takes a fast-track university job before having a child ever becomes a mother.' And as you might say, here's the kicker, 'Women who achieve tenure are more than twice as likely as their male counterparts to be single 12 years after earning the Ph.D.'"[71]

I dramatically exclaimed, "Single 12 years after tenure? Ah man!" "Actually, they're saying no man!" Sanchez replied, knowing I'd appreciate his quick wit. He added, "For men, family decisions don't tend to come at the expense of professional success. In fact, the authors explain that men who have babies within the first 5 years after earning their Ph.D. are 38% more likely to achieve tenure than women!"[72]

I admitted, "I guess I'm jumping a little ahead of myself. I have to finish the dissertation and get through graduate school first." Sanchez added, "I agree, and I still think you should put in an application. You'll be filed and done by the spring. And what a unique position, to be hired specifically to teach Chicana/o education from a sociological perspective. Plus, it doesn't start til the fall. But at the same time, I think it's important for you to think about all this, because those aren't very encouraging patterns and it's better to know what you're up against. Many of us intuitively knew something was happening. I mean, it's all around us. Our colleagues struggle to balance family with the academy, but we rarely discuss these issues openly, let alone examine them as our research focus."

I nodded in agreement and said, "But the authors' blindspot in terms of looking at race actually puts even more pressure on me as a Chicana to make sure I don't become one of those women who doesn't get tenure." Sanchez looked a little confused, so I explained further. "I feel like as a Chicana academic, I'm already dealing with racialized assumptions about whether I deserve to be a ladder-rank faculty member. And that's just me being a brown Chicana in a very White place. But a young, brown, pregnant Chicana? Or later, a Chicana with maybe a few kids? Then I'll have to not only deal with structures that discriminate against women, but also deal with racial stereotypes about Mexican women being sexually promiscuous." Sanchez added sarcastically, "or dependent on social services, and creating Spanish-speaking children who are a 'burden' on the U.S. school system?"

"But seriously," I continued, "I know I'm probably worrying too far in advance, but the article also reminded me that we need more Chicanas to earn tenure in the academy because not enough people ask the questions that we do. They just don't seem to think about us. And so that means I need to not only 'prove wrong' the ideas and assumptions my colleagues may hold about Mexican women, but I also need to succeed through the tenure track so I can contribute to the research by and about Chicanas."[73]

Sanchez began typing a few notes into the computer. "Can you say that again?" he asked. "What did I say?" I replied. I paused and said, "I feel pressure to 'prove them wrong.' To succeed in academia not just for myself, but for those who fought so I could be here and for those who will come after me." Sanchez finished typing and smiled broadly. "So your children and their children can succeed in academia." I appreciated his optimism. I could not bring myself to ask about what sacrifices he may have made to resolve the family/work conflict. I know I am a direct beneficiary of the time and energy he spends mentoring students.

Sanchez commented, "I'm typing this out because at some point, I want us to get back to the notion of 'proving them wrong.' It strikes me that you are talking about both resisting racism and being resilient in the face of inequality." He paused and so I added, "Maybe 'proving them wrong' is a form of resistance?" "Maybe," he replied. "Let's keep thinking about that."

A BRIEF ANALYSIS OF CHICANA/O DOCTORATE PRODUCTION

Sanchez dipped another bit of the zucchini bread into his coffee and asked, "Speaking of surviving and succeeding in academia, let's get to our article. I want you to be able to send a good draft of this article as part of your job application so the committee can see you're developing a publication record. The women organizing this special inaugural issue of *A Journal of Chicana and Chicano Education* have asked us to address Chicana/o doctorate production generally. So, I thought we could maybe reflect on our personal experiences on the road to the Ph.D. and draw on the social science literature to create a composite of experiences—to humanize the numbers. Where are we on our brainstorming?"

I opened my book bag and said, "OK, what I did from last time we met is to begin to examine the National Research Council's annual Survey of Earned Doctorates (SED). The survey, as you know, generates data for each doctoral recipient's field, undergraduate origins, support received during doctorate years, doctorate granting institution, postdoctoral plans, as well as race and gender.[74] A few scholars have utilized this data to identify the baccalaureate origins of African American and Chicana/o doctorates[75] for instance, but no one has really analyzed this data since 1989. So we'll extend on some of that prior research and bring it up to date to include 1990–2000. But for this article, I think we had agreed that we would just use the data to frame the discussion in the rest of the article, no?" I asked. Sanchez nodded in agreement.

I brought out a graph from my bag and wiped some of the crumbs off the table to place it where we could both see. "Alrighty," I began, "from 1990–2000, U.S. universities produced 325,573 doctorates, and Chicanas/os earned 3,403 or 1% of these degrees. By gender, of the 177,236 total male-earned doctorates, Chicano men earned 1,788 (1%). And of the 148,337 total female earned doctorates, Chicana women earned 1,615 (1.1%). So that's the overall picture, but then I started focusing just on the women."

"Now, the first assumption you said people may make is that Chicanas earned fewer degrees because there are just fewer numbers of Chicanas compared to White women. So I looked for equitable representation in terms of how many Chicanas there are in the United States and how many White women. But of course, it has to be the number of women who would be possibly eligible for a doctorate, so they can't be 15 years old or something. And so I used Sue Berryman's[76] work here because she figured out that 32 is the median age for earning a Ph.D. Using the parity index created by Berryman and Daniel Solórzano,[77] I compared women from each racial/ethnic group between the ages of 30 and 34 years old. And I put the numbers on the graph here" (figure 5.1).

I continued, "U.S. Census data shows that from 1990–2000, 6.7% of Chicanas in the United States were between the ages of 30–34. And I had already calculated that Chicanas averaged 1.1% of the female doctorates earned in that 11-year period. It's pretty dramatic to see this disproportionate underrepresentation. In contrast, 69.7% of White women were between the ages of 30–34, but they earned 81.1% of the female doctorates from 1990–2000. Clearly, the data show White women disproportionately overrepresented in the number of earned female doctorates."

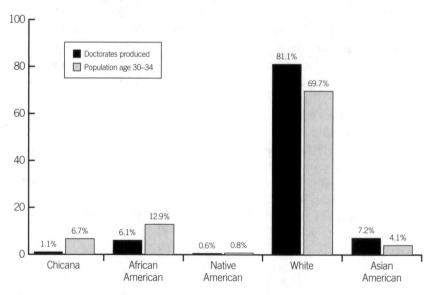

Figure 5.1. Average U.S. Female Doctoral Production Compared to Females Ages 30–34, 1990–2000[78]

Sanchez exclaimed, "To achieve parity—to even *reach* the level of their 30–34 year old age cohort—Chicana doctorate production would need to increase over 600%! And, looking at your chart, African American women earning doctorates would pretty much need to double, to go from 6.1% to 12.9% to reach parity. The data also indicate slight underrepresentation of Native American women doctorates, though that is an extremely small base." I noted, "And Asian American women doctorates appear overrepresented, though to a lesser extent than Whites."[79]

Sanchez made a few illegible notes on the side of the graph, looked up, and said, "Alright! This gives us a really good snapshot to frame the discussion. Although at some point I'd like to look at the numbers for Chicanos and African American men in comparison to their age cohort as well.[80] What did you have in mind for the best way to present this and tell a story of graduate school in the article?"

I finished off the rest of my iced coffee and said, "Good question. You mentioned creating a composite of experiences, and I'm thinking we should do a counterstory." Sanchez looked interested, so I continued, "It's very difficult to understand everything that happens to Chicana doctoral students without a critical understanding of the Chicana/o educational pipeline, but given space limits, we can only touch on that briefly. From the social science and humanities literature, we have already gathered multiple accounts of graduate school experiences from Chicanas and Women of Color, so I want to make sure to note those experiences of marginality. But I also want to mention those more personal family issues that are crucial to shaping some of the decisions Chicanas make in pursuit of the doctorate. Now that I'm looking at my notes, I'm remembering in the literature that the notion of 'proving them wrong' seemed to be a driving force for many Chicana/o scholars. And now we're thinking maybe we can conceptualize 'proving them wrong' as a form of resistance. All that to say I think the counterstory should be a discussion between a graduate student and her professor, kinda like what we're doing right now!"

THE INVISIBLE CHICANA: SILENCE AND SELF-DOUBT IN GRADUATE SCHOOL

Professor Sanchez glanced at his watch and said, "Do you want to walk over to the library then and continue this discussion?" We cleared off the table and walked out of the coffee shop to a beautiful sunny day. The slightly warm breeze caught me off guard and the graph I had shown Sanchez flew out of my hands. We finally caught up with the piece of paper about half a block down. Sanchez chided, "Are the spirits reminding us that equity is

elusive?" I retorted, "Or that we need to be more vigilant about documenting the legacy of racism?"

Agreeing it was too nice of a day to spend entirely inside the library,
we took a scenic walk through campus. As we walked, Sanchez asked me
to share some of my memories of starting graduate school. I thought for a
minute and then said, "I remember in my first year, I felt so out of place,
like I was an exotic creature on display at the zoo or something. I was the
only Chicana in my cohort, and as you know, I came straight from the B.A.,
while a lot of the students took time off school to work or raise a family
or whatever before returning to complete a Ph.D. So I definitely stuck out
as the youngest. And I had never really interacted so much with private-
school-educated students. The few Black women in my cohort pretty much
came from upper-class backgrounds and seemed to interact comfortably
right away with the White women. I remember other students talking about
their winter break plans, and one was heading to the south of France while
another was traveling to meet her fiancé's parents, who were dignitaries
somewhere in South America. What am I going to say to that? 'My plan is
to make *tamales* with my family?' Sanchez interjected, "I like *tamales*." "Me,
too," I said, "but you know what I mean." He nodded.

I continued, "Early on, the students organized themselves into groups
according to what week they had signed up to present the class readings
during the semester. I emailed my group and they told me the date, time,
and place, so I took off from work early that day to make sure I arrived
on time and ready to go. I waited for one hour, and finally one of the students from my group showed up. She casually commented that she had
only come up to that floor to make copies. It turns out the group had decided to change the location of the meeting. So I followed her downstairs
to find that the rest of the group had already planned out the presentation
and were finishing the meeting so they could head into the seminar. No one
had bothered to call or email me, but somehow they all communicated the
change in plans to each other. During the presentation, I winged my part,
but it looked choppy and the professor didn't seem too impressed. I ended
up looking unprepared."

I went on, "I also remember getting really bad migraines that first year
of grad school. But even though I felt uncomfortable, I still tried to speak
out, especially in those first few classes. I mean, as an undergraduate, I was
very outspoken, especially in my sociology or Chicana/o Studies courses.
As a graduate student, I really felt I had nothing to offer. I remember in
one of the *Intro to Urban Education* core courses, race finally came up as a
subject midway through the semester. As part of our discussion on *Brown
v. Board of Education*,[81] the professor asked the class to respond to one of
the readings that addressed the effects of desegregation on both Black and

White students. And as the discussion went on, I brought up the *Mendez v. Westminster*[82] case. I said something about *Brown* affecting Mexican students and Mexican students affecting *Brown* through the *Mendez* decision in 1946.[83] And right away, the professor responded that the *Mendez* case was only a state case and had no bearing on the *Brown* decision. I replied that *Mendez* set precedent in being the first case to strike down the 1896 *Plessy v. Ferguson*[84] 'separate but equal' doctrine, and that legal precedent provides the basis for how attorneys argue at the higher court levels. I even turned to one of the other students in the class who was a lawyer returning to get her Ph.D. And she just sat there, silent. So the professor again said my remark lacked relevance and the discussion moved on. At that moment I felt so alone, so invisible. All these students with blank stares and the professor dismissing not just my contribution, but ignoring historical fact—like writing Chicanas/os out of history right there in the classroom."

Professor Sanchez remarked, "He probably wasn't familiar enough with the case and so you inadvertently challenged his mystique as the all-knowing professor." I threw my hands up in the air and stated, "Obviously! But even though I knew he was wrong and *Mendez* did impact *Brown*, it still made me doubt myself. I went home and was so mad at myself for not saying more. I should've explained that Thurgood Marshall—the NAACP[85] attorney who argued the *Brown* case in the Supreme Court—also filed an amicus brief in the *Mendez* case 8 years earlier. I could've said that in California, the *Mendez* case led to the Andersen bill—legislation repealing all mandated racial segregation from the State's education school code.[86] Governor Earl Warren signed that bill into law—the same Warren who became Chief Justice of the U.S. Supreme Court, and ruled in the *Brown* case 8 years later!"[87]

Sanchez nodded and added, "I've been there. The professor made you second-guess yourself and that experience can kind of stun you. So you might have that delayed response, and you go home thinking, 'Oh, I could've said this, I should've said that!' I'm sure you know that you were right on about the links between *Mendez* and *Brown*. Actually, Marshall *co-authored* that amicus brief on behalf of the NAACP in the *Mendez* case. The *Mendez* case also set precedent because of the use of social science research to support legal arguments. The prosecution used social scientist expert witnesses, and the Judge used social science alongside legal precedent to make his ruling. And the NAACP picked up on that strategy and used it in *Brown* with the Kenneth Clark doll studies."[88]

Sanchez continued, "Have you read Aida Hurtado's book *The Color of Privilege: Three Blasphemies on Race and Feminism*?"[89] "Yes, a few years ago," I replied. "Well," said Sanchez, "Do you remember toward the end, where she uses a form of critical race theory counterstorytelling to construct a fable about the unspoken race and gender rules of power?" I nodded hesitantly, not sure what he was getting at.

He went on, "She is explaining how society oppresses Women of Color through an unspoken 'treaty' that includes multiple rules of race, gender, and class.[90] But she uses a 'Trickster' character to begin to reveal some of these rules. So the 'Trickster' starts out by explaining, 'If I am not the center of the universe, you do not exist. If I am not the central actor in whatever drama, I will not listen to you, I will not acknowledge your presence...my ability to not *see* you is my power. If I do not see you, you do not exist. If you only exist at my will, you are nothing without my attention. I am, therefore, the one who controls who is *real* and who is not.'"[91]

"Whoa," I took a minute to let that really sink in. "I'll have to go back and re-read that section to see if I made any notes in the margins. We walked in silence for a few moments.

Thinking to myself, I recalled legal scholar Margaret Montoya's[92] recent article on silence and silencing. Through her painful experiences of being silenced and rendered invisible, she came to believe that silence offers a pedagogical tool that can transform the courtroom and the classroom. I mentioned this to Sanchez and he agreed, "Silence can be very powerful, whether it is imposed or whether we choose silence. Audre Lorde's poem 'Litany of Silence'[93] says it's better to speak out and I think Montoya also says we need to break the silence, right?" I nodded.

Sanchez continued, "But they both recognize that it's difficult to decide when to be silent or when to speak—especially when others refuse to even see you, let alone listen.[94] You know, psychologist Olivia Espin[95] writes about maintaining silence as a form of self-preservation. Her work resonates with that research project I've been working on, examining how law school Students of Color experience and respond to the campus racial climate. In my analysis of the focus group transcripts, I found a clear pattern of students feeling very isolated, just like you. And in response, they choose to remain silent.[96] They rarely speak out in class—as a strategy—hoping that when they do comment, people will listen. But I know it's very hard to know what strategy to use and when.[97] I added, "Especially when you feel your heart practically beating in your head as you raise your hand to challenge racism and White privilege in spaces where folks haven't given those issues much thought." Sanchez agreed, "Even as they silence you, they seem blind to the ways they 'other' your experience, and recenter their White and male privilege."[98]

We continued walking and I remarked, "What also hits me about that day in class where I tried to talk about *Mendez* is like what you said about second-guessing myself. I really began to doubt myself. And it brought back the same feeling of self-doubt I remember experiencing when I was an undergraduate and I thought that someone would come up to me and say, 'You know, your application was mistakenly put in the *yes* pile, so we apologize, but this whole thing has been an error. You're going to have to pack your bags and leave. You aren't supposed to be here.'"[99]

I continued, "And that voice of self-doubt comes up time and again as I've continued through academia. I mean, how did I get through educational structures that systematically limit access to graduate school for Chicanas/os? How did I survive through the first-grade class where the teacher and school psychologist labeled me Educable Mentally Retarded because of my very low standardized exam scores? I guess they didn't have the staff to offer the exam in Spanish at that time. How did I survive being bussed to the middle school across town? It was located in a White neighborhood, but the White parents sent their kids to private schools. So instead of attending my local middle school with my Chicana/o neighbors, I spent 2 hours a day on a bus to go to a school with Chicana/o kids from all across the city.[100] How did I survive going to a high school with one college counselor for a couple thousand students, and a constant police presence? I had a better chance of getting information from the army recruiters than I did from the local college. Some of my teachers in high school told me that I wasn't really 'college material' even though I earned A's in the few Advanced Placement (AP) classes the school offered. I was one of the very few Students of Color in those predominately White AP classes, even though my high school was predominately Latina/o.[101] I graduated number five in my senior class, but when one of my classmates found out a 'prestigious' university accepted me, the first comments out of her mouth were, 'Well, they made it easier for you to get in because you're Mexican.' And I know so many of my friends from my K–12 years were actually much smarter than me, more critical and really sharp, but they didn't have the opportunity to go to college, let alone graduate school. And part of me sometimes feels guilty about being the one who's here." I paused, realizing my heart seemed like it had really started pounding from recalling all those barriers. I remarked, "So to be silenced as a doctoral student, well, it brings back a lot of memories."

"Obviously," teased Sanchez. "The literature shows us that many Chicanas and other Scholars of Color face the same self-doubt,[102] survivor's guilt[103] and imposter syndrome.[104] And few professors or other graduate students are prepared to even address these issues in a theoretical discussion, let alone deal with an actual student who has struggled through urban schools and who is already dealing with the personal aspects of internalized racism."

"Personal aspects of internalized racism?" I asked. "Yes," said Sanchez, "self-doubt, survivor's guilt, and the imposter syndrome represent three of the more personal aspects of internalized racism that Scholars of Color face in historically White institutions. We may be able to intellectualize about racial formations in the United States[105] and examine the multiple forms of racism, but we rarely examine the psychophysiological effects these racial formations and multiple forms of racism have on our bodies, minds, and spirits."[106]

RACIAL MICROAGGRESSIONS, MEES, AND RACIAL BATTLE FATIGUE

Sanchez explained, "Some scholars have begun to analyze these effects by focusing on daily, often subtle forms of racism. Take for instance the work of Chester Pierce, a psychiatrist and professor of education. Pierce has published research since at least the 1970s documenting racism occurring as subtle, stunning mini-assaults, or what he termed 'racial microaggressions.'[107] He asserts that these racialized put-downs have both immediate and long-term, cumulative effects on Blacks. A few other scholars have expanded on Pierce's research to look at some of the layers of these racial insults, like gender, phenotype, accent."[108] I nodded, remembering reading about Chicana/o scholars enduring racial microaggressions in academia.[109]

Sanchez continued, "Grace Carroll[110] extends Pierce's work to describe that being Black in the United States means living in a society permeated by mundane and extreme racism and punctuated by incessant microaggressions. So she finds that African Americans face mundane extreme environmental stress, or what she calls MEES. And William Smith[111] then focuses on the stress part of the equation, explaining that constant exposure to MEES reveals the cumulative effect of racial microaggressions. He argues that the stress associated with racial microaggressions causes African Americans to experience various forms of mental and physical strain, or what he terms 'racial battle fatigue.'"[112]

I listened intently as Sanchez added, "Your experiences confirm that Chicanas/os are very likely to experience MEES in graduate school. And the cumulative stress of dealing with racial microaggressions often results in racial battle fatigue. We may not even be aware of the connections between racism and our increased blood pressure, or headaches, nervousness, increased swearing, nightmares, or other symptoms, so the racial battle fatigue goes untreated or misdiagnosed.[113]

"Because graduate programs tend to tokenize or exoticize Chicanas, and omit, distort, or stereotype Chicana/o histories,[114] they fail to see students like you as a resource. As some of your research suggests, Chicana/o students cultivate a wealth of cultural knowledge, skills, abilities, and networks in their homes and communities. But schools rarely recognize those valuable forms of knowledge. Your work complements Dolores Delgado Bernal's research showing that Students of Color are 'holders and creators of knowledge.'[115] Delgado Bernal suggests that universities' policies should acknowledge Chicana students' *mestiza*[116] consciousness and ways of knowing as assets.[117] I'm not saying universities should *exploit* your knowledges, but they are really missing out on learning from your experiences and the historical memory you bring to this historically White, middle-class space. And they make you feel like you have nothing to contribute! There seems to be a little bit of arrogance in the dismissive way my colleagues tend to treat Chicanas."

I DIDN'T FLUNK...THEY FAILED ME

We paused in our discussion to walk up a steep flight of stairs that curved and led to a gravel-covered road. We headed toward the "top" of the campus, looking to be inspired by the incredible panoramic city view.

Maybe the heat had started to affect me or I am just really out of shape, but I felt a little out of breath as we climbed the stairs. Sanchez, who is an avid runner, continued the dialogue without any indication of physical strain. He said, "I've seen that faculty tend to treat Chicano students a little differently—as if Chicanos should be *cleaning* their office, not going to their office hours. Or Chicano students are watched with suspicion and questioned about their 'business' on campus. And of course, academic elitism and classism enable faculty to only acknowledge forms of cultural capital they see in themselves. And gender discrimination in academia privileges men, like we discussed with the issue of family/work conflict. But Chicanos do experience gendered racism and I don't think we know enough about that. We need more research on the ways race and gender intersect."[118]

I replied, "I agree. For a Chicana like me, from a working-class background, race, gender, and class link inextricably and most research doesn't really 'get' that." I caught my breath and said, "I'm not sure how this connects to MEES and racial battle fatigue, but I don't remember being so angry before graduate school. I mean, coming to my identity as a Chicana stirred up a lot of emotion, and at times, when I learned about the histories omitted from my elementary, junior high, and high school classes, I was angry. But not like this. And I really didn't feel very angry when I started graduate school either. I felt hopeful and optimistic. I started asking questions and I guess that made people uncomfortable like you said, because it showed that they might have had some blindspots in their theoretical approaches to urban schooling. Like, I asked why do we label *students* 'at risk' of failing school instead of labeling *schools* 'at risk' of failing students? Those questions earned me the 'angry

Chicana' label, and it stuck with me. But I guess it worked in my favor when the qualifying exams committee failed me."

"Oh yes, anger can be an asset sometimes," Sanchez remarked. "That might be something we can include in the article, remind me again what happened with your exams? I remember you went and respectfully asked each of the three professors to give you feedback and help you understand why they failed you?" "Yes!" I recalled, "One said that I exaggerated the issue of race and another felt that I misunderstood the concept of agency. Ironically, for someone who supposedly didn't understand the concept, I certainly ended up exercising my agency."

Sanchez asked, "It seems like they were surprised you questioned their decision." "I think so," I replied, "They asked me to bring them a copy of my exam so they could outline where I had gone wrong. The professor who had dismissed my comments about *Mendez* in his class said that I lacked critical analysis skills, but he couldn't really identify any analysis problems on my exam. It was like they were responding to their impression of me as a quiet student. It didn't even phase them that they had silenced me during their courses." Imitating the professors, I sarcastically asked, "Why is she so quiet?" Rolling my eyes, I exclaimed, "Hmmm, I wonder?!"

I continued, "So I couldn't get them to really pin down what egregious errors I had committed. I asked them what my options were and they said I would benefit from sitting in on the three core courses again the following year and then I could retake the exam." Sanchez interjected, "Another year? I thought you could retake exams within the same academic year?" I responded, "Well, maybe not in my division. At least that's not the option they gave me. They wanted me to extend my program another year, but I didn't see them offering me any real reason why."

"I asked the Department secretary if I could make copies of the other students' exams to see where I went wrong. She said that was fine, and she suggested I also speak to the Department Chair if I had questions about the exam policy. I was too embarrassed and upset to read in the student lounge—in the building where my presence was being questioned as undeserved—so I took the copies home. And as I read, I stopped being shocked and hurt and started getting angry. I outlined line by line where the exam committee found faults in my essays and praised the other students for the same things. I mean, the exam grading was supposedly a 'blind' process, but I'm the only Chicana in my cohort and the only one who cites beyond the required readings to include Scholars of Color. After reading the other students' exams, I saw that it was obvious for the committee which exam I wrote. I remember coming to you and other professors to ask you to consider my exam in comparison with the other students to make sure I wasn't just imagining the discrepancies."

Sanchez noted, "That's right, I remember I was thinking, 'Those professors in your division are asking for trouble.' They were too obvious in treating your work differently. When I assessed the exams, I clearly saw that your responses were on par—if not better than most of the other students'—just on the quality of your writing alone! Yet they all passed without question."

I recalled, "So after talking with you, I went to ask the Chair of the Department about the protocol to challenge the committee's decision and he told me to write a letter asking them to reassess my exam. But the professors who had flunked me started hearing that I had consulted some of their colleagues on the merits of my exam and I planned to appeal the committee's decision." Sanchez nodded and said, "They realized they'd have to defend their decision and explain with evidence why they failed you. But because you had copies of the other exams, you had the evidence. It was clear they failed you without cause." I remarked, "I drafted this whole letter of appeal, but they 'reassessed' my exam before I submitted the request." Sanchez said, "Those initial critiques of your exam were more telling than the committee was willing to admit. I mean, here's a student who writes about and *embodies* race, agency, and critical analysis!"[119]

I conceded, "That whole process took a month and drained me emotionally. When I first got the letter that I failed, I went home and cried. Listening to the professors tell me I needed to retake a year of coursework, I felt discouraged. After I read the other students' exams and realized my exam had merit, I still couldn't shake that self-doubt they had created in me. And I felt totally exhausted just having to go to campus each day, continue my regular work as a TA, and take on this new job of fighting back against the exam committee."

Sanchez shook his head and said, "But you didn't let them crush you. You didn't let them stamp out that fire in your spirit.[120] They may have dampened it, and they certainly *tried* to stifle it, but you used that hurt and that anger to fuel your spirit. I hope we include this as part of the article, because your experiences, that pain and anger is centuries old. It's part of our collective, historical memory of being enslaved, colonized, denied access to education, impoverished, and pushed to society's margins, whether in barrios, inner cities, on reservations, or on university campuses."[121]

"Yes, my early Ph.D. student experiences included a lot of pain and anger. Like Edward James Olmos says in the film *Selena*, 'It's exhausting being Mexican American!'"[122]

INTERNALIZING RACISM AND LASHING OUT
AT OTHER PEOPLE OF COLOR

Sanchez smiled at my effort to bring some humor to a painful discussion. He remarked, "It is exhausting! That's the racial battle fatigue.[123] And beyond the ways racism hurts us, sometimes, we take our internalized racism and our personal feelings of self-doubt, survivor's guilt, and imposter syndrome and we lash out at other People of Color. Like Paulo Freire told us in the 1970s, the oppressed can become the oppressor.[124] It's one of the saddest things that I've seen in academia."

"And one of the least talked about though," I remarked. Sanchez nodded, "We are already perceived as inferior to Whites and undeserving of our academic titles, so who wants to talk about how we begin to treat other People of Color in ways that can only be described as race and gender-based discrimination? And while I've seen some overt and very painful lashing out, sometimes we express our internalized racism in more subtle forms that reveal we are going beyond the point of 'buying into' a system that injures other People of Color—we are actually perpetuating it. Like when we resurrect 'standards' for graduate admission or faculty promotion that we *know* function as race, gender, and class barriers. We use SAT and GRE scores for admissions and we judge our junior colleagues based on whether they've published in so-called 'first-tier' journals. *Knowing* that standardized testing measures privilege White and middle-class students[125] and those 'first-tier' journals rarely publish ethnic or race-specific research.[126] So here we have Faculty of Color upholding a system that kept higher education segregated for years and continues to do so. They've become guardians of a system that treated them like imposters, gave them survivor's guilt, and instilled self-doubt in them. I don't think we'll have the space to discuss it extensively in the article, but maybe we should at least mention that the competitive nature of academia exacerbates feelings of isolation and distrust."

"And that subtle, social expression of internalized racism happens between students too," I responded. "Unfortunately, Chicana/o students sometimes act like those faculty you're describing. One of us shares an idea and then someone else will try to take credit for that idea. I've always thought that was a little crazy. How can one person own an idea? And who's to say that someone else never thought of that idea? I hate that sense of competition that creeps into these spaces. Here we are bickering among ourselves when we should be helping support each other. But what does that say for trying to increase the numbers of Students of Color in doctoral programs? We need to deal with our internalized racism before we start giving conservatives more excuses to resegregate higher education."

"Oh, they don't need any excuses," said Sanchez. He added, "But I think some of our dirty laundry so-to-speak says we actually need *more* Chicanas/os in the academy.[127] Then maybe the stakes won't seem so high, with folks trying to sabotage each other so they can get a leg up. And maybe all of our hopes and fears won't be caught up on just a few of us. So while some Chicanas/os lash out at others, there will be Chicana/o allies who are able to recognize and deal with their internalized racism in less self-defeating and less hurtful ways."

LESSONS FROM GRAD SCHOOL SURVIVORS

Sanchez turned to me and asked, "You want to head over to the café and continue this discussion over lunch?" We walked to a nearby campus café and the cool of the air conditioner provided welcome relief from the afternoon sun. I ordered a chicken salad while Sanchez asked for a turkey sandwich and chips. As I sat picking the red grapes out of my salad and piling them on a napkin to throw away, Sanchez teasingly reminded me that the United Farmworkers (UFW) grape boycott was over. I shot back that for me grapes would always be a symbol of the farm workers' struggle and that their fight for fair working conditions continues.[128] He remarked, "I agree. When I was younger, I worked briefly as an organizer with the union and my heart breaks knowing that 40 years after the historic grape boycott, the union must be so vigilant in insisting that growers treat farm workers with dignity. But Paula, those grapes were paid for as part of your salad." "I didn't know!" I exclaimed. He smiled and shook his head, seeing my stubbornness and enjoying watching me squirm. "We all live contradictions," I finally conceded with a smile.

Sanchez returned to our discussion of the article, saying, "When you've been confronted with either verbal or nonverbal racial and gender microaggressions, have you ever confronted the professor or the students about their actions?"

"A couple times. After one of my presentations that first year, this middle-age White student from New York came up to me and commented about how well I articulated myself. Then, she asked me how long I'd been speaking English. She seemed so surprised when I told her I'm a fourth-generation Chicana, born and raised here in the Southwest, so I asked her how long she'd been speaking English. She looked at me like I was crazy and said, 'I was just trying to give you a complement.' Later, the professor had us go around the room and give constructive criticism on each other's proposals, and supposedly some students didn't want to give me feedback because they felt their remarks might be misinterpreted."

I added, "Eventually, I realized that sometimes confrontation takes too much energy. To create some counterspaces where I could renew my energy, I started to reach out to family, friends, and colleagues more. But you had to remind me a lot in those first years to pick and choose my battles. And even though that was hard for me to hear, you were always right." Sanchez smiled. He often complained in a joking fashion that his students didn't listen to him, and I liked to teasingly point out that it's difficult to recognize great wisdom when you first hear it.

Sanchez commented, "It is very difficult to pick and choose our battles, and sometimes just as difficult to decide which strategy to use to engage a battle. I think I also gave you a few citations in the literature to read about other Chicanas and Women of Color who survived graduate school. Come to think of it, the reading list we're using for this article includes some of those pieces, right?"[129]

"Yes, and those articles really got me through. In the midst of reading so much research by and about Whites, I went through those articles you gave me and highlighted almost everything! Then I looked up all the other pieces those scholars cited. I became a footnote researcher! It helped me follow up on concepts they mentioned in passing and it gave me a starting place at the library. So, I read Montoya's[130] autobiographical essay about growing up as a poor, Spanish-speaking Chicana. She learned early on to disguise her background by speaking English without an 'accent,' excelling in education, and trying to acculturate. She describes how she created elaborate masks as 'defenses against racism passed on to us by our parents to help us get along in school and in society.'[131] And she specifically writes about the different 'masks' she wore at Harvard Law School, while she attempted to hide her Chicana working-class background and her cultural knowledges that others considered 'taboo.' And I really connected with the metaphor of her mother combing her hair into tight braids as a child, and later her own social and academic efforts to not look so *greñuda*.[132] Montoya finally realized that who she is informs what she brings to the academy. And her family, community history, language, and personal experiences strengthen her academic pursuits. But it took years of being silenced and experiencing invisibility for her to recognize that."

I smiled and began to speak faster, remembering the emotions I felt when reading these women's scholarship. "I also read Gloria Cuádraz and Jennifer Pierce's[133] essay on their racialized, gendered, and classed experiences as a Chicana and a White working-class woman struggling through a sociology Ph.D. program at UC-Berkeley. I really related to their stories in so many ways. They felt silenced, angry, and marginalized. They had financial burdens and felt a strong sense of responsibility to succeed to acknowledge and honor all those in their communities who didn't have the opportunity to pursue higher education. Cuádraz and Pierce echoed some of Montoya's grad school experiences, feeling the embarrassment of having their working class status exposed. And some of the scenarios they described, I had also faced. Like asserting an argument in class and having everyone give a blank stare, and then, minutes later, a male student re-phrases your statement and suddenly everyone applauds the remark as the most brilliant argument ever! Pierce says that she exploded after this had happened repeatedly in one of her courses. But by the time she defended herself, she had become so angry that her voice reflected her frustration. Instead of the professor clarifying the need for mutual respect in the class-room, he told Pierce afterward she was 'too hard' on the other graduate student.[134] And Cuádraz actually took a break from graduate school to regain her strength before finishing her degree. Speaking of taking a break, do you want another drink?"

I excused myself to refill my lemonade and Sanchez's Diet Coke. When I returned to the table I explained, "I think those two articles in particular began to help me move toward the dissertation. They encouraged me to continue, but they also showed me that I could do it on my terms. Each of those women brought various cultural knowledges to graduate school. I mean, Cuádraz and Pierce recognize the way the academy rewards cul-tural capital[135] and reproduces race, gender, and class hierarchies, but they discuss how they survived by acquiring some of that capital, which they reconceptualize as 'endurance labor.' They say 'endurance labor' refers to the 'relentless drive to persist, in spite of, and many times, because of ad-versity.'[136] Montoya initially disguised her cultural knowledges by putting on masks in an effort to look like she had acquired the 'appropriate' cul-tural capital to 'fit in' at Harvard Law School. But in the end, she realizes that to survive in the academy she needs to embrace her *greñas*,[137] to draw on those languages, histories, and experiences that are marginalized in the academy and in society."

Sanchez smiled, listened patiently, and finished the last of his chips. He said, "In the end, they choose the margin instead of being relegated to the margin. Of course, they choose from among limited options. But they recognize the contradictory nature of academia itself. Education can func-tion as a tool of oppression or empowerment. And although Chicanas/os experience extreme marginalization in graduate education, these women confirm that the margin can also be a space where we generate hope and transformational resistance. bell hooks is right in saying that we don't know enough about the margin as a site of resistance."[138]

We cleaned off our trays and gathered our bags again to walk back to-ward the main campus. Sanchez noted, "I'm glad that those articles helped you find joy in your research." I nodded and smiled, wondering to myself what I would have done if I had not come across those articles, if I did not have Sanchez's mentorship. How did Sanchez and others of his generation get through? I immediately felt a pang of worry in my stomach, thinking about my responsibility to create and maintain access and opportunities for future generations of Chicanas/os coming through the academy.[139] Will my research really make any difference for Chicanas/os making their way along the educational pipeline?

Sanchez remarked, "I am very proud of you Paula for taking on the SED data and taking a risk to engage in the process of learning a new methodology. It's exciting that we can begin to really examine the changing portrait of Chicana/o Ph.D. production over the last 20 years." I nodded and said, "I'm excited too. Though I wouldn't be able to take this risk if I didn't have you to support me. I think it will really expand my ability to reflect on the multiple transition points along the Chicana/o educational pipeline. And I hope to eventually follow up with some qualitative methods, to address some of the questions that the survey just doesn't get at."

Sanchez added, "That's really what we do, isn't it? We ask questions, but we ask about the experiences of those who, like you said earlier, are not even on the radar screen, those at the margins of society, or as Derrick Bell writes, 'those faces at the bottom of society's well.'[140] That's why Margaret Andersen's[141] piece a few years ago really spoke to me. She asks: What would sociology look like if we centered Women of Color in our teaching instead of marginalizing them? She challenges sociology as a field to decenter Whiteness and maleness and in turn, to create curriculum where People of Color can ask questions on our own terms."

I remarked, "I think Stephanie Marquez[142] extends on Andersen's argument. She explains that in *Introduction to Sociology* textbooks, Chicanas and specific subgroups of Latinas in general are basically made invisible under the generic and contradictory term 'Hispanic.' She says the experiences of Chicanas and other diverse Latina/o subgroups should be central to sociology. That brings us full circle back to why I think our article should tell a counterstory—so we can listen to and recount those experiences too often silenced and rendered invisible."

RESILIENCE AND RESISTANCE IN GRAD SCHOOL

I noticed the sun beginning to set, and said, "We'll have to go to the library next time?" "I guess so," replied Sanchez, "when we're ready to read through the draft. We'd better head back. Melinda and I are going to my brother's house for dinner. We're going to make a phone call to my niece and put her on speaker phone so she will hopefully feel a little less homesick." We walked quietly for a minute or so. Happily, it seemed much less strenuous to descend the steep staircase than it had been to climb it a few hours earlier.

I said, "We talked about this earlier, but I'm still reflecting on the literature and my own experiences with being marginalized and silenced. Chicanas/os are rendered invisible in so many ways that we may often be our only witness to mundane extreme environmental stress (MEES) and racial battle fatigue from racial microaggressions."[143] Sanchez added, "Experiencing all that in isolation, it's no wonder Chicana/o graduate students have a lot of anger, stress, and racial battle fatigue symptoms." I continued, "And you reminded me that anger fuels our spirit. Well, maybe that anger also triggers our motivation to 'prove them wrong.' I mean, racism comes at us from all angles, inside and outside classrooms, through media that's supposed to entertain us to news media that's supposed to inform us. Society seems to be repeatedly telling us that Mexicans are unintelligent, lazy, culturally deprived, and basically inferior to Whites."

Sanchez said, "Most of those messages are subtle, but sometimes people slip and 'the truth' comes out. Like Larry Summers'[144] comments recently about why women are underrepresented in the ranks of tenured science and engineering professors." I responded and paraphrased Summers, "Yes! Harvard's President saying, 'I don't really have all the data, and I hope that research can prove me wrong, but I believe women seem to lack the innate ability to do the intellectually rigorous work of science and engineering professors.' Though he later apologized and tried to clarify his comments, it strikes me that here is this White male university president who has not worked very hard to increase 'diversity' on his own campus, and he's admitting some of his stereotypical beliefs in a pretty public forum, 'hoping' that research will prove him wrong." Sanchez interjected, "Of course he hasn't read or is just ignoring the research that does challenge his remarks." "Right," I said, "But he also probably doesn't realize that women and Women of Color in particular work everyday to prove people like him wrong, to prove such stereotypical assumptions wrong. It's like 'proving them wrong' becomes part of surviving the microaggressions. It becomes almost a goal to be resilient in the face of all those layers of discrimination."

I paused and then continued, "I might seem to be resilient,[145] but at the same time, I carry battle wounds, like the internalized racism and racial battle fatigue we talked about. So sometimes I feel like I'm barely surviving. Yet in comparison to the 99.7% of Chicanas/os who don't get here,[146] it seems like I'm succeeding." Sanchez nodded, following along with my remarks. He asked, "Maybe you are surviving *and* succeeding?" I thought for a moment and said, "Huh, that's a good point. And maybe the effort to survive and succeed in the face of racism connects the process of 'proving them wrong' to resistance?"

Sanchez added, "Yes. That's the connection we were looking for. The cumulative stress of racial microaggressions triggers the resistance."[147] I explained, "As a Chicana, I'm motivated to succeed in this Ph.D. program not just to realize some of my goals and aspirations, but to show that Chicanas/os can and do succeed. And engaging in whatever way I can with the struggle for social and racial justice gives me another tool to 'prove them wrong.'"

Sanchez said, "And holding onto that passion for social and racial justice will continue to be an act of resistance as you make your way through the tenure process. Hopefully, you will work to maintain a balance between your activism and your personal, family life. That's something too often neglected and left as a last priority for many of us." "You're right," I replied, "I'm beginning to recognize even more that I need to nurture some of those counterspaces I have with family and friends. In a way, the process of writing this article is serving as another counterspace. It gives me a place to reveal the many forms of racism that continue to shape Chicana/o experiences in graduate school." Sanchez commented, "And hopefully, the article will also function as a counterspace for those who read it. I think it can add to the literature that challenges the oppressive silences of academia, and let other Chicanas/os know that they are not alone. That we don't need to look any further than our own Chicana/o communities to find the strength and cultural tools we need to be resilient and resistant to racism."

We had arrived back at our cars near the coffee shop, and Sanchez thanked me for what had turned into a marathon meeting. I told him I really enjoyed our discussion and felt it was a very productive meeting. I also said that I appreciated him buying me lunch, even though I accidentally made him pay for grapes. He shook his head with a grin, gave me a hug, and told me to be safe driving home in traffic. I assured him I would have a draft of the article before we met again in 2 weeks. He asked me to email him a reminder to send the references we had discussed. Maybe he saw that I looked a little overwhelmed, because as I was starting my car, he signaled for me to roll down my window, and he yelled out, "Remember, you're bad!"

PAULA'S REFLECTIONS

That night, I tried to veg out in front of the television, but the conversation of the day kept replaying in my head. I thought about all of the concepts we discussed. The personal and social expressions of internalized racism were most painful to think about. It's amazing that we continue to uncover more effects of racism along the educational pipeline, like how racism leads to self-doubt, survivor's guilt, impostor syndrome, and causes some Chicanas/os to lash out in subtle and overt ways toward other Chicanas/os. I made myself a mental note that I needed to confirm the references for the scholars who built on Pierce's racial microaggressions and developed the concepts of mundane extreme environmental stress and racial battle fatigue.[148] I don't know exactly how to feel knowing that some of the psychophysiological symptoms I've experienced over the last few years likely connect with the stress of being a Chicana in graduate school.

I hoped I didn't freak Sanchez out too much by sharing my concerns about being a single Chicana headed for an academic lifestyle where my hopes of having a family may conflict with my desire to "give back" to my community as a scholar. Although I'm still not sure I'll make it to tenure or that my work will make a difference for Chicana/o communities, I am encouraged by the role model I have in Sanchez. He certainly has helped me survive and succeed through graduate school. And my survival is connected to my process of struggle—my process of resilient resistance. I feel a sense of responsibility not just to myself or to Sanchez, but to my family and to so many Chicanas/os who never had the opportunity to attend college, let alone graduate school. Their spirits of resistance fuel my own 'prove them wrong' efforts.

I turned off the TV and brushed my teeth to get ready for bed. Thinking about our conversation about the multiple effects of racism, I rinsed the toothpaste from my mouth and put on my plastic mouthguard. The dentist said that I grind my teeth at night and if my stress level remained high, then the least I could do was ease the damage to my teeth by wearing a protective guard.

I tried to straighten up my desk space before heading to bed so I could get a fresh start on writing the article draft in the morning. As I reshelved a stack of books, I found *This Bridge Called My Back: Radical Writings by Women of Color*.[149] I had checked it out from the library a few months ago and hadn't even had a chance to look at it yet. I flipped through the pages and saw that other library users had underlined and put stars next to many of the passages. One section in particular had hot pink highlighter all over it. As I began to read the highlighted passage, the voice of self-doubt quieted down and my eyes welled with tears:

> Why am I compelled to write?… Because I have no choice. Because I must keep the spirit of my revolt and myself alive. Because the world I create in writing compensates for what the real world does not give me… I write because life does not appease my appetite and hunger. I write to record what others erase when I speak, to rewrite the stories others have miswritten about me, about you… To discover myself, to preserve myself, to make myself, to achieve self-autonomy… To convince myself that I am worthy and that

what I have to say is not a pile of shit. To show that I *can* and that I *will* write, never mind their admonitions to the contrary. And I will write about the unmentionables, never mind the outraged gasp of the censor and the audience. Finally I write because I am scared of writing but I'm more scared of not writing.[150]

I miss you, Gloria.[151] Thanks again for the reminder that I'm never alone.

NOTES

1. "It's exhausting being Mexican American" is borrowed from Esparza & Katz, prds., 1997. University of the Southwest is a composite Research I institution located in an unidentified city in the southwestern United States.
2. Gándara, 1995; Vasquez, 1982
3. For 1980–1990 Chicana/o data, see Solórzano, 1993, 1994, 1995. From 1980-2000, the data for Latina/o doctorate production has included three subgroup options: Chicana/o, Puerto Rican, and Other Latina/o (e.g., Central American, Cuban, or other Latina/o). Chicanas/os earned the least numbers of doctorate degrees within the Latina/o category and in comparison to other race/ethnicity groups. For 1990–2000 Latina/o data, see Watford, Rivas, Burciaga, & Solórzano, in press.
4. Source: NSF/NIH/USED/NEH/USDA/NASA, Survey of Earned Doctorates, 1990–2000.
5. Flores, 1988; Noboa-Rios, 1981/82; Simoniello, 1981; Solórzano, 1993, 1994, 1995a
6. Zuckerman, 1977
7. McGrayne, 1993
8. Berger, 1990; Riley, 1988
9. O'Connell & Russo, 1983, 1988, 1990
10. Ryan & Sackrey, 1984
11. See Bernal, 1988. Research that did focus on the graduate school experience of underrepresented minority groups emphasized the declining enrollment of African Americans in graduate school (particularly Black males). See Arce & Manning, 1984; Blackwell, 1991; Noboa-Rios, 1981/82; Thomas, 1987, 1992
12. See Bowen & Rudenstine 1992; Brown, 1987, 1988; Carter & Wilson, 1993; Chipman & Thomas, 1984; Clewell, 1987; Dix, 1987; National Science Foundation, 1990; Nettles, 1990a, 1990b; Oakes, 1990; Task Force on Women, Minorities, and the Handicapped in Science and Technology, 1989; Thomas, 1986, 1992. In fact, most studies do not recognize the importance of examining Latina/o subgroups separately (see Gimenez, 1989; Hayes-Bautista & Chapa, 1987; Oboler, 1992; Portes & Truelove, 1987). This is also an issue when discussing Asian American doctoral production, as the data rarely allow for subgroup disaggregation (see Nakanishi & Yamano Nishida, 1995).
13. Gándara, 1979, 1982, 1993, 1995
14. Gándara, 1982
15. Morales, 1988
16. Anchor & Morales, 1990
17. Cuádraz, 1992, 1993
18. Solórzano, 1993, 1994, 1995a
19. Urrieta, 2003
20. Margolis & Romero, 1997/98
21. Villalpando, 1996
22. Heimlich, 2001
23. Ponce, 2002
24. Burciaga, in press

25. *Nepantla* is a Nahuatl word referring to a place or space of in between (see Anzaldúa & Keating 2002).

26. Padilla & Chavez, 1995

27. Latina Feminist Group, 2001

28. Cuádraz & Pierce, 1994

29. Johnson, 1999

30. Flores-Niemann, 1999

31. Delgado-Gaitan, 1997

32. Montero-Sieburth, 1997

33. Montoya, 1994

34. Espinoza, 1990

35. Matute-Bianchi, 1982

36. Bernal, 1988

37. Indeed, autobiographical and biographical reflections of African American women scholars confirm the patterns evidenced in Chicana/o, Latina/o accounts of academia (see for example Caldwell,1991; Williams, P., 1991; Winfield, 1997; Ladson-Billings, 1997). Legal scholar Derrick Bell's (2002) autobiographical *Ethical Ambition: Living a Life of Meaning and Worth* and the biography of psychiatrist and education professor Chester Pierce (Griffith & Pierce, 1998) add to this scholarship recounting personal struggles of African American men in academia.

38. Of Chicanas/os who earned their Ph.D. from 1990–2000, 22.7% attended community colleges. On average overall, only 10% of U.S. citizen and permanent residents who earned Ph.D.s from 1990–2000 attended a community college. Asian Americans 2.7%, Puerto Ricans, 5.7%, African Americans 10.3%, Whites 10.5%, Latinas/os 13.5%, Native Americans 19.3%, and Chicanas/os, 22.7%. Source: National Science Foundation Survey of Earned Doctorates.

39. Ornelas, 2002; Ornelas & Solórzano, 2004

40. See Hurtado & Faye Carter, 1997

41. See generally Hall, 1984a, 1984b; Hardy, 1974; Holland, 1957; Knapp & Goodrich, 1951. For educational origins of White women scientists, see Tidball, 1986; Tidball & Kistiakowsky, 1976. For baccalaureate origins of African American men scientists, see Brazziel, 1983; Conyers, 1986; Pearson & Pearson, 1985. For undergraduate origins Black women and men in doctoral science, see Jay, 1971; Pearson, 1985.

42. See Solórzano, 1993, 1994, 1995a

43. Lisa Wolf-Wendel (1998) examined undergraduate origins of women Ph.D.s, identifying European Americans, African Americans, and Latinas from the National Research Council's doctoral records data from 1975–1991 in conjunction with data gathered from *Who's Who in America*, *Who's Who Among Black Americans*, and *Who's Who Among Hispanic Americans*. In this research on baccalaureate origins Wolf-Wendel also identifies "women friendly colleges" (see Wolf-Wendel, 2000). Though she analyzes the data based on gender and race, she does not specify Chicanas.

44. The Latina Equity Education Project (LEEP) at UCLA conducted much of this preliminary data analysis (Solórzano, Rivas, Velez, 2005; Watford, Rivas, Burciaga, & Solórzano, in press).

45. Anchor & Morales, 1990

46. See Pierce, 1974, 1989, 1995; See also chapter 4 for further discussion and p. 113 for a definition of racial microaggressions.

47. See Solórzano, 1998

48. See Montoya, 1994

49. See Collins, 1986

50. See Solórzano, 1998

51. Solórzano, Ceja, & Yosso, 2000

52. See Solórzano, 1998 for more discussion on the marginality of Chicana/o scholars; See Yosso, 2000 for more on Chicana/o students "proving them wrong."

53. See Montoya, 2000

54. See Allen & Solórzano, 2001 for more discussion on strategic silence, strategic separation, social and academic counterspaces, and campus racial climate.
55. See hooks, 1990
56. Data for U.S. citizens and permanent residents.
57. These focus groups were part of a study on campus racial climate conducted for the Student of Color Intervenors' case in *Grutter v. Bollinger*, decided by the Supreme Court June 13, 2003.
58. Paula and Professor Sanchez are composite characters based on information from numerous interviews, focus groups, biographical, humanities, and social science literature, and personal experiences. Sanchez also appears in Solórzano & Yosso, 2000, 2001a, 2001c.
59. Do you drink coffee with milk?
60. See chapter 2
61. See Solórzano & Yosso, 2001c, 2002a, 2002b
62. In speaking to one of his dear friends and counterstory characters, renowned legal scholar Derrick Bell (1992) admits he shares this frustration. He says, "You know, Geneva, when I agreed to become Harvard's first black faculty member back in 1969, I did so on the express commitment that I was to be the first, but not the last, black hired. I was to be the pioneer, the trailblazer. And Lord knows there was plenty of brush to clear away—all of it steeped in tradition designed to make it easy for smart young white men from privileged backgrounds, and impossible for everyone else. To look back now, after more than twenty years of clearing the trail and see it all grown over—well, it's a feeling not easy to describe" (p. 138).
63. Mason & Goulden, 2002
64. Mason & Goulden, 2004a. To contextualize some of their national data, the researchers also conducted a survey for UC–Berkeley faculty, see http://ucfamilyedge.berkeley.edu/workfamily/htm. See also Mason & Goulden, 2004b.
65. Mason & Goulden, 2002, p. 24. The SDR is a national biennial longitudinal study of U.S. doctoral recipients dating back to 1973. Sponsored by the National Science Foundation and others, for each biennial survey, the SDR includes (1) a nationally representative subsample of Ph.D. recipients drawn from the Survey of Earned Doctorates (SED), roughly 10 percent of the SED survey population; and (2) all individuals previously included in earlier SDR survey cycles who are younger than seventy-six years of age and live in the United States. Starting in 1981, the SDR included questions about both marriage and children younger and older than age six living in the household. Mason and Goulden utilize SDR data to provide a full picture of career and family patterns over the life cycle and to identify characteristics associated with career issues and family patterns (see Mason & Goulden, 2004b).
66. Mason & Goulden, 2002, p. 24
67. Mason & Goulden, 2002, p. 25
68. Mason & Goulden, 2002, p. 25
69. Mason & Goulden, 2002, p. 23
70. Mason & Goulden, 2002, p. 27
71. Mason & Goulden, 2004a, p. 12
72. Mason & Goulden, 2004a, pp. 11–12
73. In 2005, Chicana doctoral students Raquel Olmos and Jackie Villareal created a website dedicated to addressing many of the same concerns Paula raises in this counterstory. Through reflective and humorous writings, poetry, photos, artwork, and music, Olmos and Villareal express their hopes, fears, worries, and dreams about being single Chicana graduate students and future academics. They describe themselves as "Chicanas on the verge of a nervous breakthrough." Retrieved August 8, 2005 from, http://chicanasontheverge.com
74. The data are collected in the seven broad fields of physical science, engineering, life science, social science, humanities, education, and professional. In addition, the survey identifies those Ph.D.s who attended community colleges.
75. See Solórzano, 1994, 1995a, 1995b
76. Berryman, 1983
77. Solórzano, 1994, 1995a, 1995b

78. Compiled from NSF/NIH/USED/NEH/USDA/NASA, Survey of Earned Doctorates, 1990–2000. U.S. Census Bureau, 1990 Census of Population, United States Summary (CP-1-1), U.S. Census Bureau, Census 2000 Summary File 4 (SF4). Doctorates shown in data are U.S. citizens or permanent U.S. residents. Census data includes those who may not be U.S. citizens or permanent U.S. residents.

79. See also Table 1 in Watford, Rivas, Burciaga, & Solórzano, in press

80. The patterns of underrepresentation are very similar for Chicano and African American men.

81. *Brown v. Board of Education*, 347 U.S. 483 (1954).

82. *Mendez v. Westminster*, 64 F. Supp. 544 (S.D. Cal. 1946).

83. See Perea, 2004; Valencia, 2005; See also Haro & Bermudez, 2004

84. *Plessy v. Ferguson*, 163 U.S. 537 (1896)

85. National Association for the Advancement of Colored People

86. On appeal, the Ninth Circuit court upheld the district court opinion. See *Mendez v. Westminster*, 161 F. 2d 744 (9th Cir. 1947). See also chapter 3, endnote 79 for text of California education codes repealed in 1947.

87. See Aguirre, 2005

88. Wollenberg, 1976, 2004

89. Hurtado, 1996

90. Similar to what Charles Mills (1997) calls, *The Racial Contract*.

91. Hurtado, 1996, p. 133; See also Ralph Ellison's *Invisible Man* (1952/2002). Legal scholar Kim Taylor (1993) adapts Ellison's work to introduce how invisibility functions for Women of Color. She writes: "I am an invisible [wo]man. No I am not a spook like those who haunted Edgar Alan Poe; nor am I one of your Hollywood-movie ectoplasms. I am a [wo]man of substance, of flesh and bone, fiber and liquids-and I might even be said to possess a mind. I am invisible, understand, simply because people refuse to see me. Like the bodiless heads you see sometimes in circus sideshows, distorting glass. When they approach me they see only my surroundings, themselves, or figments of their imagination-indeed, everything and anything except me" (p. 443).

92. Margaret Montoya (2000) explains that discourse in courtrooms and classrooms maintains silence about race and that race-neutral approaches to the law have a silencing, oppressive effect on People of Color, especially those who speak languages other than English. Yet she also shares a story of her own experience being a hate crime victim as a young professor, when she chose not to break silence to challenge her anonymous aggressor. In retrospect, Montoya asserts that alongside its power as an oppressive force, silence can be an empowering and transformative pedagogical tool. Steven Bender (2000) draws on Montoya's work to challenge the silencing of Latina/o communities in legal education and to argue the need to be persistent in speaking to those pedagogical and curricular silences. Dorothy Roberts (2000) critically reflects on Montoya's article, wondering whether maintaining silence is a form of resistance or accommodation.

93. See Lorde,1978, pp. 31–32

94. In a testimony of her experiences as an untenured Black female professor, Pamela Smith (2000) asserts that speaking out about racism and sexism is a form of resistance necessary to challenge the tyrannies of silence. She finds that maintaining silence disrupts the potential for community building and exacerbates isolation and self-doubt.

95. Espin, 1993

96. Suzanne Homer and Lois Schwartz (1989–90) speak to an alternative interpretation of classroom silence as a: "counter-code of classroom ethics … one that affirmatively endorses the silence of female students and students of color. Reluctance to participate may have originated in an instinct for self-protection" (p. 37).

97. Lani Guinier (1990–91) recalls her experience as a law student at the Yale Law School: "I had no personal anecdotes for the profound senses of alienation and isolation caught in my throat every time I opened my mouth … In law school I resisted through silence. Only later did I learn to question out loud" (p. 94).

98. For more discussion on White and male privilege, see Carbado, 2002; McIntosh, 1989; Tatum, 1997

99. In asking his students to gage the value of being White, Andrew Hacker (1992) poses a similar scenario wherein a White person is told, "sorry, there was a mistake, you were supposed to be born Black." Margaret Montoya (2001) notes that too often, legal education overlooks Latina/o histories, and many people may assume "Chicanas/os have no claim upon desegregation as a public policy to remove the vestiges of the *de jure* and *de facto* discriminatory policies and practices of the past" (p. 162). This type of academic erasure distorts historical accounts, ignores current realities, and it further alienates Chicana/o students.

100. See Wells & Serna, 1996

101. For more discussion of AP courses, see chapter 3 and Solórzano & Ornelas, 2002, 2004

102. See Espinoza, 1990

103. See Piorkowski, 1983

104. Solórzano, 1998

105. See Omi & Winant, 1994

106. See Malcolm X, 1972

107. Pierce, 1969, 1970, 1974, 1980, 1989, 1995

108. See Davis, 1989; Solórzano, Allen, & Carroll, 2002; Solórzano, Ceja, & Yosso, 2000

109. See Solórzano, 1998

110. Carroll, 1998

111. Smith, 1993–2004, 2004

112. See also, Smith, Yosso, & Solórzano, in press

113. See Smith, Allen, & Land, 2005

114. See Gay, 2004; Margolis & Romero, 1998

115. Delgado Bernal, 2002

116. Margaret Montoya (1994) draws on the work of Gloria Anzaldúa (1987) to define *mestiza* as "a woman whose identity is a product of at least two cultures" (p. 31). Anzaldúa (1987) argues that a *mestiza* consciousness is forged by Chicanas living in, among, and between socially constructed borderlands, and resisting against race, gender, class, sexual, linguistic, and cultural oppressions.

117. See Delgado Bernal, 2001

118. See Figueroa & Garcia, in press

119. See Cruz, 2001

120. Patricia Williams refers to this as "spirit murder," see Williams, 1997; See also Caughey, 1973.

121. Audre Lorde (1984) writes: "Women of color in America have grown up within a symphony of anger, at being silenced, at being chosen, at knowing that when we survive, it is in spite of a world that takes for granted our lack of humanness, and which hates our very existence outside of its service. And I say symphony rather than cacophony because we have had to learn to orchestrate those furies so that they do not tear us apart. We have had to learn to move through them and use them for strength and force and insight within our daily lives. Those of us who did not learn this difficult lesson did not survive. And part of my anger is always libation for my fallen sisters" (p.119). See also Carroll 1998, pp. 121–122; hooks, 1995.

122. Olmos' character (Abraham Quintanilla) uses this phrase out of exasperation while explaining the struggles of growing up Mexican American. Written and directed by Gregory Nava, *Selena* portrays a biography of the late Grammy-award-winning Tejana vocalist, Selena Quintanilla Perez (Esparza & Katz, prds., 1997).

123. Smith, 2004

124. See Freire, 1973. Grace Carroll (1998) also notes that in response to living with mundane extreme environmental stress (MEES), some African Americans begin to "identify with the oppressor" (p. 121).

125. See Rosner, 2001

126. For example, Sandra Graham (1992) found that over a twenty-year period, "first-tier" journals of the American Psychological Association published very few articles about African Americans.

127. To help each other survive through graduate school and academia, a small group of Chicana/ Latina women from several northern California universities founded *Mujeres Activas en Letras*

y Cambio Social (MALCS) in 1982. Today, MALCS serves as a national network for faculty, administrators, community workers, and graduate and undergraduate students who are working toward four common goals: (1) To recruit and support Chicana/Latina women in higher education and advanced studies; (2) To encourage and promote the distribution of research on Chicana/Latina women; (3) To promote the development and institutionalization of Chicana/Latina Studies; and (4) To address issues of concern to Chicana/Latina communities. Each year, MALCS organizes a summer institute, which serves as a forum for presenting research while it also functions as a place/space for Chicana/Latina community activists and scholars to encourage and mentor each another (see http://www.malcs.org).

128. For example, at this writing, the United Farmworkers are struggling to ensure that growers provide adequate toilet facilities in the fields (see http://www.ufw.org).

129. See appendix of Solórzano & Yosso, 2001a; Gloria Cuádraz (2005) also outlines some of this scholarship in her essay, "Chicanas and higher education: Three decades of literature and thought."

130. Montoya, 1994

131. Montoya, 1994, pp. 6–7

132. Uncombed.

133. Cuádraz & Pierce, 1994

134. See Cuádraz & Pierce, 1994, p. 28

135. Bourdieu & Passeron, 1977

136. Cuádraz & Pierce, 1994, p. 31

137. Messy hair.

138. hooks, 1990

139. Lani Guinier's book *Becoming Gentlemen: Women, Law School, and Institutional Change* describes in a footnote the motto of the National Association of Colored Women's Clubs as, "lifting as I rise." bell hooks (1994) mentions this in her book *Teaching to Transgress*, as a promise to "lift as we climb."

140. Bell, 1992, p. v

141. Andersen, 1988

142. Marquez, 1994

143. See Carroll, 1998; Smith 2004; Smith, Yosso, & Solórzano, in press

144. Summers, 2005

145. See also the concept of invulnerability, Alva, 1991, 1995; Arrellano & Padilla, 1996

146. See U.S. Bureau of the Census, 2000

147. For more on triggers of resistance, see Talavera-Bustillos, 1998

148. See Grace Carroll's 1998 book *Environmental Stress and African Americans: The Other Side of the Moon* for further discussion of MEES. See William A. Smith (2004; Smith & Allen, 2004; Smith, Yosso, & Solórzano, in press) for more discussion of racial battle fatigue and its connection to racial microaggressions (Pierce, 1970, 1974, 1980, 1989, 1995) and MEES. Smith's work draws primarily on a longitudinal national study of African Americans (Smith, 1993–2004).

149. Moraga & Anzaldúa, 1981

150. Anzaldúa, 1981, pp. 168–169

151. Chicana author and activist Gloria E. Anzaldúa passed away in May 2004, but lives on through her writing. Anzaldúa's major published works as well as her unpublished manuscripts, notebooks, correspondence, lectures, and audio/video interviews can be accessed in her archive at the University of Texas, Austin as part of the Nettie Lee Benson Latin American Collection (archive opening anticipated in Fall 2006).

EPILOGUE

How will historians judge our efforts a hundred years hence? The question cannot be answered for the future, but it is essential for our work today that we pose it regularly to ourselves, and to one another.[1]

In this brief epigraph, Derrick Bell challenges critical race scholars to consider how their work might contribute to lasting societal change. Bell's remarks resonate with the counterstories in this volume, as they seek to (1) cultivate community among socially and racially marginalized groups, (2) challenge the perceived wisdom of majoritarian stories, (3) nurture community memory and resistance, and (4) encourage readers to continue working toward social and racial justice with determined urgency.

As noted earlier in this volume, only 44 of every 100 Chicana/o students graduate high school, seven earn a baccalaureate degree, and less than one earns a doctorate degree. This compares to 83 of every 100 White students graduating high school, 26 earning a baccalaureate degree, and 10 earning a doctorate. To explain these disparate outcomes, majoritarian stories claim that U.S. social institutions function well, and problems originate from Chicana/o students, parents, and communities. On the other hand, critical race counterstories argue that supposed biological or cultural deficits in Chicana/o communities cannot account for these persistent unequal outcomes. Instead, counterstories assert that these racialized disparities reveal an appalling level of institutionalized failure accepted by mainstream U.S. society.

If the civil rights gains of the last century occurred in large part because White mainstream society held a vested interest in showcasing itself as a pluralistic society during the Cold War,[2] what will it take to progress toward social and racial justice in this century? Researchers David Hayes-Bautista, Werner Schink, and Jorge Chapa have warned that underpreparing the youngest, fastest growing racial/ethnic minority in the United States will cause long-term consequences for U.S. society.[3] In their 1988 book, these scholars explain that by 2030, undereducated Chicanas/os working low-wage service jobs will bear *The Burden of Support* for an aging White society. The authors suggest this potential crisis necessitates a major shift in U.S. public policy to educate Chicanas/os for high-tech, high-wage jobs, increase access to quality healthcare, and ensure sufficient political representation for Chicana/o communities. Have the public policies and educational reform efforts over the last decade addressed Hayes-Bautista, Schink, and Chapa's warnings? Will mainstream society's concerns over the solvency of Social Security benefits lead to making equality along the Chicana/o educational pipeline a national priority? How does undereducating Chicanas/os further or hinder mainstream society's interests?

In the spirit of students, parents, teachers, and communities who engage in Bell's call to work,[4] I offer the following counterstory, which takes place on September 16 in a future year.[5] Based on current realities along the Chicana/o educational pipeline, and inspired by historical and contemporary examples of resistance against racism, this scenario looks to the future of the Chicana/o educational pipeline.

EL PUEBLO UNIDO...

"Good afternoon ladies and gentlemen, this is a special breaking news report. I'm John Smith here in the studio and we're going straight to our live team coverage in East Los Angeles."

"Thanks, John, this is Alma Tejeda reporting live from the corner of Atlantic and Whittier Boulevard, in the heart of East Los Angeles. We're not too far from some of the main high schools at the heart of the controversy. As our camera is trying to show, thousands of Mexican American students have walked out of their schools and are now in the streets. I'm learning that a group called *Students Who Care,* have been organizing for at least a few years, leading up to this event. We found one of those students to explain what's happening here. Miss?"

My name is América and I'm here because historically, this is the only way people listen to us—it takes the schools losing millions in per pupil monies to see that they are here to serve us, and they're failing us. We're demanding equal schools. We're demanding schools, not jails.[6] We're tired of being tracked away from college. Chicanas/os have a 56% pushout rate from the K–12 system and this blatant racism has gone on for far too long.

"Thank you for speaking with us. Now John, I'm learning that many of these teenagers participated in what they call a *Strike School,*[7] which is a training center for youth organizing. But as our camera pans around, you can see that this protest is not limited to these young activists. Moments ago, I saw hundreds of Catholic school students joined by their teachers walking here in solidarity with their public school counterparts.[8] A large group of religious leaders from many faiths followed behind these students. I should note that hundreds of Black, Asian/Pacific Islander, and White students also walked out in solidarity with the Mexican American students. There are large contingents here from the hotel and restaurant unions, the Justice for Janitors union,[9] the bus drivers union, and construction workers who are part of the AFL-CIO. Some of the *Mothers of East Los Angeles* spoke with me a few minutes ago about their support for the students' demands. These mothers joined the protest along with *Parent U-Turn* and *Familias Unidas* volunteers. Apparently, these parents have spent a few years trying to make their schools accountable to the *Williams v. State of California* settlement agreement and have filed numerous complaints about unsafe facilities, a lack of trained bilingual teachers, and not enough textbooks. It seems some of their complaints remain unresolved, John."

"I also saw a group of urban planning students from UC-Oceanview with a sign reading, 'Got schools?'[10] And a group of law school students marched behind a large banner that read, 'Black and Brown v. Board of Unequal Education.' Disbursed throughout the crowd, a multiracial team of legal monitors observes carefully, ready to witness and document any encroachment of these protestors' rights. But so far, the only police I've seen are the Mexican American and Black Peace Officers Associations marching in support of the students alongside their Police Activities League mentees. Just a moment ago, I also saw most of the infamous Chicano 'Los Angeles 13,' who were arrested for supposedly organizing the 1968 walkouts. They walked side-by-side with many of the Chicana student leaders from back then. A few of these folks must be nearing their 70s, but their voices remain strong. They loudly chanted, '*Ya Basta!*' meaning 'Enough is enough already!' So far, no incidents of violence have been reported. Thousands of folks organized caravans from all over the southern California area, John. I've also heard some reports I have yet to confirm. It seems, a group of students, parents, and educator activists calling themselves *Californians for Justice*[11] may be coordinating simultaneous demonstrations in San Jose, San Diego, and Sacramento."

"Thank you Alma, now we're going to go to our sister station in Chicago, Illinois, where we've found another large-scale protest?"

"That's right, John, Patricia Murphy reporting from Pilsen, on the corner of Ashland Avenue and Division, here on the West side of Chicago. Pilsen is a historically Mexican community and the third largest Mexican community in the nation since 1960. We had heard rumors about a potential action being planned for a while now, but we weren't sure whether it would materialize. I'd estimate that this crowd now includes at least 40,000 people, John, and hundreds continue to de-board the trains and join the protest. Apparently, this morning, thousands of Mexican American students walked out of Chicago public schools. Then, teachers and students from the Dr. Pedro Albizu Campos High School[12] walked out in solidarity, followed by a few thousand Puerto Rican students and families from that neighboring community. Another couple thousand African American students from the South side of Chicago also joined the protest, and apparently convinced their parents and many of their teachers to support the Chicana/o students' list of demands. What are those demands? Well, reading from the talking-points sheet here, they demand that Chicago's public education system engage in immediate action to: build new schools, hire trained bilingual/bicultural teachers, provide all students access to Gifted and Talented Education and Advanced Placement, and well, the list goes on here, John. I have asked this young woman, Esmeralda, from Midwestern University to share why she is here today. Esmeralda?"

> I'm here supporting the students because there's an uneven playing field from elementary through high school and without taking affirmative action to address the legacy of racism in this country, generations of Chicanas/os have been and will continue to be denied access to college. At the university, Chicanas/os often face a negative campus racial climate where we are assaulted with subtle and overt discrimination everyday. We're tired of asking for access and opportunity. We're demanding equality.

"John, I have also seen a fairly large contingent of White men under a banner that reads "Angry White Guys for Affirmative Action."[13] Following that group, quite a number of Black and Latino firefighters echoed demands for affirmative action to create equality within and beyond schools. Community organizations such as *The Instituto De Progreso Latino*[14] and *The Resurrection Project*[15] spoke to me earlier, expressing their solidarity with the Chicana/o youth of Pilsen. And hundreds of agricultural workers who traveled from other parts of Illinois joined the protest with red flags bearing the black eagle symbol of the *United Farm Workers*.[16] These laborers support the students' demands to increase funding for Migrant Education programs. And this protest includes so many trade union members that some major Chicago hotels and restaurants are beginning to shut down, due to lack of staff. I'm not sure if schools have officially closed or how long they could remain open without most of their students attending. I see Chicana/o artists from *Casa Aztlan*[17] now engaging some of the youth in the creation of an impromptu graffiti mural and many youth continue to document this event with digital video cameras. So far, no incidents of violence have been reported. Those cheers you're hearing now are in response to a poet performer from the *Zocalo Urbano*.[18] He just finished a spoken word piece describing the struggle for educational justice as central to the fight for social and racial justice."

"Thank you Patricia, now if you're just tuning in, we've been receiving reports of widespread walkouts and mass demonstrations and we're trying to keep our viewers updated to the greatest extent possible, so please bear with us. We now go live to Tucson, Arizona."

"Yes, this is Carole Evans, and I'm here on the Southside of Tucson, where demonstrators have gathered at Joaquin Murrieta Park. Thousands of Mexican American and Native American teenagers from across Arizona walked out of their schools this morning. I have just seen their press release explaining why they're protesting, and it begins with a demand that the State stop building prisons and start rebuilding the school system. Since I arrived on the scene, I've heard a lot of chanting: 'Educate, Don't Incarcerate.'[19] These students also demand that public schools in Arizona be prohibited from using Native American terms such as 'Redskins' or 'Chiefs' as a school or athletic team name, mascot, or nickname.[20] The *Coatique Danza Group* will soon perform a ceremonial blessing for these students and their supporters. I spoke earlier with a member of Tucson Unified School District's *Raza Studies Team*[21] who reiterated students' demands, citing that schools suspend and expel Chicana/o students at higher rates than they grant these youngsters access to academic enrichment opportunities. I also saw members of *Chicanos Por La Causa*[22] from Phoenix and faculty and students from Tucson's *Salt of Earth Labor College*[23] demonstrating their solidarity with the students. And a group called *Derechos Humanos* set up an information tent so they can prepare protestors for how to respond nonviolently should the police try to start a riot. This appears to be a peaceful gathering, John. Some of the many supporting groups here include the *Southern Arizona Cesar E. Chavez Coalition*. They began marching several days ago from various rural communities right along the U.S. border with Mexico, in the spirit of the nonviolent organizer Cesar E. Chavez, and under a large banner of *La Virgen de Guadalupe*. Thousands of elementary schoolchildren and their parents also paraded today through the streets of Northside, predominately White and middle-class communities, making their cause known there before arriving to the park here. These very young students echo the demands of their high school counterparts, and insist that the state repeal Proposition 203 and reinstate bilingual education. This reminds me of those fifth graders who camped outside the State Capitol building back in 2000 and organized with local Native American tribes to stop the passage of Prop 203.[24] It seems they're back and they've brought thousands with them. We have here a mother of one of these children. Why are you here today, ma'am?"

My name is Carmen and I am here with *Madres Por La Educación* in support of these brave students, because Mexican parents value education. It's not fair that Chicana/o communities are blamed for the failures of the school system. And schools ignore the cultural strengths our children bring to the classroom. They say our children are slow? They are too slow in treating us with respect. We have a strong history of resisting racism and today we're walking with our children to make sure to pass on that legacy. *Sí se puede*!

"I'm sorry, Carole, we have to go to Texas, where Kim Tijerina is reporting from the Westside of San Antonio."

"Yes, thank you, John, that's right, Kim Tijerina coming to you live in front of the *Guadalupe Cultural Arts Center*,[25] here in San Antonio Texas. Students walked out of their schools a few hours ago, demanding some big changes in the educational system. Thousands have joined this demonstration, filling the streets with various artistic statements of protest. As you can see behind me, a number of lowriders, organized by the *Centro Cultural de Aztlan*,[26] are driving low and slow so folks can read their large posters questioning the Texas high school exit exam. Many of the signs and speeches here focus on stopping the recruitment of Mexican American and Black students into the armed forces. I've heard a recurring chant echoing through the crowd, '*Al Colegio Si, A La Guerra No!*' My camera operator confirmed that phrase means send us 'To College, Not To War.' And Teachers Union members from most of the urban and rural districts in the state have joined this student-led protest in full force. A representative from the union noted that districts tend to place the least prepared teachers in the schools with the highest levels of poverty, the largest percentages of racial minorities, and the highest numbers of English Language Learners. A group of university students and a few professors tied a banner reaching from one street light to another that reads: 'History Shouldn't Be a Mystery.[27] We Need Chicana/o Studies K–16.' And numerous churches and grassroots organizations, such as the *Esperanza Peace and Justice Center*,[28] line the streets here, demonstrating in solidarity with this nonviolent student protest. Some folks have remarked that today's actions resonate with the high school walkouts in San Antonio and Crystal City, Texas, in 1968. John? John?"

"Sounds like we just lost our connection there in Texas, we'll work to get it back. As we round this half-hour of special breaking news coverage on this September 16, we have witnessed massive walkouts in multiple states led by Mexican American students who identify themselves as Chicanas/os. We're not sure exactly what the protestors' plans entail, but they have articulated a series of demands to change inequalities they claim to experience along the educational pipeline. Here in the studio, we just received a text message from a student named Marisela, who reports that she and a few thousand other students walked out of her high school in New York..."

* * *

Does this massive mobilization instigate the transformation of the Chicana/o educational pipeline? Does mainstream society finally recognize the ways they benefit from ensuring equal educational opportunities for all communities? Stay tuned. As Bell's remarks remind us at the opening of this epilogue, persistent social and racial injustice requires our action. We need to recommit ourselves each day to keep struggling toward a more fair, just society.

I am honored and humbled to recount social science research through the composite characters and counterstories in this book. The sweat, tears, struggles, laughter, and aspirations of *mucha gente*[29] created these counterstories. These counterstories have passed through many lives. I gave them what I could, and now the time has come for me to pass them on—to you.[30] Critical race counterstories ask difficult questions that sometimes have no answers; questions about what it means to be marginalized, rendered invisible, and treated as an intruder in the place you call home. Counterstories challenge social and racial injustice by listening to and learning from experiences of racism and resistance, despair and hope at the margins of society.

So please, take these counterstories and make them your own. Retell them, add new characters, speak your truth, and take action to transform the Chicana/o educational pipeline.[31] Storytelling is a "genre of action."[32] How the story continues is up to each of us.

NOTES

1. Bell, 2002, p. 412
2. See Bell, 1976, 1980, 2004; Delgado, 2002; Dudziak, 1988, 2000
3. Hayes-Bautista, Schink, & Chapa, 1988
4. See Parker & Stovall, 2004; Pizarro, 2005
5. The 1969 *Plan Espiritual de Aztlán*, offers six main points of action. Number 2 reads: "September 16, on the birthdate of Mexican Independence, a national walkout by all Chicanos of all colleges and schools to be sustained until the complete revision of the educational system: its policy makers, administrators, its curriculum, and its personnel meet the needs of our community."
6. See http://SchoolsNotJails.com. To challenge a 2001 California ballot initiative lowering the age of when minors can be tried as adults and altering the definition of a felony, high school students used this organizing phrase. They created a website reflecting their efforts to oppose Proposition 21 and other measures that criminalize youth, and to organize across the state for educational change. See also Lee & Fernandez, 1998
7. Inner City Struggle is an independent center building community leadership to improve the quality of life in Boyle Heights and East Los Angeles. Three of their organizing projects include *United Students, Familias Unidas,* and the *Strike School.* See http://SchoolsNotJails.com.
8. U.S. Catholic Bishops have written about the pervasive and persistence evils of racism in U.S. society in at least three letters, from 1958, 1968, and 1979. In their 1979 letter, they note, "the

ugly external features of racism which marred our society have in part been eliminated. But …
too often what has happened has only a covering over, not a fundamental change… Because it
is less blatant, this subtle form of racism is in some respects even more dangerous—harder to
combat and easier to ignore… Racism is not merely one sin among many; it is a radical evil that
divides the human family and denies the new creation of a redeemed world. To struggle against
it demands an equally radical transformation, in our own minds and hearts as well as in the
structure of our society. See "Brothers and Sisters to Us: U.S. Catholic Bishops Pastoral Letter on
Racism," 1979.

9. See http://www.seiu.org/building/janitors/
10. See websites designed by UCLA urban planning students outlining that magnet schools and
    academic-enriched charter schools are located outside of neighborhoods that are predominately
    populated by low-income People of Color. These websites are interactive and allow the upload-
    ing of data to interface with county and state-wide data. Neighborhood Knowledge Los Angeles,
    http://www.nkla.ucla.edu; Neighborhood Knowledge California, http://www.nkca.ucla.edu
11. Californians for Justice (CFJ) is a statewide grassroots organization working for racial jus-
    tice by building power in low-income communities of color. CFJ's current major program is
    the Campaign for Quality Education, which brings together youth, parents, and community
    members to organize for better schools and racial justice in public education. See http://www
    .caljustice.org/
12. See http://prcc-c.fatcow.com/pachs.htm
13. Paul Rockwell (2003) writes, "As white men whose own families got free medical care, or un-
    questioned access to higher education through the GI Bill, who shared in the social uplift of the
    New Deal, we support affirmative action for those who are still left out."
14. Established in 1975, the *Instituto del Progreso Latino* works to contribute to the fullest devel-
    opment of Latino immigrants and their families in Chicago through education, training, and
    employment that fosters full participation in the changing U.S. society while preserving cultural
    identity and dignity. See http://www.idpl.org/
15. Founded in 1990 by a coalition of parishioners from six Catholic parishes, *The Resurrection Project*
    is an institution-based neighborhood organization whose mission is to build relationships and
    challenge people to act on their faith and values to create healthy communities through education,
    organizing, and community development. See http://www.resurrectionproject.org/home.html
16. See http://www.ufw.org
17. *Casa Aztlán* is a nonprofit community organization that since 1970 has sought to sustain the
    strong cultural identity of the Mexican Pilsen community by organizing and educating residents
    and providing supportive services in order to combat social violence, discrimination, and pov-
    erty. See http://www.neiu.edu/~casaaztl/index.htm
18. The *Zocalo Urbano* is a space for Chicana/o, Latina/o, and cultural expression (spoken word,
    music, performance, etc.). See http://www.pilsenlittlevillage.org/forcommunity.htm
19. San Diego-based Mexicano-Chicano musicians *Los Alacranes* also sing this refrain in their
    song, "Rising Souls" (Los Alacranes, 1999). See also newspaper account of high school students
    protesting educational inequality in San Leandro, California (Lee & Fernandez, 1998).
20. See legislation being considered in California (April 2005). Assembly Bill 13 "Racial Mascots
    Act" (sponsored by Assembly member Jackie Goldberg). The Act would "prohibit public schools
    from using the term 'Redskins' as a school or athletic team name, mascot, or nickname."
21. The Mexican American/Raza Studies Department at Tucson Unified School District is dedicated
    to the empowerment and strengthening of a community of learners. See http://instech.tusd.k12
    .az.us/Raza/index.asp
22. Since 1969, *Chicanos Por La Causa, Inc.* (CPLC), has been a statewide community develop-
    ment corporation in Arizona, committed to building stronger, healthier communities as a lead
    advocate, coalition builder, and direct service provider. Its first major campaign in 1969 brought
    attention to the unfair treatment of Chicano students in Phoenix's public school system. The
    committee announced that Chicano students would not attend classes until the Phoenix school
    system hired more Latino teachers and counselors and permitted Mexican American parents to

have a voice in matters that affected their children. Forty days after the boycott was launched, school officials agreed to meet the demands. See http://www.cplc.org/

23. Salt of the Earth Labor College was founded in the early 1990s in Tucson, Arizona, in the copper mining belt and seeks to build solidarity and critical awareness among working people. The school was inspired by the Empire Zinc Strike in the 1950s, when Mexican American zinc miners in Hanover, New Mexico, walked off their jobs to demand better working conditions. See http://www.saltearthlaborcollege.org/

24. See newspaper headlines: Associated Press, "Tribes rally against anti-bilingual education initiative," October 14, 2000, *Arizona Republic*; Associated Press, "March protests English immersion," October 18, 2000, *Arizona Republic*; see also "Children protesting against an anti-bilingual education proposition in Arizona" email communication from Carole Edelsky (Phoenix), October 28, 2000 (on file with author). See also Schevitz, 1998

25. Founded in 1980 and located on the west side of San Antonio, TX, the Guadalupe Cultural Arts Center offers public and educational programming to preserve, develop, present, and promote the art and culture of the Chicano, Latino, and indigenous peoples. See http://www.guadalupeculturalarts.org/

26. The *Centro Cultural de Aztlan* is a nonprofit organization committed to developing, maintaining, and promoting the consciousness of Chicana/o art and culture. See http://www.centroculturalaztlan .50megs.com/

27. This phrase is also part of the rap group Public Enemy's song, "Brother's Gonna Work It Out," on the 1990 album *Fear of a Black Planet*.

28. *Esperanza* works to create bridges between people through education, empowerment, and sharing visions of hope. See http://www.esperanzacenter.org/

29. Many people.

30. Adapted from *Visions: El Corrido* (1978). Luis Valdez and El Teatro Campesino. Los Angeles: KCET. At the end of the film, two characters dialogue on the back of a truck about *El Corrido*:

> Beto: There's got to be more to it than that…. Who wrote this *corrido* anyway? You?
> Alberto: Yeah, part of it. Nah, Beto, this *corrido* has passed through many lives. *Mucha gente* wrote this *corrido*. Ah, I gave it what I could. Now I think it's time for me to pass it on—to you.
> Beto: To me?
> Alberto: Eh, It's your *corrido* now. *Te lo regalo.*
> Beto: Gracias, but I don't want it. I don't even know if I like it!
> Alberto: Then change it!
> Beto: How am I gonna change it?
> Alberto: *Pues como*, Write new *versos. Con esto. (Hands him guitar)*
> Beto: You're gonna give me your *guitarra*? … Gracias!
> Alberto: *Mira*, just don't forget, eh, this *guitarrita* is used to being among the poor, *los pobres.*
> Beto: And what if I take this *guitarrita* and pawned it?
> Alberto: You won't.
> Beto: What makes you think I won't.
> Alberto: Because I have faith.
> Beto: In what?
> Alberto: In you…

31. Robert A. Williams (1995) explains, "Our lives are the stories we are ultimately responsible for telling, and the richness of the stories we tell will be a reflection of the richness of the lives we live" (p. xiv).

32. See Lomas, 2003

REFERENCES

Abney, E. R. (1974). The status of Florida's Black school principals. *The Journal of Negro Education, 43*(1), 3–8.

Acuña, R. F. (1972). *Occupied America: A history of Chicanos.* New York, NY: Harper Collins Publishers.

Acuña, R. F. (1996). *Anything but Mexican: Chicanos in contemporary Los Angeles.* London: Verso.

Acuña, R. F. (2004). *Occupied America: A history of Chicanos* (5th ed.). New York: Pearson Longman.

Aguirre, A. (2000). Academic storytelling: A critical race theory story of affirmative action. *Sociological Perspectives, 43,* 319–339.

Aguirre, F. P. (2005). *Mendez v. Westminister School District:* How it effected *Brown v. Board of Education. Orange County Lawyer, 47,* 30–37.

Allen, A. (1990/91). On being a role model. *Berkeley Women's Law Journal, 6,* 22–42.

Allen, W., Epps, E., & Haniff, N. (Eds.). (1991). *College in black and white: African American students in predominantly White and in historically Black public universities.* Albany, NY: State University of New York Press.

Allen, W., & Solórzano, D. (2001). Affirmative action, educational equity, and campus racial climate: A case study of the University of Michigan law school. *Berkeley La Raza Law Journal, 12*(2), 237–363.

Allport, G. W. (1979). *The nature of prejudice.* Reading, MA: Addison-Wesley Publishing Company.

Alschuler. A. (1980). *School discipline: A socially literate solution.* New York: McGraw-Hill.

Alva, S. (1991). Academic invulnerability among Mexican American students: The importance of protective resources and appraisals. *Hispanic Journal of Behavioral Sciences, 13,* 18–34.

Alva, S. (1995). Academic invulnerability among Mexican American students: The importance of protective resources and appraisals. In A. Padilla (Ed.), *Hispanic Psychology: Critical Issues in Theory and Research* (pp. 288–302). Thousand Oakes, CA: Sage.

Alvarez, F. (2005, February 21). Is upward bound headed for a fall? Participants defend the college prep program that President Bush is seeking to eliminate. *Los Angeles Times,* p. B1.

Alvarez v. Lemon Grove School District (1931). Superior Court of the State of California, County of San Diego, petition for Writ of Mandate, No. 66625.

Anchor, S., & Morales, A. (1990). Chicanas holding doctoral degrees: Social reproduction and cultural ecological approaches. *Anthropology and Education Quarterly, 21,* 269–287.

Andersen, M. L. (1988). Moving our minds: Studying women of color and reconstructing sociology, *Teaching Sociology, 16*(2), 123–132.

Anyon, J. (1980). School class and the hidden curriculum of work. *Journal of Education, 162,* 67–92.

Anzaldúa, G. E. (1981). Speaking in tongues: A letter to third world women writers. In C. Moraga & G. Anzaldúa (Eds.), *This bridge called my back: Radical writings by women of Color* (pp. 165–174). Watertown, MA: Persephone Press.

Anzaldúa, G. E. (1987). *Borderlands/la frontera: The new mestiza.* San Francisco, CA: Aunt Lute Books.

Anzaldúa, G. (1990). Haciendo caras: Una entrada. In G. Anzaldúa (Ed.), *Haciendo caras/ making face, making soul: Creative and critical perspectives by women of color* (pp. xv–xxviii). San Francisco, CA: Aunt Lute Press.

Anzaldúa, G. E., & Keating, A. (2002). *This bridge we call home: Radical visions for transformation.* New York: Routledge.

Arce, C., & Manning, W. (1984). Minorities in academic careers: The experience of the ford fellows. Report to the Ford Foundation. New York: Ford Foundation.

Arce, C., Murgia, E., & Frisbie, W. (1987). Phenotype and the life chances among Chicanos. *Hispanic Journal of Behavioral Sciences, 9*(1), 19–32.

Arias, B. (1986). The context of education for Hispanic students: An overview. *American Journal of Education, 95*(1), 26–57.

Arrellano, A. R., & Padilla, A. M. (1996). Academic invulnerability among a select group of Latino university students. *Hispanic Journal of Behavioral Sciences, 18*(4), 485–507.

Arriola, E. R. (1997). LatCrit theory, international human rights, popular culture, and the faces of despair in ins raids. *Inter-American Law Review, 28*(2), 245–262.

Arriola, E. R. (1998). March! *Chicano-Latino Law Review, 19,* 1–67.

Astin, A. (1963). Undergraduate institutions and the production of scientists. *Science, 141,* 334–338.

Astin, A. W. (1984). Student involvement: A developmental theory for higher education. *Journal of College Student Development, 25*(4), 297–308.

Astin, A. W. (1990). Educational assessment and educational equity. *American Journal of Education, 98*(4), 458–478.

Astin, A. W. (1996). Involvement in learning: Lessons we have learned. *Journal of College Student Development, 37*(2), 123–134.

Auerbach, S. (2001). *Under co-construction: Parent roles in promoting college access for students of color.* Unpublished doctoral dissertation, University of California, Los Angeles.

Auerbach, S. (2004). From moral supporters to struggling advocates: Reconceptualizing parent involvement through the experience of Latino families. Paper presented at annual meeting of the American Educational Research Association, San Diego, CA.

Baca Zinn, M. (1989). Family, race, and poverty in the eighties. *Signs: Journal of Woman in Culture and Society, 14,* 856–874.

Bailey, K. M., & Galvan, J. L. (1977). Accentedness in the classroom. *Aztlan: A Journal of Chicano Studies, 8,* 83–98.

Bakke v. Regents of the University of California, 438 U.S. 265 (1978).

Banks, T. (1990/91). Two life stories: Reflections of one Black woman law professor. *Berkeley Women's Law Journal, 6,* 46–56.

Banfield, E. C. (1970). Schooling versus education. *The unheavenly city: The nature and future of our urban crisis* (pp. 132–157). Boston: MA: Little Brown and Company.

Barnes, L., Christensen, C., & Hansen, A. (1994). *Teaching and the case method: Test, cases, and readings* (3rd ed.). Boston, MA: Harvard Business School Press.

Baron, R., Tom, D., & Cooper, H. (1985). Social class, race, and teacher expectations. In J. B. Dusek (Ed.), *Teacher expectancies* (pp. 251–259). Hillsdale, NJ: Lawrence Erlbaum.

Barrera, M. (1979). *Race and class in the southwest: A theory of inequality.* London: University of Notre Dame Press.

Barrera, M. (1997). A theory of racial inequality. In A. Darder, R. D. Torres, & H. Gutierrez (Eds.), *Latinos and education: A critical reader* (pp. 3–44). New York: Routledge.

Becerra, R. (2004). 2003/04 diversity statistics—Regular rank faculty, UCLA. *UCLA Chancellor's Office, Faculty Diversity.* Retrieved September 25, 2004, from http://www .faculty.diversity.ucla.edu

Bell, D. A. (1976). Serving two masters: Integration ideals and client interests in school desegregation litigation. *The Yale Law Journal, 85*(4), 470–516.

Bell, D. A. (1980). *Brown v. Board of Education* and the interest-convergence dilmenna. *Harvard Law Review, 93*(3), 518–533.

Bell, D. A. (1986). Application of the "tipping point" principle to law faculty hiring policies. *Nova Law Journal, 10,* 319–327.

Bell, D. A. (1987). *And we will not be saved: The elusive quest for racial justice.* New York: Basic Books.

Bell, D. A. (1992). *Faces at the bottom of the well: The permanence of racism.* New York: Basic Books.

Bell, D. A. (1996). *Gospel choirs: Psalms of survival for an alien land called home.* New York: Basic Books.

Bell, D. A. (2002a). Afterword: The handmaid's truth. In F. Valdes, J. McCristal Culp, & A. P. Harris (Eds.), *Crossroads, directions, and a new critical race theory* (pp. 411–412). Philadelphia: Temple.

Bell, D. A. (2002b). *Ethical ambitions: Living a life of meaning and worth.* New York: Bloomsbury.

Bell, D. A. (2004). *Silent covenants: Brown v. board of education and the unfulfilled hopes for racial reform.* New York: Oxford University Press.

Bell, L. A. (1997). Theoretical foundations for social justice education. In M. Adams, L. A. Bell, & P. Griffin (Eds.), *Teaching for diversity and social justice: A sourcebook* (pp. 3–15). New York: Routledge.

Bell, L. A. (2003). Telling tales: What stories can teach us about racism. *Race Ethnicity and Education, 6*(1), 3–28.

Bender, S. W. (2000). Commentary: Silencing culture and culturing silence: A comparative experience of centrifugal forces in ethnic studies curriculum. *Michigan Journal of Race and Law, 5,* 913–926.

Benjamin, L. (Ed.). (1997). *Black women in the academy: Promises and perils.* Gainesville, FL: University Press of Florida.

Berger, B. (Ed.). (1990). *Authors of their own lives: Intellectual autobiographies by twenty American sociologists.* Berkeley, California: University of California Press.

Bergin, D. A., & Cooks, H. C. (2002). High school students of color talk about accusations of "acting white." *The Urban Review, 34*(2), 113–134.

Bernal, M. E. (1988). Martha E. Bernal. In A. O'Connell & N. Russo (Eds.), *Models of achievement: Reflections of Eeminent women in psychology* (2nd ed.) (pp. 262–276). Hillsdale, NJ: Erlbaum.

Berryman, S. (1983). *Who will do science? Minority and female attainment of science and mathematics degrees: Trends and causes.* New York: Rockefeller Foundation.

Bernstein, B. (1977). *Class, Codes, and Control: Vol. 3 Towards a Theory of Educational Transmission.* London, England: Routledge and Kegan Paul.

Bettis, P. J. (1994). Deindustrialization and urban schools: Some theoretical considerations. *Urban Review, 26*(2), 75–94.

Bettis, P. J. (1996, April). Urban students, liminality, and the postindustrial context. *Sociology of Education, 69*(2), 105–125.

Blackwell, J. (1981). *Mainstreaming outsiders: The production of Black professionals.* Bayside, NY: General Hall.

Blackwell, J. (1991). Graduate and professional education for Blacks. In C. Willie, A. Garibaldi, & W. Reed (Eds.), *The education of African-Americans* (pp. 103–109). New York: Auburn House.

Bloom, B. (1966). The role of the educational sciences in curriculum development. *International Journal of Educational Sciences, 1*(1), 5–16.

Bloom, B. (Ed.). (1969). *Taxonomy of educational objectives.* New York: D-McKay Co., Inc.

Bobbitt, F. (1918). *The curriculum.* New York: Houghton Mifflin.

Bobbitt, F. (1924). *How to make a curriculum.* Boston, MA: Houghton Mifflin.

Bouchard, T., Lykken, D., McGue, M., Segal, N., & Tellegen, A. (1990). Sources of human psychological differences: The Minnesota study of twins reared apart. *Science, 250,* 223–250.

Bourdieu, P., & Passeron, J. (1977). *Reproduction in education, society, and culture.* London: Sage.

Bowen, W. G., & Bok, D. (1998). *The shape of the river: Long-term consequences of considering race in college and university admissions.* New Jersey: Princeton University Press.

Bowen, W., & Rudenstine, N. (1992). *In pursuit of the PhD.* Princeton, NJ: Princeton University Press.

Bowles, S., & Gintis, H. (1976). *Schooling in capitalistic America: Educational reform and the contradictions of economic life.* New York: Basic Books, Inc.

Brayboy, B. M. J. (2004, November). *Those Indians are taking over: A tribal critical theory analysis of a legal challenge to Indian education.* Invited session, presented at the annual meeting of the American Anthropological Association and the Council of Anthropology and Education. San Francisco, California.

Brayboy, B. M. J. (in press). Toward a tribal critical race theory. *The Urban Review.*

Brazziel, W. (1983). Baccalaureate college of origin of Black doctorate recipients. *Journal of Negro Education, 52,* 102–109.

Breggin, P., & Breggin, G. (1993, April). The federal violence initiative: Threats to Black children (and others). *Psych Discourse, 24,* 8–11.

Brookover, W. (1985). Can we make schools effective for minority students? *Journal of Negro Education, 54,* 257–268.

Brooks, R. (1986). Life after tenure: Can minority law professors avoid the Clyde Ferguson syndrome. *University of San Francisco Law Review, 20,* 419–427.

Brown, S. (1987). *Minorities in the education pipeline.* Princeton, NJ: The Educational Testing Service.

Brown, S. (1988). *Increasing minority faculty: An elusive goal.* Princeton, NJ: Educational Testing Service.

Brown v. Board of Education, 347 U.S. 483 (1954).

Brown v. Board of Education, 349 U.S. 294 (1955).

Buendia, E., Ares, N., Juarez, B. D., & Peercy, M. (2004). The geographies of difference: The production of the east side, west side, and central city school. *American Educational Research Journal, 41*(4), 833–863.

Bulman, R. C. (2002). Teachers in the 'hood: Hollywood's middle-class fantasy. *The Urban Review, 34*(3), 251–276.

Burciaga, R. (in press). *Living* nepantla: *Chicana education doctoral students' personal and professional aspirations.* Unpublished doctoral dissertation, University of California, Los Angeles.

Cabrera, A. M. (1997). (Ed.). LatCrit theory: Naming and launching a new discourse of critical legal scholarship. *Harvard Latino Law Review, 2*(1), 1–501.

Caldwell, P. (1991). A hair piece: Perspectives on the interaction of race and gender. *Duke Law Journal, 1991,* 365–396.

Californians for Justice Education Fund. (2003, May 17). *First things first: Why we must stop punishing students and fix California's schools: A report on school inequality and the impact of the California High School Exit Exam.* Oakland: Author.

Calmore, J. (1992). Critical race theory, Archie Shepp, and fire music: Securing an authentic intellectual life in a multicultural world. *Southern California Law Review, 65,* 2129–2231.

Carbado, D. W. (2002). Straight out of the closet: Race, gender, and sexual orientation. In F. Valdes, J. McCristal Culp, & A. P. Harris (Eds.), *Crossroads, directions, and a new critical race theory* (pp. 221–242). Philadelphia: Temple.

Carnegie Foundation for the Advancement of Teaching. (1987). *A classification of institutions of higher education.* Princeton, NJ: Author.

Carrasco, E. (1996). Collective recognition as a communitarian device: Or, of course we want to be role models! *La Raza Law Journal, 9,* 81–101.

Carroll, G. (1998). *Environmental stress and African Americans: The other side of the moon.* Westport: Praeger.

Carter, D., & Wilson, R. (1993). *Minorities in higher education: 1992 eleventh annual status report.* Washington, DC: American Council on Education.

Carter, P. (2003). "Black" cultural capital, status positioning, and schooling conflicts for low-income African American youth. *Social Problems, 50*(1), 136–155.

Carter, T. (1970). *Mexican Americans in school: A history of educational neglect.* New York: College Entrance Examination Board.

Carter, T. P., & Segura, R. D. (1979). *Mexican Americans in school: A decade of change.* New York: College Entrance Examination Board.

Castañeda, A. (1998). Language and other lethal weapons: Cultural politics and the rites of children as translators of culture. *Chicano-Latino Law Review, 19,* 229–241.

Castañeda v. Regents of the University of California, (1999). United States District Court, Northern District of California, Case No. C99-0525SI (Plaintiff Complaint).

Castañeda v. Regents of the University of California, (2003). United States District Court, Northern District of California, Case No. C99-0525SI (Consent Decree).

Caughey, J. (1973). *To kill a child's spirit: The tragedy of school segregation in Los Angeles.* Itasca, IL: F.E. Peacock Publishers, Inc.

Cave, D. (2005, June 3). Growing problem for military recruiters: Parents. *New York Times.* Retrieved June 25, 2005, from http://www.nytimes.com/2005/06/03/nyregion/03recruit.html?ex=1119412800&en=7b408a433eba9ff&ei=5070

Cazenave, N. (1988). From a committed achiever to a radical social scientist: The life course dialectics of a 'marginal' Black American sociologist. *American Sociologist, 19,* 347–354.

Ceja, M. (2001). *Applying, choosing, and enrolling in higher education: Understanding the college choice process of first-generation Chicana students.* Unpublished doctoral dissertation, University of California, Los Angeles.

Chang, R. (1993). Toward an Asian American legal scholarship: Critical race theory, poststructuralism, and narrative space. *California Law Review, 81,* 1243.

Chang, R. (1998). Who's afraid of Tiger Woods? *Chicano-Latino Law Review, 19,* 223–227.

Chapa, J., & Valencia, R. (1993). Latino population growth, demographic characteristics, and educational stagnation: An examination of recent trends. *Hispanic Journal of Behavioral Sciences, 15,* 165–187.

Chapman, T. K. (2005). Peddling backwards: Reflections of *Plessy* and *Brown* in the Rockford public schools *de jure* desegregation efforts. *Race Ethnicity and Education, 8*(1), 29–44.

Chavez, L. (1992). *Out of the barrio: Toward a new politics of Hispanic assimilation.* New York: Basic Books.

Chipman, S., & Thomas, G. (1984). *The participation of women and minorities in mathematical, scientific, and technical fields.* Washington, DC: Howard University Institute for Urban Affairs and Research.

Chon, M. (1995). On the need for Asian American narratives in law: Ethnic specimens, native informants, storytelling, and silences. *Asian Pacific American Law Journal, 3*(1), 4–32.

Clark, B. (1960). The "cooling-out" function of higher education. *American Journal of Sociology 65*(6), 569–576.

Clark, J. (1985). The status of science and mathematics in historically Black colleges and universities. *Science Education, 69,* 673–679.

Clark, M. (1983). Mamie Phipps Clark. In A. O'Connell and N. Russo (Eds.), *Models of achievement: Reflections of eminent women in psychology* (Vol. 1). New York: Columbia University Press.

Clewell, B. (1987). *Retention of Black and Hispanic doctoral students* (Parts I and II). Princeton, New Jersey: Educational Testing Service.

Collins, P. H. (1986). Learning from the outsider within: The sociological significance of Black feminist thought. *Social Problems, 33,* S14–S32.

Collins, P. H. (1998). *Fighting words: Black women & the search for justice.* Minneapolis: University of Minnesota Press.

Conyers, J. (1986). Black American doctorates in sociology: A follow-up study of their social and educational origins. *Phylon, 47,* 303–317.

Cortés, C. E. (2000). *The children are watching: How the media teach about diversity.* New York: Teachers College Press.

Cope, R. D. (1994). *The Limits of racial domination: Plebeian society in colonial Mexico City, 1660–1720.* Madison: University of Wisconsin Press.

Cota-Robles de Suárez, C. (1971). Skin color as a factor of racial identification and preference of young Chicano children. *Aztlán: A Journal of Chicano Studies, 2*(1), 107–150.

Council on Interracial Books for Children. (1977). *Stereotypes, distortions, and omissions in U.S. history textbooks.* New York: Author.

Crawford v. Board of Education of the City of Los Angeles, 17 Cal. 3d 280 (1976).

Crawford v. Board of Education of the City of Los Angeles, 458 U.S. 527 (1982).

Crenshaw, K. (1989). Demarginalizing the intersection of race and sex: A black feminist critique of antidiscrimination doctrine, feminist theory, and antiracist politics. *University of Chicago Legal Forum, 1989,* 139–167.

Crenshaw, K. (1991). Mapping the margins: Intersectionality, identity politics, and the violence against women of color. *Stanford Law Review, 43*(6), 1241–1299.

Crenshaw, K. (2002). The first decade: Critical reflections, or 'A foot in the closing door.' In F. Valdes, J. McCristal Culp, & A. Harris (Eds.), *Crossroads, directions, and a new critical race theory* (pp. 9–31). Philadelphia, PA: Temple University Press.

Crenshaw, K., Gotanda, N., Peller, G., & Thomas, K. (Eds.). (1995). *Critical race theory: The key writings that formed the movement.* New York: The New Press.

Cruz, C. (2001). Toward an epistemology of a brown body. *International Journal of Qualitative Studies in Education, 14*(5), 657–669.

Cuádraz, G. H. (1992). Experiences of multiple marginality: A case study of Chicana 'scholarship women.' *Association of Mexican American Educators Journal,* 31–43.

Cuádraz, G. H. (1993). *Meritocracy (un)challenged: The making of a Chicano and Chicana professoriate and professional class.* Unpublished doctoral dissertation, University of California, Berkeley.

Cuádraz, G. H. (1997). Chicana academic persistence: Creating a university-based community. *Education and Urban Society, 30,* 107–121.

Cuádraz, G. H. (2005). Chicanas and higher education: Three decades of literature and thought. *Journal of Hispanic Higher Education, 4*(3), 215–234.

Cuádraz, G. H., & Pierce, J. (1994). From scholarship girls to scholarship women: Surviving the contradictions of class and race in academe. *Explorations in Ethnic Studies, 17,* 21–44.

Cummins, J. (1986). Bilingual education and anti-racist education. *Interracial Books for Children Bulletin, 17*(3 & 4), 9–12.

Daniels v. State of California, (1999). Superior Court of the State of California, Los Angeles Superior Court Case No. BC 214156 (Plaintiff Complaint).

Daniels v. State of California, (2003). Superior Court of the State of California, Los Angeles Superior Court Case No. BC 214156 (Consent Decree).

Darby, J. T., & Fitzgerald, S., (Eds.). (2003). *Keepers of the morning star: An anthology of native women's theater.* Los Angeles, CA: UCLA American Indian Studies Center.

Darder, A. (1991). *Culture and power in the classroom: A critical foundation for bicultural education.* New York: Bergin & Garvey.

Darder, A., & Torres, R. D. (2000). Mapping the problematics of "race": A critique of Chicano education discourse. In C. Tejeda, C. Martinez, & Z. Leonardo (Eds.), *Charting new terrains of Chicana(o), Latina(o) education* (pp. 161–172). Cresskill, NJ: Hampton Press.

Darder, A., & Torres, R. D. (2004). *After race: Racism after multiculturalism.* New York University Press.

Darder, A., Torres, R. D., & Gutierrez, H. (Eds.). (1997). *Latinos and education: A critical reader.* New York: Routledge.

Darling-Hammond, L. (1988). *Teacher quality and equality.* Manuscript presented at the Colloquium on Access to Knowledge, Educational Equity Project, College Board, Oakland, CA.

Darling-Hammond, L. (1988). *The evolution of teacher policy.* Washington D.C: U.S. Dept. of Education, Office of Educational Research and Improvement, Educational Resources Information Center.

Davis, P. (1989). Law as microaggression. *The Yale Law Journal, 98*(8), 1559–1577.

de la Luz Reyes, M., & J. Halcon. (1988). Racism in academia: The old wolf revisited. *Harvard Educational Review, 58,* 299–314.

DeCuir, J. T., & Dixson, A. D. (2004). "So when it comes out, they aren't that surprised that it is there:" Using critical race theory as a tool of analysis of race and racism in education. *Educational Researcher, 33*, 26–31.

Delgado, R. (1984). The imperial scholar: Reflections on a review of civil rights literature. *University of Pennsylvania Law Review, 132*, 561–578.

Delgado, R. (1989). Storytelling for oppositionists and others: A plea for narrative. *Michigan Law Review, 87*, 2411–2441.

Delgado, R. (1990). When a story is just a story: Does voice really matter? *Virginia Law Review, 76*(1), 95–111.

Delgado, R. (1992). The imperial scholar revisited: How to marginalize outsider writing, ten years later. *University of Pennsylvania Law Review, 140*, 1349–1372.

Delgado, R. (1993). On telling stories in school: A reply to Farber and Sherry. *Vanderbilt Law Review, 46*, 665–676.

Delgado, R. (Ed.). (1995a). *Critical race theory: The cutting edge*. Philadelphia, PA: Temple University Press.

Delgado, R. (1995b). *The Rodrigo chronicles: Conversations about America and race*. New York: New York University Press.

Delgado, R. (1996). *The coming race war: And other apocalyptic tales of American after affirmative action and welfare*. New York: New York University Press.

Delgado, R. (1999). *When equality ends: Stories about race and resistance*. Boulder, CO: Westview Press.

Delgado, R. (2001). Two ways to think about race: Reflections on the id, the ego, and other reformist theories of equal protection. *Georgetown Law Journal, 89*, 2279–2296.

Delgado, R. (2003a). *Justice at war: Civil liberties and civil rights during times of crisis*. New York: New York University Press.

Delgado, R. (2003b). Crossroads and blind alleys: A critical examination of recent writing about race. *Texas Law Review, 82*, 121–152.

Delgado, R. (2005). Rodrigo and revisionism: Relearning the lessons of history. *Northwestern University Law Review, 99*, 805–837.

Delgado, R., & Stefancic, J. (1993). Critical race theory: An annotated bibliography. *Virginia Law Review, 79*, 461–516.

Delgado, R., & Stefancic, J. (Eds.). (1997). *Critical White studies: Looking behind the mirror*. Philadelphia: Temple University Press.

Delgado Bernal, D. (1997). *Chicana school resistance and grassroots leadership: Providing an alternative history of the 1968 east Los Angeles blowouts*. Unpublished doctoral dissertation, University of California, Los Angeles.

Delgado Bernal, D. (1998a). Grassroots leadership reconceptualized: Chicana oral histories and the 1968 east Los Angeles school blowouts. *Frontiers: A Journal of Women Studies, 19*, 113–142.

Delgado Bernal, D. (1998b). Using a Chicana feminist epistemology in educational research. *Harvard Educational Review, 68*(4), 555–582.

Delgado Bernal, D. (2001). Living and learning pedagogies of the home: The mestiza consciousness of Chicana students. *International Journal of Qualitative Studies in Education, 14*(5), 623–639.

Delgado Bernal, D. (2002). Critical race theory, LatCrit theory, and critical raced-gendered epistemologies: Recognizing students of color as holders and creators of knowledge. *Qualitative Inquiry, 8*(1), 105–126.

Delgado Bernal, D., & Villalpando, O. (2002). An apartheid of knowledge in academia: The struggle over the "legitimate" knowledge of faculty of color. *Equity and Excellence in Education, 35*(2), 169–180.

Delgado-Gaitan, C. (1992). School matters in the Mexican-American home: Socializing children to education. *American Educational Research Journal, 29,* 495–513.

Delgado-Gaitan, C. (1994). Socializing young children in Mexican-American families: An intergenerational perspective. In P. Greenfield & R. Cocking. (Eds.), *Cross-Cultural roots of minority development* (pp. 55–86). New Jersey: Lawrence Erlbaum Associates.

Delgado-Gaitan, C. (1997). Dismantling borders. In A. Neumann & P. L. Peterson (Eds.), *Learning from our lives: Women, research, and autobiography in education* (pp. 37–51). New York: Teachers College Press.

Delgado-Gaitan, C. (2001). *The power of community: Mobilizing for family and schooling.* Boulder, CO: Rowman and Littlefield Publishers.

Deloria, V. (1969). *Custer died for your sins: An Indian manifesto.* New York: Avon.

Diaz, R. (2000). *Latina parent educational participation: A pro-active approach.* Unpublished doctoral dissertation, University of California, Los Angeles.

Diaz v. San Jose Unified School District, 412 F. Supp. 310 (N.D. Cal. 1976).

Diaz v. San Jose Unified School District, 733 F.2d 660 (9th Cir. 1984).

Dix, L. (Ed.). (1987). *Minorities: Their underrepresentation and career differentials in science and engineering.* Washington, DC: National Academy Press.

Dixson, A. D., & Rousseau, C. K. (Eds.). (2005). Special issue on critical race theory in education. *Race Ethnicity and Education, 8*(1), 1–127.

Donato, R. (1997). *The other struggle for equal schools: Mexican Americans during the civil rights era.* New York: State University of New York Press.

Donato, R., Menchaca, M., & Valencia, R. R. (1991). Segregation, desegregation, and integration of Chicano students: Problems and prospects. In R. R. Valencia (Ed.), *Chicano school failure and success: Research and policy agenda for the 1990s* (pp. 27–63). New York: The Falmer Press.

Donoso, R. F., & Reyes, C. (2002). *Taking action: Confronting the health, social, and environmental factors associated with asthma in the Latino community.* San Francisco, CA: Latino Issues Forum.

DuBois, W. E. B. (1903/1994). *The Souls of Black Folk.* New York: Dover Publications.

DuBois, W. E. B. (1920/2003). *Darkwater: Voices from within the veil.* Amherst, NY: Humanity Books.

DuBois, W. E. B. (1935). Does the Negro need separate schools? *The Journal of Negro Education, 4*(3), 328–335.

Dudziak, M. L. (1988). Desegregation as a cold war imperative. *Stanford Law Review, 41*(1), 61–120.

Dudziak, M. L. (2000). *Cold War Civil Rights: Race and the Image of American Democracy.* Princeton, NJ: Princeton University Press.

Duncan, G. (2002a). Beyond love: A critical race ethnography of the schooling of adolescent Black males. *Equity and Excellence in Education, 35*(2), 131–143.

Duncan, G. (2002b). Critical race theory and method: Rendering race in urban ethnographic research. *Qualitative Inquiry, 8*(1), 85–104.

Duncan, G. (2005). Critical race ethnography in education: Narrative, inequality and the problem of epistemology. *Race Ethnicity and Education, 8*(1), 93–114.

Dunn, L. (1987). *Bilingual Hispanic children on the mainland: A review of research of their cognitive, linguistic, and scholastic development.* Circle Pines, MN: American Guidance Service.

Durán, A. (2003, August 31). *Exigen escuelas para el este de LA. La Opinión.*

Duster, T. (1976). The structure of privilege and its universe of discourse. *American Sociologist, 11,* 73–78.

Edmonds, R. (1979). Effective schools for the urban poor. *Educational Leadership, 37,* 15–24.

Edmonds, R. (1984). School effects and teacher effects. *Social Policy, 15,* 37–39.

Edmonds, R. (1986). Characteristics of effective schools. U. Neisser (Ed.), *The school achievement of minority children: New perspectives* (pp. 93–104). Hillsdale, NJ: Lawrence Erlbaum Associates.

Elenes, C. A., Gonzalez, F., Delgado Bernal, D., & Villenes, S. (2001). Introduction: Chicana/ Mexicana feminist pedagogies: Consejos, respeto, y educación. *International Journal of Qualitiative Studies in Education, 14*(5), 595–602.

Ellison, R. (1952/2002). *Invisible Man.* New York: Random House.

Empowerment Project. (Producer). (1992). *The Panama deception.* [Film]. (Available from Empowerment Project, 8218 Farrington Mill Rd. Chapel Hill, NC 27517).

Esparza, M., & Katz, R. (Producers). Nava, G. (Writer/Director). (1997). *Selena* [Film]. United States: Warner Bros.

Espin, O. (1993). Giving voice to silence: The psychologist as witness. *American Psychologist, 48,* 408–414.

Espinoza, P. (Producer/Writer). (1986). *The Lemon Grove Incident.* [Film]. San Diego: KPBS Television. (Available from Teaching for Change, P.O. Box 73038, Washington, DC 20056).

Espinosa, R. W., Fernández, C., Dornbusch, S. M. (1977). Chicano perceptions of high school and Chicano performance. *Aztlan: A Journal of Chicano Studies, 8,* 133–155.

Espinoza, L. G. (1990). Masks and other disguises: Exposing legal academia. *Harvard Law Review, 103,* 1878–1886.

Espinoza, L. G. (1998). Latino/a identity and multi-identity: Community and culture. In R. Delgado & J. Stefancic (Eds.), *The Latino/a condition: A critical reader* (pp. 17–23). New York: New York University Press.

Espinoza, L., & Harris, A. (1998). Embracing the tar-baby: LatCrit theory and the sticky mess of race. *La Raza Law Journal, 10*(1), 499–559.

Estrada, L. (1993). The dynamic demographic mosaic called America: Implications for education. *Education and Urban Society, 25,* 231–245.

Etter-Lewis, G. (1993). *My soul is my own: Oral narratives of African American women in the professions.* New York: Routledge.

Etter-Lewis, G., & M. Foster (Eds.). (1996). *Unrelated kin: Race and gender in women's personal narratives.* New York: Routledge.

Falcone, M. (2002, May 16). Former Chancellor Kerr remembers UC history. *UCLA Daily Bruin.* Retrieved September 25, 2004, from http://www.dailybruin.ucla.edu/news/articles .asp?ID=19827

Fanon, F. (1967). *Black skin, White masks.* New York: Grove. Reprint of *Peau noire, masques blancs.* Paris, 1952.

Faulstich Orellana, M. (2003). *In other words: En otras palabras: Learning from bilingual kids' translating/interpreting experiences.* Evanston, IL: School of Education and Social Policy, Northwestern University.

Fernández, L. (2002). Telling stories about school: Using critical race and Latino critical theories to document Latina/Latino education and resistance. *Qualitative Inquiry,* (8)1, 45–65.

Fernandez, R. (Ed.). (1988). Special issue, achievement testing: Science v. ideology (response to Lloyd Dunn). *Hispanic Journal of Behavioral Sciences, 10,* 179–323.

Figueroa, J. L., & Garcia, E. E. (in press). Tracing institutional racism in higher education: Academic practices of Latino male undergraduates. In M. G. Constantine & D. Wing Sue (Eds.), *The effects of institutional racism in higher education settings.* New York: Teachers College.

Fischel, W. (1989). Did *Serrano* cause Proposition 13? *National Tax Journal, 42,* 465.

Fischel, W. A. (1996). How *Serrano* caused Proposition 13. *Journal of Law and Politics, 12,* 607.

Fischel, W. A. (2004). Did John Serrano vote for Proposition 13? A reply to Stark and Zasloff, 'Tiebout and Tax Revolts: Did Serrano Really Cause Proposition 13?' *UCLA Law Review, 51*(4), 887–932.

Fleming, J. (1984). *Blacks in College: A comparative study of students' success in Black and White institutions.* San Francisco, CA: Jossey-Bass.

Flores, J. (1988). Chicana doctoral students: Another look at educational equity. In H. S. Garcia & R. Chavez (Eds.), *Ethnolinguistic issues in education* (pp. 90–99). Lubbock, TX: College of Education, Texas Tech University.

Flores-Niemann, Y. F. (1999). The making of a token: A case study of stereotype threat, stigma, racism, and tokenism in academe. *Frontiers: A Journal of Women Studies, 20*(1), 111–135.

Foley, D. E. (1997). Deficit thinking models based on culture: The anthropological protest. In R. Valencia (Ed.), *The evolution of deficit thinking: Educational thought and practice* (pp. 113–131). London: The Falmer Press.

Fordham, S. (1988). Racelessness as a factor in black students' school success: Pragmatic strategy or pyrrhic victory? *Harvard Educational Review, 58,* 54–84.

Fordham, S., & Obgu, J. (1986). Black students' school success: Coping with the 'burden of acting white.' *The Urban Review, 18,* 176–206.

Foster, J., Miller, R. P., & Renzi, M. (Producers). Sayles, J. (Writer/Director). (1996). *Lone star.* [Film]. United States: Castle Rock Entertainment.

Freedman, S. G. (2005, January 26). At Stanford, tutoring helps make a janitor less invisible, *The New York Times.* Retrieved March 26, 2005, from http://www.nytimes.com/2005/01/26/education/26education.html

Freire, P. (1970). *Education for critical consciousness.* New York: Continuum Publishing Company.

Freire, P. (1973). *Pedagogy of the oppressed.* New York: The Seabury Press.

Fry, R. (2004). *Latino youth finishing college: The role of selective pathways.* A report of the Pew Hispanic Center. Washington, DC: June 23, 2004.

Fuller, C. (1985). *An analysis of leading undergraduate sources of PhD's, adjusted for institutional size.* Ann Arbor, MI: Great Lakes College Association.

Fuller, C. (1989). *Baccalaureate sources of 1975–1986 doctorates earned by American Indian, Asian, Black, Hispanic and White men and women who received baccalaureate degrees 1975–1982: Total numbers adjusted for institutional size.* New York: Ford Foundation.

Gándara, P. (1979). *Early environmental correlates of high academic attainment in Mexican Americans from low socio-economic backgrounds.* Unpublished doctoral dissertation, University of California, Los Angeles.

Gándara, P. (1982). Passing through the eye of the needle: High-achieving Chicanas. *Hispanic Journal of Behavioral Sciences 4*, 167–179.

Gándara, P. (1993). *Choosing higher education: The educational mobility of Chicano students.* Berkeley, California: The California Policy Seminar.

Gándara, P. (1995). *Over the ivy walls: The educational mobility of low income Chicanos.* Albany, NY: State University of New York Press.

Garcia, E. E. (1987/88). Effective schooling for language minority students. National Clearinghouse for Bilingual Education, Occasional Papers in Bilingual Education, Number 1.

Garcia, E. E. (1999). Chicanos/as in the United States: Language, bilingual education, and achievement. In J. Moreno (Ed.), *The elusive quest for equality: 150 Years of Chicano/ Chicana education.* Cambridge, MA: Harvard Educational Review.

Garcia, E. E. (2001). *Hispanic education in the United States: Raíces y alas.* New York: Rowman & Littlefield.

Garcia, E. E., & Padilla, R. V. (Eds.). (1985). *Advances in bilingual education research.* Tucson: University of Arizona Press.

Garcia, I. M. (1997). *Chicanismo: The forging of a militant ethos among Mexican Americans.* Tucson: University of Arizona Press.

Garcia, J. (1980). Hispanic perspective: Textbooks and other curricular materials. *The History Teacher, 14*(1), 105–120.

García, O., & Baker, C. (Eds.). (1995). *Policy and practice in bilingual education: A reader extending the foundations.* Philadelphia: Multilingual Matters.

Garcia, P. (2003). The use of high school exit examinations in four southwestern states. *Bilingual Research Journal, 27*(3), 431–450.

García, P. A., & Gopal, M. (2003). The relationship to achievement on the California high school exit exam for language minority students. *NABE Journal of Research and Practice, 1*(1), 123–137.

Garcia, R. (1995). Critical race theory and proposition 187: The racial politics of immigration law. *Chicano-Latino Law Review, 17*, 118–148.

García, S. B., & Guerra, P. L. (2004). Deconstructing deficit thinking: Working with educators to create more equitable learning environments. *Education and Urban Society, 36*(2), 150–168.

Garibaldi, A. (1984). *Black colleges and universities: Challenges for the future.* New York: Praeger.

Garibaldi, A. (1991). The role of historically Black colleges in facilitating resilience among African-American students. *Education and Urban Society, 24*, 103–112.

Gay, G. (2004). Navigating marginality en route to the professoriate: Graduate Students of Color learning and living in academia. *International Journal of Qualitative Studies in Education, 17*(2), 265–288.

Gee, H. (1997). Changing landscapes: The need for Asian Americans to be included in the affirmative action debate. *Gonzaga Law Review, 32*, 621–658.

Gee, H. (1999). Beyond Black and White: Selected writings by Asian Americans within the critical race theory movement. *St. Mary's Law Journal, 30*, 759–799.

Gilbert, M. J. (1980a). *Los parientes: Social structural factors and kinship relations among second generation Mexican Americans in two southern California communities.* Unpublished doctoral dissertation, University of California, Santa Barbara.

Gilbert, M. J. (1980b). Communities within communities: Social structural factors and variation in Mexican-American communities. *Hispanic Journal of Behavioral Sciences, 2*(3) 241–268.

Giménez, M. E. (1989). 'Latino/Hispanic'—who needs a name? The case against a standardized terminology. *International Journal of Health Services, 19*, 557–571.

Ginorio, A., & Huston, M. (2001). *Sí se puede! Yes we can!: Latinas in education report.* Washington, DC: American Association of University Women Educational Foundation.

Giroux, H. (1983). Theories of reproduction and resistance in the new sociology of education: A critical analysis. *Harvard Educational Review, 55*, 257–293.

Giménez, M. E. (1989). 'Latino/Hispanic'—Who needs a name? The case against a standardized terminology. *International Journal of Health Services, 19*, 557–571.

Glaser, B., & Strauss, A. (1967). *The discovery of grounded theory.* Chicago, IL: Aldine.

Gómez-Quiñones, J. (1973). The first steps: Chicano labor conflict and organizing 1900–1920. *Aztlan: A Journal of Chicano Studies, 3*(1), 13–49.

Gómez-Quiñones, J. (1994). *Roots of Chicano politics, 1600–1940.* Albuquerque, NM: University of New Mexico Press.

González, G. G. (1990). *Chicano education in the era of segregation.* Philadelphia: Balch Institute Press.

González, G. G. (1997). Culture, language, and the Americanization of Mexican children. In A. Darder, R. Torres, & H. Gutierrez (Eds.), *Latinos and education: A critical reader* (pp. 158–173). New York: Routledge.

Gonzalez, G. G. (1999). "Segregation and the education of Mexican children, 1900–1940." In J. Moreno (Ed.), *The elusive quest for equality: 150 years of Chicano/Chicana education* (pp. 53–76). Cambridge, MA: Harvard Educational Publishing Group.

Gonzalez, N., & Moll, L. C. (2002). Cruzando el puente: Building bridges to funds of knowledge. *Educational Policy, 16*(4), 623–641.

Gonzalez, N., Moll, L. C., Tenery, M. F., Rivera, A., Rendon, P., Gonzales, R., & Amanti, C. (1995). Funds of knowledge for teaching in Latino households. *Urban Education, 29*(4), 443–470.

Goodstein, D. (1993). Scientific PhD problems. *The American Scholar, 62*, 215–220.

Gordon, M. M. (1981). *America as a multicultural society.* Philadelphia: American Academy of Political and Social Science.

Graham, S. (1992). 'Most of the subjects were White and middle class': Trends in published research on African Americans in selected APA journals, 1970–1989. *American Psychologist, 47*, 629–639.

Gratz v. Bollinger, 539 U.S. 244 (2003).

Greene, L. (1990/91). Tokens, role models, and pedagogical politics: Lamentations of an African American female law professor. *Berkeley Women's Law Journal, 6*, 81–92.

Gregory, S. (1995). *Black women in the academy: The secrets to success and achievement.* New York: University Press of America.

Griffith, E. E. H., & Pierce, C. M. (1998). *Race and Excellence: My dialogue with Chester Pierce.* University of Iowa Press.

Grutter v. Bollinger, 539 U.S. 306 (2003).

Guinier, L. (1990/91). Of gentleman and role models. *Berkeley Women's Law Journal, 6*, 93–106.

Guinier, L., Fine, M., & Balin, J. (1997). *Becoming gentlemen: Women, law school, and institutional change.* Boston, MA: Beacon Press.

Gutierrez, K. (2002). Studying cultural practices in urban learning communities. *Human Development, 45*(4), 312–321.

Gutierrez, K., Rymes, B., & Larson, J. (1995). Script, counterscript, and underlife in the classroom: Brown, James versus Brown v. Board of Education. *Harvard Educational Review, 65*(3), 445–471.

Gutiérrez-Jones, C. (2001). *Critical race narratives: A study of race, rhetoric, and injury.* New York: New York University Press.

Gutman, H. (1976). *The Black family in slavery and freedom, 1750–1925.* New York: Pantheon Books.

Hacker, A. (1992). *Two nations: Black and White, separate, hostile, unequal.* New York: Ballantine.

Hackford, T., & Borden, B. (Producers) & Valdez, L. (Writer/Director). (1987). *La Bamba* [Film]. United States: Columbia Pictures.

Hakeem, F. (2005, March 2). *Teens take on military recruiters: High school students win right to counter-recruitment table.* Retrieved June 20, 2005, from http://www.pulsetc.com/article.php?sid=1678

Hakuta, K. (1991). Distinguishing between proficiency, choice, and attitudes in questions about language for bilinguals. Working Paper series, no. 32. Stanford Center of Chicano Research.

Hall, A. (1984a, April). Starting from the beginning: The baccalaureate origins of doctorate recipients, 1920–1980. *Change, 16,* 40–43.

Hall, A. (1984b, September). Baccalaureate origins of doctorate recipients in chemistry. *Change, 16,* 47–49.

Haney Lopez, I. F. (1994). Social construction of race: Some observations on illusion, fabrication, and choice. *Harvard Chicano Latino Law Review, 29,* 1–62.

Haney Lopez, I. F. (1996). *White by law: The legal construction of race.* New York University Press.

Hardy, K. (1974). Social origins of American scientists and scholars. *Science, 185,* 497–506.

Haro, C. M. (1977). *Mexicano/Chicano concerns and school desegregation in Los Angeles. Monograph no. 9.* Chicano Studies Center Publications. University of California, Los Angeles.

Harris, A. (1990/91). Women of color in legal education: Representing *la mestiza. Berkeley Women's Law Journal, 6,* 107–122

Harris, A. (1995). Race and essentialism in feminist legal theory. In R. Delgado (Ed.), *Critical race theory: The cutting edge* (pp. 253–266). Philadelphia, PA: Temple University Press.

Harris, C. I. (1993). Whiteness as property. *Harvard Law Review, 106,* 1707–1791.

Harris, L. (2002). A survey of the status of equality in public education in California: A survey of a cross-section of public school teachers. Public Advocates, Inc.

Hayasaki, E. (2003, May 21). Schools see "an awakening" of student activism. *Los Angeles Times,* p. B2.

Hayasaki, E. (2005, June 15). College prep idea approved in L.A.: School board votes to require students, with some exceptions, to take classes needed to enter state universities. Some teachers object. *Los Angeles Times,* p. B1.

Haycock, K., & Navarro, S. (1988). *Unfinished business: Fulfilling our children's promise.* Oakland, CA: The Achievement Council.

Hayes-Bautista, D., & Chapa, J. (1987). Latino terminology: Conceptual bases for standardized terminology. *American Journal of Public Health, 77,* 61–68.

Heidenreich, L. (in press). Against the grain: Confronting hispanic service organizations in times of increasing inequalities, 1930 and 2005. *Journal of Latinos and Education, 5*(2).

Heimlich, S. M. (2001). *Through the eyes of aspiring scientists: Mexican Americans in pursuit of the phd.* Unpublished doctoral dissertation, University of California, Los Angeles.

Helfand, D. (2000, December 15). South LA pupils demand more college prep classes. *Los Angeles Times*, p. B4.

Helfand, D. (2001, February 2). Pupils press demands for prep classes. *Los Angeles Times*, p. B1.

Helfand, D. (2002, May 29). Schools challenge mandatory testing: L.A. and San Francisco districts seek to alter or scrap Stanford 9 and exit exams. *Los Angeles Times*, p. B1.

Heller, C. S. (1966). *Mexican American youth: Forgotten youth at the crossroads.* New York: Random House.

Henderson, P., Clark, J., & Reynolds, M. (1996). *Summary report 1995: Doctorate recipients from United States universities.* Washington, D.C.: National Academy Press.

Hernandez, D. (2003, December 20). Backers of prop. 187 push for new initiative: Proposed measure to deny services to illegal immigrants raises fears of divisive racial politics. *The Los Angeles Times*, p. A1.

Herrnstein, R., & Murray, C. (1994). *The bell curve: Intelligence and class structure in American life.* New York: Free Press.

Higginbotham, L. (1992). An open letter to Justice Clarence Thomas from a federal judicial colleague. In T. Morrison (Ed.), *Race-ing justice, en-gendering power: Essays on Anita Hill, Clarence Thomas, and the construction of social reality* (pp. 3–39). New York: Random House.

Hirsch, E. D., Jr. (1988). *Cultural literacy: What every American needs to know.* New York: Vintage Books.

Hirsch, E. D., Jr. (1996). *The schools we need and why we don't have them.* New York: Doubleday.

Hispanic Association of Colleges and Universities. (1991). *Hispanic Association of Colleges and Universities: 1991 annual report.* San Antonio, TX: Author.

Hispanic Policy Development Project. (1984). *Make something happen: Hispanics and urban high school reform* (Vols. 1 & 2). Washington, DC: Hispanic Development Policy Project.

Holland, J. (1957). Undergraduate origins of American scientists. *Science, 126*, 433–437.

Homer, S., & Schwartz, L. (1989–90). Admitted but not accepted: Outsiders take an inside look at law school. *Berkeley Women's Law Journal, 5*, 1–74.

Hong Kingston, M. (1976). *The woman warrior: Memoirs of a girlhood among ghosts.* New York: Knopf, distributed by Random House.

hooks, B. (1990). *Yearnings: Race, gender, and cultural politics.* Boston, MA: South End Press.

hooks, B. (1994). *Teaching to transgress: Education as the practice of freedom.* New York, NY: Routledge.

hooks, B. (1995). *Killing rage: Ending racism.* New York: Henry Holt and Company.

hooks, B. (2002). *Communion: The female search for love.* New York: William Morrow.

Hopfenberg, W., Levin, H., Meister, G., & Rodgers, J. (1990). *Accelerated schools.* Stanford, CA: Center for Educational Research at Stanford.

Humez, J. M. (2003). *Harriet Tubman: The life and the life stories.* University of Wisconsin Press.

Hunter, M. (2002). If you're light you're alright: Light skin color as social capital for women of color. *Gender and Society, 16*(2), 175–193.

Hunter, M., Allen, W., & Telles, E. (2000). Skin color, income and education: A comparison of African Americans and Mexican Americans. *National Journal of Sociology 12*(1), 129–180.

Hurtado, A. (1996). *The color of privilege: Three blasphemes on race and feminism.* Ann Arbor: University of Michigan Press.

Hurtado, A. (1997). Understanding multiple group identities: Inserting women into cultural transformations. *Journal of Social Issues, 53*(2), 299–328.

Hurtado, S., & Carter, D. F. (1997). Effects of college transition and perceptions of the campus racial climate on Latino college students' sense of belonging. *Sociology of Education, 70*, 324–346.

Hurtado, S., Milem, J., Clayton-Pederson, A., & Allen, W. (1999). *Enacting diverse learning environments: Improving the climate for racial/ethnic diversity in higher education.* ASHE-ERIC Higher Education Report Volume 26, No. 8. Washington, D.C.: The George Washington University, Graduate School of Education and Human Development.

Hurtado, S., & Ponjuan, L. (2005). Latino educational outcomes and the campus climate. *Journal of Hispanic Higher Education, 4*(3), 235–251.

Hutchinson, D. L. (2004). Critical race histories: In and out. *American University Law Review, 53*, 1187–1215.

Ikemoto, L. (1992). Furthering the inquiry: Race, class, and culture in the forced medical treatment of pregnant women. *Tennessee Law Review, 59*(3), 487–519.

Irvine, J. J. (1988). Urban schools that work: A summary of relevant factors. *Journal of Negro Education, 57*, (3), 236–242.

James, J., & R. Farmer (Eds.). (1993). *Spirit, space, and survival: African American women in (White) academe.* New York: Routledge.

Jay, J. (1971). *Negroes in science: Natural science doctorates, 1876–1969.* Detroit, MI: Balamp Publishing.

Jay, M. (2003). Critical race theory, multicultural education, and the hidden curriculum of hegemony. *Multicultural Perspectives, 5*, 3–10.

Jensen, A. (1969). How much can we boost I.Q. and scholastic achievement? *Harvard Educational Review, 39*, 1–123.

Johnson, K. R. (1998). 'Melting pot' or 'ring of fire'? Assimilation and the Mexican-American Experience. *La Raza Law Journal, 10*(1), 173–227.

Johnson, K. R. (1999). *How did you get to be Mexican? A White/Brown man's search for identity.* Philadelphia, PA: Temple University Press.

Johnson, K. R. (2004). Roll over Beethoven: 'A critical examination of recent writing about race.' *Texas Law Review, 82*, 717–734.

Jones-Johnson, G. (1988). The victim-bind dilemma of Black female sociologists in academe. *American Sociologist, 19*, 312–322.

Jordan, Emma. (1990/91). Images of Black women in the legal academy: An introduction. *Berkeley Women's Law Journal, 6*, 1–21.

Kamin, L. J. (1974). *The science and politics of I.Q.* New York: Potomac, MD., L. Erlbaum Associates, distributed by Halsted Press.

Knapp, R., & Goodrich, H. (1951). The origins of American scientists. *Science, 113*, 543–545.

Kozol, J. (1991). *Savage inequalities. Children in America's schools.* New York: Crown Publications.

Kretovics, J., & Nussel, E.J. (1994). *Transforming urban education.* Boston: Allyn and Bacon.

Kretzman, J., & McKnight, J. (1993). *Building communities from the inside out: A path toward finding and mobilizing a community's assets.* Chicago: ACTA.

Ladson-Billings, G. (1997). For Colored girls who have considered suicide when the academy's not enough: Reflections of an African American woman scholar. In A. Neumann & P. L. Peterson (Eds.), *Learning from our lives: Women, research, and autobiography in education* (pp. 52–69). New York: Teachers College Press.

Ladson-Billings, G. (1998). Preparing teachers for diverse student populations: A critical race theory perspective. *Review of Research in Education, 24,* 211–247.

Ladson-Billings, G. (2000). Racialized discourses and ethnic epistemologies. In N. Denzin & Y. Lincoln (Eds.), *Handbook of qualitative research* (2nd ed.) (pp. 257–277). Thousand Oaks, CA: Sage.

Ladson-Billings, G., & Tate, W. (1995). Toward a critical race theory of education. *Teachers College Record, 97,* 47–68.

Lamphere, L. (Ed.) (1992). *Structuring diversity: Ethnographic perspectives on the new immigration. Chicago: University of Chicago Press.*

Laosa, L. M. (1977). Inequality in the classroom: Observational research on teacher-student interactions. *Aztlan: A Journal of Chicano Studies, 8,* 51–67.

Laosa, L. M. (1990). Psychosocial stress, coping, and development of Hispanic immigrant children. In F. C. Serafica, A. I. Schwebel, R. K. Russell, P. D. Isaac, & L. B. Meyers (Eds.), *Mental health of ethnic minorities* (pp. 38–65). New York: Praeger.

Laslett, B., & B. Thorne (Eds.). (1997). *Feminist sociology: Life histories of a movement.* New Brunswick, NJ: Rutgers University Press.

Latina Feminist Group, The. (2001). *Telling to live: Latina feminist testimonios.* Durham, IN: Duke University Press.

Lau v. Nichols, 94 S.Ct. 786 (1974).

Lawrence, C. (1992). The word and the river: Pedagogy as scholarship as struggle. *Southern California Law Review, 65*(5), 2231–2298.

Lawrence, C., & Matsuda, M. (1997). *We won't go back: Making the case for affirmative action.* Boston, MA: Houghton Mifflin.

Lawrence-Lightfoot, S. (1994). *I've known rivers: Lives of loss and liberation.* Reading, Massachusetts: Addison-Wesley.

Lee, H. K., & Fernandez, M. (1998, October 2). Youths want more money for schools: Rally in San Leandro. *The San Francisco Chronicle,* p. A21.

Leggon, C. (1987). Minority underrepresentation in science and engineering graduate education and careers: A critique. In L. Dix (Ed.), *Minorities: Their underrepresentation and career differentials in science and engineering* (pp. 151–157). Washington, DC: National Academy Press.

Leonardo, Z. (2004). The color of supremacy: Beyond the discourse of 'White privilege.' *Educational Philosophy and Theory, 36*(2), 138–152.

Levin, H. (1986). *Educational reform for disadvantaged students: An emerging crisis.* West Haven, CT: National Educational Association.

Levin, H. (1987a). Accelerated schools for disadvantaged students. *Educational Leadership, 44,* 19–21.

Levin, H. (1987b). New schools for the disadvantaged. *Teacher Education Quarterly, 14,* 60–83.

Levin, H. (1989). Accelerated schools: A new strategy for at-risk students. *Policy Bulletin* (6), 1–6.

Lewis, A. E. (2003). *Race in the schoolyard: Negotiating the color line in classrooms and communities.* New Brunswick, NJ: Rutgers University Press.

Lewis, O. (1968). The culture of poverty. In D. Moynihan (Ed.), *On understanding poverty: Perspectives from the social sciences.* New York: Basic Books.

Litowitz, D. (1997). Some critical thoughts on critical race theory. *Notre Dame Law Review, 72,* 503–529.

Lockheed, M., Thorpe, M., Brooks-Gunn, J., Casserly, P., & McAloon, A. (1985). *Sex and ethnic differences in mathematics, science, and computer science: What do we know?* A Report to the Ford Foundation. Princeton, NJ: Educational Testing Service.

Loewen, J. W. (1995). *Lies my teacher told me: Everything your American history textbook got wrong.* New York: New Press.

Lomas, C. (2003). Latina feminisms: Reflections on theory, practice, and pedagogy emerging in *Telling to live.* Paper presented at MALCS Summer Institute, San Antonio, Texas.

Lomotey, K. (Ed.). (1990). *Going to school: The African-American experience.* New York: State University of New York Press.

Lopez, G. (2003). Parental involvement as racialized performance. In G. Lopez & L. Parker (Eds.), *Interrogating racism in qualitative research methodology* (pp. 71–95). New York: Peter Lang Publishing.

Lopez, G., & Parker, L. (Eds.). (2003). *Interrogating racism in qualitative research methodology.* New York: Peter Lang Publishing.

Lopez-Garza, M. (1992). Los Angeles: Ascendant Chicano power. *NACLA Report on the Americas, 26*(2), 34–38, 45–46.

Lorde, A. (1978). *The black unicorn: Poems.* New York: Norton.

Lorde, A. (1984). *Sister Outsider.* Trumansburg, NY: Crossing Press.

Lorde, A. (1992). Age, race, class, and sex: Women redefining difference. In M. Anderson & P. H. Collins (Eds.), *Race, class, and gender: An anthology* (pp. 495–502). Belmont, CA: Wadsworth.

Los Angeles County Office of Education. (1994). *The condition of public education in Los Angeles County 1994.* Los Angeles, CA: Author.

Los Alacranes (Producer). Sanchez, R. (Writer). (1999). Rising souls. [Recorded by Los Alacranes]. On *Rising Souls* [CD]. San Diego, CA: Los Alacranes Publishing.

Los Tigres del Norte. Producer (1988). America. [Recorded by Los Tigres del Norte]. On *16 super exitos.* [CD]. México: Fonovisa.

Love, B. J. (2004). Brown plus 50 counter-storytelling: A critical race theory analysis of the "majoritarian achievement gap" story. *Equity and Excellence in Education, 37,* 227–246.

Lucas, T., Henze, R., & Donato, R. (1990). Promising the success of Latino language minority students: An exploratory study of six high schools. *Harvard Educational Review, 60,* 315–340.

Lynn, M. (1999). Toward a critical race pedagogy: A research note. *Urban Education, 33,* 606–626.

Lynn, M. (2002). Critical race theory and the perspectives of black men teachers in the Los Angeles public schools. *Equity and Excellence in Education, 35*(2), 119–130.

Lynn, M., & Adams, M. (Eds.). (2002). Special issue of critical race theory in education. *Equity and Excellence in Education, 35*(2), 87–199.

Lynn, M., Yosso, T., Solórzano, D., & Parker, L. (Eds.). (2002). Special issue: Critical race and qualitative research. *Qualitative Inquiry, 8*(1), 3–126.

Lyons, J. L. (1990). The past and future directions of federal bilingual education policy. *Annals of the American Academy of Political and Social Science, 508*, 66–80. Newbury Park: Sage.

Macedo. D., & Bartolomé, L. (1999). *Dancing with bigotry: Beyond the politics of tolerance.* New York: Palgrave.

Malcom, S. (1990a). Reclaiming our past. *Journal of Negro Education, 59*, 246–259.

Malcom, S. (1990b). Who will do science in the next century? *Scientific American, 262*(2), 112.

Mandel, R. (Director). Frumkes, R., Simonelli, R., & Ormsby, A. (Writers). (1996). *The substitute.* [Film]. Live Entertainment.

Marable, M. (1992). *Black America.* Westfield, NJ: Open Media.

Margolis, E., & Romero, M. (1998). 'The department is very male, very White, very old, and very conservative': The functioning of the hidden curriculum in graduate sociology departments. *Harvard Educational Review, 68*, 1–32.

Marquez, S. (1994). Distorting the image of 'Hispanic' women in sociology: Problematic strategies of presentation in the introductory text. *Teaching Sociology, 22*, 231–236.

Mason, M. A., & Goulden, M. (2002). Do babies matter? The effects of family formation on the lifelong careers of academic men and women. *Academe, 88*(6), 21–27.

Mason, M. A., & Goulden, M. (2004a). Do babies matter (Part II)? Closing the baby gap. *Academe*, 90(6), 11–15.

Mason, M. A., & Goulden, M. (2004b). Marriage and baby blues: Redefining gender equity in the academy. *Annals of American Political and Social Scientists. 596*, 86–103.

Martinez, C. (2000). Rethinking literacy & curriculum reform for Chicana/Chicano students. In C. Tejeda, C. Martinez, & Z. Leonardo (Eds.), *Charting new terrains of Chicana(o)/Latina(o) education* (pp. 193–212). Cresskill, NJ: Hampton Press.

Martínez, C., & Reyna, J. (1998). (Eds.). Difference, solidarity and law: Building Latina/o communities through latcrit theory. *Chicano-Latino Law Review, 19*, 1–612.

Martinez, E. (1998). *De colores means all of us: Latina views for a multi-colored century.* Cambridge, MA: South End Press.

Marx, S. (Ed.). (2003). Special issue of critical White studies in education. *International Journal of Qualitative Studies in Education, 16*(1), 1–140.

Mathews, J. (2000, December 21). High school students protest poor facilities, programs in Compton. *Los Angeles Times*, p. B5.

Matsuda, M. (1989). When the first quail calls: Multiple consciousness as jurisprudential method. *Women's Rights Law Reporter, 11*, 7–13.

Matsuda, M. (1991). Voices of America: Accents, antidiscrimination and a jurisprudence for the last reconstruction. *Yale Law Journal, 100*, 1329–1407.

Matsuda, M., Lawrence, C., Delgado, R., & Crenshaw, K. (Eds.). (1993). *Words that wound: Critical race theory, assaultive speech, and the first amendment.* Boulder, CO: Westview Press.

Matute-Bianchi, M. E. (1982). A Chicana in academe. *Women's Studies Quarterly, 10*(1), 14–17.

McGrayne, S. (1993). *Nobel prize women in science: Their lives, struggles, and momentous discoveries.* New York: Birch Lane Press.

McIntosh, P. (1989). White privilege: Unpacking the invisible knapsack. *Peace and Freedom, July/August*, 10–12.

McLaren, P. (1994). *Life in schools: An introduction to critical pedagogy in the foundations of education* (2nd ed.). White Plains, NY: Longman.

McWhorter, J. (2000). *Losing the Race: Self-sabotage in Black America*. New York: Free Press.

Menchaca, M. (1995). *The Mexican outsiders: A community history of marginalization and discrimination in California*. Austin, TX: University of Texas Press.

Menchaca, M. (1998). Early racist discourses: Roots of deficit thinking. In R. Valencia (Ed.), *The evolution of deficit thinking: Educational thought and practice* (pp. 13–40). Washington, DC: Falmer Press.

Mendez v. Westminster, 64 F. Supp. 544 (S.D. Cal. 1946).

Mendez v. Westminster, 161 F. 2d 744 (9th Cir. 1947).

Merton, R. (1968). The Matthew effect in science. *Science, 159*, 56–63.

Merton, R. (1973). *The sociology of science: Theoretical and empirical investigations* (E. Storer, Ed.). Chicago, IL: University of Chicago Press.

Merton, R. (1977). *The sociology of science: An episodic memoir*. Carbondale, IL: Southern Illinois University Press.

Mickelson, R., & Oliver, M. (1991). The demographic fallacy of the Black academic: Does quality rise to the top. In W. Allen, E. Epps, & N. Haniff (Eds.), *College in Black and White: African American students in predominantly White and in historically Black public universities* (pp. 177–195). Albany, NY: State University of New York Press.

Mills, C. W. (1997). *The racial contract*. Ithaca, NY: Cornell University Press.

Moll, L. C., Amanti, C., Neff, D., & Gonzalez, N. (1992). Funds of knowledge for teaching: Using a qualitative approach to connect homes and classrooms. *Theory into Practice, 31*(2), 132–141.

Montecinos, C. (1995). Culture as an ongoing dialog: Implications for multicultural teacher education. In C. E. Sleeter & P. L. McLaren (Eds.), *Multicultural education, critical pedagogy, and the politics of difference* (pp. 269–308). Albany, NY: State University of New York Press.

Montero-Sieburth, M. (1997). The weaving of personal origins and research: Reencuentro y reflexión en la investigación. In A. Neumann & P. L. Peterson (Eds.), *Learning from our lives: Women, research, and autobiography in education* (pp. 124–149). New York: Teachers College Press.

Montoya, M. E. (1994). *Mascaras, trenzas, y grenas*: Un/Masking the self while un/braiding Latina stories and legal discourse. *Chicano-Latino Law Review, 15*, 1–37.

Montoya, M. E. (2000, Summer). Silence and silencing: Their centripetal and centrifugal forces in legal communication, pedagogy, and discourse. *Michigan Journal of Race and Law, 5*, 847–911.

Montoya, M. E. (2001). A brief history of Chicana/o school segregation: One rationale for affirmative action. *La Raza Law Journal, 12*, 159–172.

Montoya, M. E. (2002). Celebrating racialized legal narratives. In F. Valdes, J. McCristal-Culp, & A. Harris (Eds.), *Crossroads, directions, and a new critical race theory* (pp. 243–250). Philadelphia, PA: Temple University Press.

Moore, J., & Vigil, J. D. (1993). Barrios in transition. In J. Moore & R. Pinderhughes (Eds.), *In the barrios: Latinos and the underclass debate* (pp. 27–49). New York: Russell Sage Foundation.

Moraga, C. (1983). La güera. In C. Moraga & G. E. Anzaldúa (Eds.), *This bridge called my back: Writings by radical Women of Color* (2nd ed., pp. 27–34). New York: Kitchen Table Women of Color Press.

Moraga, C., & Anzaldúa, G. E. (Eds.). (1981). *This bridge called my back: Radical writings by Women of Color*. Watertown, MA: Persephone Press.

Morales, A. (1988). *Barriers, critical events, and support systems affecting Chicanas in their pursuit of an academic doctorate.* Unpublished doctoral dissertation, East Texas State University.

Moreno, J. (Ed.). (1999). *The elusive quest for equality: 150 Years of Chicano/Chicana education.* Cambridge, MA: Harvard Educational Review.

Morris, J. (1999). A pillar of strength: An African-American school's communal bonds with families and community since *Brown. Urban Education, 33*(5), 584–605.

Morris, J. (2004). Can anything good come from Nazareth? Race, class, and African American schooling and community in the urban south and midwest. *American Educational Research Journal, 41*(1), 69–112.

Moses, Y. (1989). *Black women in academe: Issues and strategies.* Washington D.C.: Association of American Colleges.

Muñoz, C. (1989). *Youth, identity, power: The Chicano movement.* New York: Verso.

Muñoz, D. G. (1986). Identifying areas of stress for Chicano undergraduates. In M. A. Olivas (Ed.), *Latino College Students* (pp. 131–156). New York: Teachers College Press.

Murgia, E., & Telles, E. (1990). Phenotypic discrimination and income differences among Mexican Americans. *Social Science quarterly, 71*(4) 682–696.

Murgia, E., & Telles, E. (1992). The continuing significance of phenotype among Mexican Americans. *Social Science Quarterly, 73*(1), 120–122.

Murgia, E., & Telles, E. (1996). Phenotype and schooling among Mexican Americans. *Sociology of Education, 69*, 276–289.

Nakanishi, D. T., & Nishida, T. Y. (Eds.). (1995). *The Asian American educational experience: A source book for teachers and students.* New York: Routledge.

National Science Foundation. (1990). *Women and minorities in science and engineering.* Washington, DC: National Science Foundation.

Nelson, S., & Pellet, G. (Producers, Writers, Directors). (1997). *Shattering the silences: Minority professors break into the ivory tower.* [Film]. United States: PBS.

Nettles, M. (1990a). *Black, Hispanic, and White doctoral students: Before, during, and after enrolling in graduate school.* Princeton, NJ: Educational Testing Service.

Nettles, M. (1990b). Success in doctoral programs: Experiences of minority and White students. *American Journal of Education, 98*, 494–522.

Neumann, A., & Peterson, P. (Eds.). (1997). *Learning from our lives: Women, research, and autobiography in education.* New York: Teacher College Press.

Nicolaides, B. M. (2002). *My blue heaven: Life and politics in the working-class suburbs of Los Angeles, 1920–1965.* Chicago: University of Chicago Press.

Nieves-Squires, S. (1991). *Hispanic women: Making their presence on campus less tenuous.* Washington D.C.: Association of American Colleges.

Noboa-Rios, A. (1981/82). An analysis of Hispanic doctoral recipients from U.S. universities, 1900–1973: With special emphasis on Puerto Rican doctorates. *Metas, 2*, 1–108.

Nugiel, N. R. (Producer). Wolfe, G. C. (Director). Santiago-Hudson, R. (Writer). (2005). *Lackawanna Blues* [Film]. United States: HBO Films.

Oakes, J. (1985). *Keeping track: How schools structure inequality.* New Haven, CT: Yale University Press.

Oakes, J. (1986, September). Tracking: Part 1: The policy and practice of curriculum inequality. *Phi Delta Kappan, 68*(1), 12–17.

Oakes, J. (1990). *Lost talent: The underrepresentation of women, minorities, and disabled students in science.* Santa Monica, CA: The Rand Corporation.

Oakes, J. (1990). *Multiplying inequalities: The effects of race, social class, and tracking on opportunities to learn mathematics and science.* Santa Monica, CA: RAND.

Oakes, J., & Lipton, M. (2004). "Schools that shock the conscience": Williams v. California and the struggle for education on equal terms fifty years after Brown. *La Raza Law Journal, 15,* 25–48.

Oakland, D., & Valenzuela, M. (Eds.). (1998). LatCrit: Latinas/os and the Law. *La Raza Law Journal, 10*(1), 1–600).

Oboler, S. (1992). The politics of labeling: Latina/o cultural identities of self and others. *Latin American Perspectives, 19*(4), 18–36.

O'Connell, A. N., & Russo, N. F. (Eds.). (1983). *Models of achievement: Reflections of eminent women in psychology.* New York: Columbia University Press.

O'Connell, A. N., & Russo, N. F. (Eds.). (1988). *Models of achievement: Reflections of eminent women in psychology* (vol. 2). Hillsdale, NJ: Erlbaum.

O'Connell, A. N., & Russo, N. F. (1990). *Women in psychology: A bio-bibliographical sourcebook.* New York: Greenwood Press.

Ogbu, J. (1990). Minority education in comparative perspective. *Journal of Negro education, 59,* 45–57.

O'Halloran, C. S. (1995) Mexican American female students who were successful in high school science courses. *Equity and Excellence in Education, 28*(2), 57–63.

Olivas, M. (1990). The chronicles, my grandfather's stories, and immigration law: The slave traders chronicle as racial history. *Saint Louis University Law Journal, 34,* 425–441.

Oliver, M., & Shapiro, T. (1995). *Black wealth/White wealth: A new perspective on racial inequality.* New York: Routledge.

Olmedo, I. M. (1997). Voices of our past: Using oral history to explore funds of knowledge within a Puerto Rican family. *Anthropology and Education Quarterly, 28*(4), 550–573.

Olmedo-Williams, I. (1981). Functions of code-switching in a Spanish/English bilingual classroom. National Dissemination and Assessment Center, California State University, Los Angeles.

Omi, M., & Winant, H. (1994). *Racial formation in the United States: From the 1960s to the 1990s* (2nd ed.). New York: Routledge.

Ong Hing, B. (1997). *To be an American: Cultural pluralism and the rhetoric of assimilation.* New York: New York University Press.

Orfield, G. (1996). *Dismantling desegregation: The quiet reversal of Brown v. Board of Education.* New York: New Press.

Orfield, G., & Monfort, F. (1992). *Status of school desegregation: The next generation.* Cambridge, MA: Metropolitan Opportunity Project, Harvard University.

Orlans, K., & Wallace, R. (Eds.). (1994). *Gender and the academic experience: Berkeley women sociologists.* Lincoln, NE: University of Nebraska Press.

Ornelas, A. O. (2002). *An examination of the resources and barriers in the transfer process for Latina/o community college students: A case study analysis of an urban community college.* Unpublished doctoral dissertation, University of California, Los Angeles.

Ornelas, A. O., & Solórzano, D. G. (2004). Transfer conditions of Latina/o community college students: A single institution case study. *Community College Journal of Research and Practice, 28,* 233–248.

Ortiz, F. I. (1977). Bilingual education program practices and their effect upon students' performance and self-identity. *Aztlan: A Journal of Chicano Studies, 8,* 157–174.

Oseguera, L. (2004). *Individual and institutional influences on the baccalaureate degree attainment of African American, Asian American, Caucasian, and Mexican American undergraduates.* Unpublished doctoral dissertation, University of California, Los Angeles.

Ozomatli Music (Producer). 2na, C., Sierra, A., & Pacheco, R. (Writers). (1998). *Cumbia de los Muertos* (Cumbia of the Dead). [Recorded by Ozomatli]. On Ozomatli [CD]. Los Angeles, CA: Almo Sounds.

Pachon, H., & de la Garza, R. (1996). *Differential access to advanced placement courses: Implications for the University of California admissions policies.* Claremont, CA: The Tomas Rivera Policy Institute.

Pachon, H. P., & Tokofksy, D. (2000, May 5). AP program—A big step up if you can get it. *Los Angeles Times*, p. B9.

Padilla, L. M. (2001). 'But you're not a dirty Mexican': Internalized oppression, Latinos & law. *Texas Hispanic Journal of Law & Policy, 7*, 59–133.

Padilla, R., & Chavez, R. (1995). *The leaning ivory tower: Latino professors in American universities.* Albany, NY: State University of New York Press.

Pardo, M. (1990). Mexican American women grassroots community activists: Mothers of east Los Angeles. *Frontier: A Journal of Women Studies, 11*, 1–7.

Pardo, M. (1991). Creating community: Mexican American women in eastside Los Angeles. *Aztlan: A Journal of Chicano Studies, 20*(1–2), 39.

Pardo, M. (1998). *Mexican American women activists: Identity and resistance in two Los Angeles communities.* Philadelphia, PA: Temple University Press.

Paredes, A. (1958). *With his pistol in his hand: A border ballad and its hero.* Austin, TX: University of Texas Press.

Parker, L., Deyhle, D., & Villenas, S. (Eds.). (1999). *Race is...race isn't: Critical race theory and qualitative studies in education.* Boulder, CO: Westview Press.

Parker, L., Deyhle, D., Villenas, S., & Crossland, K. (Eds.). (1998). Special issue: Critical race theory and education. *International Journal of Qualitative Studies in Education, 11*(1), 1–184.

Parker, L., & Stovall, D. (2004). Actions following words: Critical race theory connects to critical pedagogy. *Journal of Educational Philosophy and Theory, 36*(2), 159–174.

Paton, D. (2005, May 18). Rift over recruiting at public high schools: A Seattle high school bars military solicitation, touching off debate over Iraq war and free speech. *Christian Science Monitor*, Retrieved June 25, 2005, from http://www.csmonitor.com/2005/0518/p02s01-ussc.html.

Payton, C. (1988). Carolyn Robertson Payton. In A. N. O'Connell & N. F. Russo (Eds.), *Models of achievement: Reflections of eminent women in psychology* (Vol. 2). Hillsdale, NJ: Erlbaum.

Pearl, A. (1991). Systemic and institution factors in Chicano school failure. In R. Valencia (Ed.), *Chicano school failure and success: Research and policy agenda for the 1990s* (pp. 273–320). New York: Falmer Press.

Pearl, A. (2002). The big picture: Systemic and institution factors in Chicano school failure. In R. Valencia (Ed.), *Chicano school failure and success: Past, present, and future* (2nd ed., pp. 335–364). New York: Routledge.

Pearson, W., & Pearson, L. C. (1985). Baccalaureate origins of Black American scientists: A cohort analysis. *Journal of Negro Education 54*(1), 24–34.

Pearson, W. (1985). *Black scientists, White society, and colorless science: A study of universalism in American science.* New York: Associated Faculty Press.

Pearson, W., & Bechtel, K. (Eds.). (1989). *Blacks, science, and American education*. New Brunswick, New Jersey: Rutgers University Press.

People Who Care v. Rockford Board of Education, 246 F.3d 1073 (7th Cir. 2001).

Perea, J. F. (1998). The Black/White binary paradigm of race: The 'normal science' of American racial thought. *La Raza Law Review, 10*(1), 127–172.

Perea, J. F. (2004). Why integration and equal protection fail to protect Latinos. *Harvard Law Review, 117,* 1420–1469.

Perea, J. F., Delgado, R., Harris, A., & Wildman, S. (Eds.), (2000). *Race and races: Cases and resources for a multiracial America*. St. Paul, MN: West Group.

Persell, C. H. (1977). *Education and inequality: A theoretical and empirical synthesis.* New York: Free Press.

Peters, W. (Producer/Director). (1970). *Eye of the Storm* [Film]. United States: ABC News.

Peters, W. (Producer/Director). (1985). *A Class Divided* [Film]. Boston: WGBH. Frontline, PBS. (Available from PBS Video, PO Box 751089, Charlotte, NC 28275)

Pew Hispanic Research Center (2004, June). *Latino youth finishing college: The role of selective pathways.*Washington, DC: Fry, R.

Pierce, C. M. (1969). Is bigotry the basis of the medical problems of the ghetto? In J.C. Norman (Ed.), *Medicine in the ghetto* (pp. 301–314). New York: Meredith Corporation.

Pierce, C. M. (1970). Offensive mechanisms. In F. B. Barbour (Ed.), *The Black '70s*, (pp. 265–282). Boston, MA: Porter Sargent.

Pierce, C. M. (1974). Psychiatric problems of the Black minority. In S. Arieti (Ed.), *American handbook of psychiatry* (pp. 512–523). New York: Basic Books.

Pierce, C. M. (1975). Poverty and racism as they affect children. In I. N. Berlin. (Ed.), *Advocacy for child mental health* (pp. 92–109). New York: Brunner/Mazel Publishers.

Pierce, C. M. (1980). Social trace contaminants: Subtle indicator of racism in tv. In S. B. Withey & R. P. Abeles (Eds.), *Television and social behavior: Beyond violence and children. A report of the committee on television and social behavior social science research council* (pp. 249–257). Hillsdale, NJ: Lawrence Erlbaum Associates.

Pierce, C. M. (1989). Unity in diversity: Thirty-three years of stress. In G. Berry & J. Asamen (Eds.), *Black students: Psychological issues and academic achievement* (pp. 296–312). Newbury Park, Sage.

Pierce, C. M. (1995). Stress analogs of racism and sexism: Terrorism, torture, and disaster. In C. V. Willie, P. P. Rieker, B. M. Kramer, & B. S. Brown (Eds.), *Mental health, racism, and sexism* (pp. 277–293). Pittsburgh, PA: University of Pittsburgh Press.

Piorkowski, G. (1983). Survivor guilt in the university setting. *Personnel and Guidance Journal, 61,* 620–622.

Pizarro, M. (1998). Chicano power!: Epistemology and methodology for social justice and empowerment in Chicana/o communities. *International Journal of Qualitative Studies in Education, 11*(1), 57–80.

Pizarro, M. (2005). *Chicanas and Chicanos in school: Racial profiling, identity battles, and empowerment*. Austin: University of Texas Press.

Plessy v. Ferguson, 163 U.S. 537 (1896).

Ponce, P. A. (2002). *Pioneer Chicana and Chicano doctorates: An examination of their educational journey and success*. Unpublished doctoral dissertation, University of California, Los Angeles.

Portes, A., & Truelove, C. (1987). Making sense of diversity: Recent research on Hispanic minorities in the United States. *Annual Review of Sociology, 13,* 359–385.

Quintana, S. (1999). Mexican American children's ethnic pride and internalized racism. JSRI Occasional Paper, 41. East Lansing, MI: Julian Samora Research Institute.

Racho, S. (Producer). (1996). *Chicano! The Mexican American Civil Rights Movement. Episode 3: Taking Back the Schools.* Sal Castro Interview [Film]. Los Angeles: KCET-TV PBS.

Ragland, J. (2002, January 28). Schools grow from new 'core.' *Los Angeles Times*, pp. B1, B8.

Rangel, Y. (2001) *College immigrant students: How undocumented female Mexican immigrant students transition into higher education.* Unpublished doctoral dissertation, University of California, Los Angeles.

Ramos, M. (1996). Unqualified to be voiceless: Inaudible screams falling on deaf ears of a not so color-blind society. *Berkeley Women's Law Journal, 11*, 1–18.

Reed, D. (1998). Twenty-five years after Rodriguez; School finance litigation and the impact of new judicial federalism. *Law and Society Review, 32*(1), 175–220.

Rendon, L. (1992, Winter). From the barrio to the academy: Revelations of a Mexican American 'scholarship girl.' *New Directions for Community Colleges, 80*, 55–64.

Revilla, A. T. (2001). LatCrit and crt in the field of education: A theoretical dialogue between two colleagues. *Denver University Law Review, 78*(4), 623–632.

Revilla, A. T. (2003). Inmensa fe en le victoria (Immense faith in victory). Social Justice through Education. *Frontiers: A Journal of Women Studies 24*(2&3), 282–301.

Revilla, A. T. (2004a). Muxerista pedagogy: Raza womyn teaching social justice through activism. *The High School Journal, 87*(4), 80–94.

Revilla, A. T. (2004b). *Raza womyn re-constructing revolution: Exploring the intersections of race, class, gender and sexuality in the lives of Chicana/Latina student activists.* Unpublished doctoral dissertation, University of California, Los Angeles.

Reynolds, K. (Director). Yagemann, S. (Writer). (1997). *187*. [Film]. Warner Bros.

Richardson, R., & Skinner, E. (1990). Adapting to diversity: Organizational influences on student achievement. *Journal of Higher Education, 61*, 485–511.

Riley, M. (Ed.). (1988). *Sociological Lives.* Newbury Park, CA: Sage.

Roberts, D. E. (2000, Summer). Commentary: The paradox of silence: Some questions about silence as resistance. *Michigan Journal of Race and Law, 5*, 927–941.

Robinson, T., & Ward, J. (1991). A belief in self far greater than anyone's belief: Cultivating resistance among African American female adolescents. In C. Gilligan, A. Rogers, & D. Tolman (Eds.), *Women, girls, and psychotherapy: Reframing resistance* (pp. 87–103). New York: Haworth.

Rockwell, P. (2003). Why angry white guys for affirmative action are marching to the supreme court. Retrieved March 29, 2005 from http://www.inmotionmagazine.com/rocka.html

Rodriguez v. Los Angeles Unified School District, C611 358. (1986).

Rodriguez, R. (1982). *Hunger of memory: The education of Richard Rodriguez.* Boston, MA: D. R. Godine.

Rogers, J. (2004a). *School segregation and educational opportunity in Los Angeles.* Paper presented at C. Haro & N. Bermudez "Symposium: Mendez v. Westminster School District: Paving the Path for School Desegregation and Brown v. Board of Education." March 14, 2004. University of California, Los Angeles Chicano Studies Research Center.

Rogers, J. (2004b, March 27). Shining a light on the journey to educational justice. In S. Cooper & M. Welsing (Eds.), *On equal terms: Advancing educational justice in Los Angeles* (pp. 8–9). Los Angeles, CA: The Southern California Library for Social Studies and Research.

Rosaldo, R. (1994). Whose cultural studies? *American Anthropologist, 96*, 524–529.

Rosner, J. (2001). Disparate outcomes by design: University admission tests. *Berkeley La Raza Law Journal, 12*(2), 377–395.

Rueda, R., Artiles, A. J., Salazar, J., & Higareda, I. (2002). An analysis of special education as a response to the diminished academic achievement of Chicano students: An update. In R. R. Valencia (Ed.), *Chicano school failure and success: Past, present, and future* (2nd ed, pp. 310–332). London: Routledge Falmer.

Rueda, R., Monzo, L. D., & Higareda, I. (2004). Appropriating the sociocultural resources of Latino paraeducators for effective instruction with Latino students: Promises and problems. *Urban Education, 29*(1) 52–90.

Rumberger, R. W. (1991). Chicano dropouts: A review of research and policy issues. In R. R. Valencia (Ed.), *Chicano school failure and success: Research and policy agendas for the 1990s* (pp. 64–89). The Stanford Series on Education and Public Policy. London: Falmer Press.

Russell, J. (1993). On being a gorilla in your mist, or, the life of one Black woman in the legal academy. *Harvard Civil Rights-Civil Liberties Law Review, 28*, 259–262.

Ryan, J. E. (1999). The influence of race on school finance reform. *Michigan Law Review, 98*(2), 432–481.

Ryan, J., & Sackrey, C. (1984). *Strangers in paradise: Academics from the working class.* Boston, MA: South End Press.

Salvucci, L. K. (1991). Mexico, Mexicans, and Mexican Americans in secondary-school United States history textbooks. *The History Teacher, 24*, (2), 203–222.

San Antonio Independent School District v. Rodriguez, 411 U.S. 1 (1973).

Sánchez, G. J. (1993). *Becoming Mexican American: Ethnicity, culture, and identity in Chicano Los Angeles, 1900–1945.* Oxford: Oxford University Press.

Sánchez, G. J. (1997). History, culture, and education. In A. Darder, R. O. Torres, & H. Gutiérrez. (Eds.), *Latinos and education: A critical reader* (pp. 117–134). New York: Routledge.

Sassen, S. (1992). Why migration? *NACLA Report on the Americas, 26*(1), pp. 13–19, 46–47.

Schevitz, T. (1998, April 23). Students hold march in Concord: Protestors target lack of educational access. *The San Francisco Chronicle*, p. A20.

Schwartz, N. (2000, November 27). High school students organize 'union' to work for change. *Los Angeles Times*, p. B3.

Scott-Heron, G. (1971). The revolution will not be televised. On *Pieces of Me* [Album]. Flying Dutchman/RCA.

Serrano v. Priest, 487 P.2d 1241 (Cal. 1971).

Serrano v. Priest, 557 P.2d 929 (Cal. 1976).

Shapiro, T. (2004). *The hidden cost of being African American: How wealth perpetuates inequality.* New York: Oxford University Press.

Shuit, D. P. (1998, March 26). Despite all odds, poly still excels. *Los Angeles Times*, p. A1.

Silva, F., & Sonstelie, J.C. (1995). Did Serrano cause a decline in school spending? *National Tax Journal, 48*(2), 199–215.

Simoniello, K. (1981). On investigating the attitudes toward achievement and success in eight professional U.S. Mexican women. *Aztlan: A Journal of Chicano Studies, 12*, 121–137.

Simpson, D., & Bruckheimer, J. (Producers). Smith, J. N. (Director). Johnson, L., & Bass, R. (Writers). (1995). *Dangerous Minds.* [Film]. Hollywood Pictures.

Sleeter, C. E., & Delgado Bernal, D. (2004). Critical pedagogy, critical race theory, and anti-racist education: Implications for multicultural education. In J. A. Banks & C. M. Banks

(Eds.), *The handbook of research on multicultural education* (2nd ed., pp. 240–258). New York: Macmillan.

Smith, D. (1999, September 11). Students protest in walkout at Fremont High. *Los Angeles Times*, p. B1.

Smith, P. J. (2000, Summer). Forging our identity: Transformative resistance in the areas of work, class, and the law: The tyrannies of silence of the untenured professors of color. *UC Davis Law Review, 22*, 1105–1133.

Smith, W. A. (1993–2004). *National study on African Americans.* Unpublished interview database. University of Illinois at Chicago and the University of Utah.

Smith, W. A. (2004). Black faculty coping with racial battle fatigue: The campus racial climate in a post-civil rights era. In D. Cleveland (Ed.), *A long way to go: Conversations about race by African American faculty and graduate students at predominately White institutions* (pp. 171–190). New York: Peter Lang Publishers.

Smith, W. A., & Allen, W. (2004). *Surviving with racial battle fatigue: African Essex Americans fighting weapons of mass destruction on historically White campuses.* Paper presented at The Association of Black Sociologists, San Francisco, CA.

Smith, W. A., Allen, W. R., & Land, L. D. (2005). *"Assume the position... you fit the description": Campus racial climate and the psychoeducational experiences of African American male college students.* Manuscript submitted for publication.

Smith, W. A., & Alschuler, A. S. (1976). *How to measure Freire's stages of conscientizacão: The C code manual.* Amherst, MA: University of Massachusetts, Social Literacy Project.

Smith, W. A., Yosso, T. J., & Solórzano, D. G. (in press). Challenging racial battle fatigue on historically White campuses: A critical race examination of race-related stress. In C. A. Stanley (Ed.), *Faculty of Color teaching in predominantly White colleges and universities.* Bolton, MA: Anker Publishing.

Smith-Maddox, R., & Solórzano, D. (2002). Using critical race theory, Paulo Freire's problem-posing method, and case study research to confront race and racism in education. *Qualitative Inquiry, 1*(8), 66–84.

Social Justice in Education Project. (Producer). (2004). *Questions for answers.* [Film]. (Available from Mexican American/Raza Studies 1010 E. Tenth St. Tucson, AZ 85719).

Soja, E. W. (1987). Economic restructuring and the internationalization of the Los Angeles region. In M. P. Smith & J. Feagin (Eds.), *The capitalist city: Global restructuring and community politics* (pp. 178–198). New York: Basil Blackwell.

Soja, E. W. (1989). It all comes together in Los Angeles. In E. Soja, *Postmodern geographies: The reassertion of space in critical social theory* (pp. 190–221). New York: Verso.

Solórzano, D. G. (1986). *A study of social mobility values: The determinants of Chicano parents' occupational expectations for their children.* Unpublished doctoral dissertation, The Claremont Graduate University.

Solórzano, D. G. (1989). Teaching and social change: Reflections on a Freirean approach in a college classroom. *Teaching Sociology, 17*, 218–225.

Solórzano, D. G. (1992). Chicano mobility aspirations: A theoretical and empirical note. *Latino Studies Journal, 3*, 48–66.

Solórzano, D. G. (1993). *The career paths of Chicana and Chicano doctorates: A study of Ford Foundation minority fellows in California.* Berkeley, California: The California Policy Seminar.

Solórzano, D. G. (1994). The baccalaureate origins of Chicana and Chicano doctorates in the physical, life, and engineering sciences: 1980–1990. *Journal of Women and Minorities in Science and Engineering, 1*, 253–272.

Solórzano, D. G. (1995a). The baccalaureate origins of Chicana and Chicano doctorates in the social sciences. *Hispanic Journal of Behavioral Sciences, 17*, 3–32.

Solórzano, D. G. (1995b). The doctorate production and baccalaureate origins of African Americans in the sciences and engineering. *Journal of Negro Education, 64*, 15–32.

Solórzano, D. G. (1996). A talent development approach to determining the goals of a university minority retention program. *Studies in Educational Evaluation, 22*, 245–261.

Solórzano, D. G. (1997). Images and words that wound: Critical race theory, racial stereotyping, and teacher education. *Teacher Education Quarterly, 24*, 5–19.

Solórzano, D. G. (1998). Critical race theory, racial and gender microaggressions, and the experiences of Chicana and Chicano scholars. *International Journal of Qualitative Studies in Education, 11*, 121–136.

Solórzano, D. G. (1999). *Navigating through college: The stages of passage for Chicana and Chicano students.* Latino Higher Education Focus Group Study. Research report prepared for Inter-University Program for Latino Research, University of Texas, Austin, August, 1999.

Solórzano, D. G., Allen, W., & Carroll, G. (2002). A case study of racial microaggressions and campus racial climate at the University of California, Berkeley. *UCLA Chicano/ Latino Law Review, 23*, 15–111.

Solórzano, D. G., Burciaga, R., Calderón, D., Ledesma, M. C., Ochoa, V., Rivas, M. A., Sanchez, M., Velez, V., Watford, T., Ortega, L., & Pineda, J. (2004). Unlocking GATE: A case study of Student of Color (under)representation in a Southern California school district's Gifted and Talented Education program. A report to the Latina Rights Project of the American Civil Liberties Union.

Solórzano, D. G., Ceja, M., & Yosso, T. (2000). Critical race theory, racial microaggressions, and campus racial climate: The experiences of African American college students. *Journal of Negro Education, 69*(1/2), 60–73.

Solórzano, D. G., & Delgado Bernal, D. (2001). Critical race theory, transformational resistance, and social justice: Chicana and Chicano students in an urban context. *Urban Education, 36*, 308–342.

Solórzano, D. G., Ledesma, M. C., Pérez, J., Burciaga, M. R., & Ornelas, A. (2003). *Latina equity in education: Gaining access to academic enrichment programs.* Latino Policy & Issues Brief. (no. 4). Los Angeles, CA: UCLA Chicano Studies Research Center.

Solórzano, D. G., & Ornelas, A. (2002). A critical race analysis of advanced placement classes: A case of educational inequality. *Journal of Latinos and Education, 1*(4), 215–229.

Solorzano, D. G., & Ornelas, A. (2004, February/March). A critical race analysis of Latina/o and African American advanced placement enrollment in public high schools. *The High School Journal*, 15–26. University of North Carolina Press.

Solórzano, D. G., Rivas, M. A., & Velez, V. (2005). *Community College as a pathway to Chicana/o doctorate production.* Latino Policy and Issues Brief (no. 11). Los Angeles, CA: UCLA Chicano Studies Research Center.

Solórzano, D. G., & Solórzano, R. (1995). The Chicano educational experience: A proposed framework for effective schools in Chicano communities. *Educational Policy, 9*, 293–314.

Solórzano, D. G., & Villalpando, O. (1998). Critical race theory, marginality, and the experience of minority students in higher education. In C. Torres & T. Mitchell, (Eds.), *Emerging issues in the sociology of education: Comparative perspectives* (pp. 211–224). New York: SUNY Press.

Solórzano, D. G., Villalpando, O., & Oseguera, L. (2005). Educational inequities and Latina/o undergraduate students in the United States: A critical race analysis of their educational progress. *Journal of Hispanic Higher Education, 4*(3), 272–294.

Solórzano, D. G., & Yosso, T. J. (2000). Toward a critical race theory of Chicana and Chicano education. In C. Tejeda, C. Martinez, Z. Leonardo, & P. McLaren (Eds.), *Charting new terrains of Chicana(o)/Latina(o) education* (pp. 35–65). Cresskill, NJ: Hampton Press.

Solórzano, D. G., & Yosso, T. J. (2001a). Critical race and LatCrit theory and method: Counterstorytelling Chicana and Chicano graduate school experiences. *International Journal of Qualitative Studies in Education, 14*(4), 471–495.

Solórzano, D. G., & Yosso, T. J. (2001b). From racial stereotyping toward a critical race theory in teacher education. *Multicultural Education, 9*(1), 2–8.

Solórzano, D. G., & Yosso, T. J. (2001c). Maintaining social justice hopes within academic realities: A Freirean approach to critical race/Latcrit pedagogy. *Denver University Law Review, 78*(4), 595–621.

Solórzano, D. G., & Yosso, T. J. (2002a). A critical race counterstory of race, racism, and affirmative action. *Equity and Excellence in Education, 35*(2), 155–168.

Solórzano, D. G., & Yosso, T. J. (2002b). Critical race methodology: Counterstorytelling as an analytical framework for education research. *Qualitative Inquiry, 8*(1), 23–44.

Sowell, T. (1981). *Ethnic America: A history.* New York: Basic Books.

Spring, J. (2001). *Deculturalization and the struggle for equality: A brief history of the education of dominated cultures in the United States.* Boston: McGraw Hill.

Stanford Center for Chicano Research. (1991). *Distinguishing between proficiency, choice and attitudes in questions about language for bilinguals.* (Working Paper no. 32). Stanford, CA: Hakuta, K.

Stanton-Salazar, R. D. (2001). *Manufacturing hope and despair: The school and kin support networks of U.S. - Mexican youth.* New York: Teachers College Press.

Stanton-Salazar, R., & Spina, S. U. (2000). The network orientations of highly resilient urban minority youth: A network-analytic account of minority socialization and its educational implications. *The Urban Review, 32*(3), 227–261.

Steele, C., & Aronson, J. (1995). Stereotype threat and the intellectual test performance of African Americans. *Journal of Personality and Social Psychology, 69,* 797–811.

Stefancic, J. (1998). Latino and Latina critical theory: An annotated bibliography. *La Raza Law Journal, 10,* 423–498.

Stevenson, B. (1996). *Life in Black and White: Family and community in the slave south.* New York: Oxford University Press.

Stovall, D. O. (2005). Forging communities in race and class: Critical race theory and the quest for social justice in education. Manuscript submitted for publication.

Strauss, A., & Corbin, J. (1990). *Basics of qualitative research: Grounded theory procedures and techniques.* Newbury Park, CA: Sage Publications.

Summers, L. H (2005). Remarks at NBER Conference on Diversifying the Science and Engineering Workforce. January 14, 2005. Cambridge, MA. Retrieved March 14, 2005, from http://www.president.harvard.edu/speeches/2005/nber.html

Talavera-Bustillos, V. (1998). *Chicana college choice and resistance: An exploratory study of first-generation Chicana college students.* Unpublished doctoral dissertation, University of California, Los Angeles.

Task Force on Women, Minorities, and the Handicapped in Science and Technology. (1989). *Changing America: The new face of science and engineering.* (Final Report). Washington DC: Author.

Tate, W. (1994). From inner city to ivory tower: Does my voice matter in the academy? *Urban Education, 29*(3), 245–269.

Tate, W. (1997). Critical race theory and education: History, theory, and implications. *Review of Research in Education, 22*, 191–243.

Tatum, B. D. (1997). *Why are all the Black kids sitting together in the cafeteria?: And other conversations about race.* New York: Basic Books.

Taylor, E. (1998). A primer on critical race theory: Who are the critical race theorists and what are they saying? *The Journal of Blacks in Higher Education, 19*, 122–124.

Taylor, F. (1911). *The principles of scientific management.* New York: Harper.

Taylor, K. (1993). Invisible women: Reflections on the Clarence Thomas confirmation hearings. *Stanford Law Review, 45*(2), 443–452.

Tedin, K. L. (1994). Self-interest, symbolic values, and the financial equalization of public schools. *Journal of Politics, 56*(3), 628–249.

Tejeda, C., Martinez, C., & Leonardo, Z. (Eds.). (2000). *Charting new terrains of Chicana(o)/ Latina(o) education.* Cresskill, NJ: Hampton Press.

Terman, L. M. (1916). *The measurement of intelligence: An explanation of and a complete guide for the use of the standard revision and extension of the Binet-Simon intelligence scale.* Boston: Houghton Mifflin Company.

Thomas, G. (1986). *The access and success of Blacks and Hispanics in U.S. graduate and professional education.* Washington, DC: National Academy of Science.

Thomas, G. (1987). Black students in U.S. graduate and processional schools in the 1980s: A national and institutional assessment. *Harvard Educational Review, 57*, 261–282.

Thomas, G. (1992). Participation and degree attainment of African-American and Latino students in graduate education relative to other racial and ethnic groups: An update from office of civil rights data. *Harvard Educational Review, 62*, 45–65.

Tidball, M. (1986). Baccalaureate origins of recent natural science doctorates. *Journal of Higher Education, 57*, 606–620.

Tidball, M., & Kistiakowsky, V. (1976). Baccalaureate origins of American scientists and scholars. *Science, 193*, 646–652.

Tinto, V. (1993). *Leaving college: Rethinking the causes and cures of student attrition.* (2nd Ed.) Chicago: The University of Chicago Press.

Tokarczyk, M., & Fay, E. (Eds.). (1993). *Working-class women in the academy: Laborers in the knowledge factory.* Amherst, MA: University of Massachusetts Press.

Tomas Rivera Center. (1993). Resolving a crisis in education: Latino teachers for tomorrow's classrooms. Claremont, CA: Author.

Trujillo, C. B. (1990). *Soldados: Chicanos in Viet Nam.* San Jose, CA: Chusma House Publications.

Turner, C., & Thompson, J. (1993). Socializing women doctoral students: Minority and majority experiences. *Review of Higher Education, 16*, 355–370.

Tyler, R. (1949). *Basic principles of curriculum and instruction.* Chicago, IL: University of Chicago Press.

Urrieta, L. (2003). *Orchestrating the selves: Chicana and Chicano negotiations of identity, ideology, and activism in education.* Unpublished doctoral dissertation, University of North Carolina, Chapel Hill.

United States Commission on Civil Rights. (1971). *Ethnic isolation of Mexican Americans in the public schools of the southwest.* Report I: Mexican American Education Study. Washington DC: U.S. Government Printing Office.

United States Commission on Civil Rights. (1973). *Teachers and students: Differences in teacher interaction with Mexican American and Anglo students*. Report V: Mexican American Education Study. Washington, DC: U.S. Government Printing Office.

U.S. Bureau of the Census. (2000). *2000 census of the population: General population characteristics, United States summary*. Washington, DC: U.S. Government Printing Office.

U.S. Department of Education, Office for Civil Rights (OCR). (2000). *Elementary and secondary school survey (e&s survey), 2000* [data file]. Retrieved September 26, 2004, from http://www.ed.gov/about/offices/list/ocr/data.html?src=rt

Valdes, F. (1997). Poised at the cusp: LatCrit theory, outsider jurisprudence and Latina/o self-empowerment. *Harvard Latino Law Review, 2*(1), 1–59.

Valdes, F. (1998). Under construction: LatCrit consciousness, community and theory. *La Raza Law Journal, 10*(1), 1–56.

Valdes, F., McCristal-Culp, J., & Harris, A. (Eds.). (2002). *Crossroads, directions, and a new critical race theory*. Philadephia, PA: Temple University Press.

Valdés, G., & Figueroa, R. A. (1994). *Bilingualism and testing: A special case of bias*. Norwood, NJ: Ablex.

Valdés-Fallis, G. (1978). Code switching and the classroom teacher. Prepared by ERIC Clearinghouse on Languages and Linguistics. Arlington, VA: Center for Applied Linguistics.

Valdez, L. (1971). *Early works, actos, bernabé, and pensamiento serpentino*. Houston, TX: Arte Público Press.

Valencia, R. R. (1991). (Ed.). *Chicano school failure and success: Research and policy agenda for the 1990s*. New York: Falmer Press.

Valencia, R. R. (Ed.). (1997). *The evolution of deficit thinking: Educational thought and practice*. Washington, DC: Falmer Press.

Valencia, R. R. (1999). Educational testing and Mexican American students: Problems and prostpects. In J. Moreno (Ed.), *The elusive quest for equality: 150 years of Chicano/ Chicana education*, (pp. 123–139). Harvard University, Harvard Educational Review.

Valencia, R. R. (2002a). (Ed.). *Chicano school failure and success: Past, present, and future* (2nd ed.) New York: Routledge/Falmer.

Valencia, R. R. (2002b). The plight of Chicano students: An overview of schooling conditions and outcomes. In R. R. Valencia (Ed.), *Chicano school failure and success: Past, present, and future* (2nd ed., pp. 3–51). London: Routledge/Falmer.

Valencia, R. R. (2005). The Mexican American struggle for equal educational opportunity in Mendez v. Westminster: Helping pave the way for Brown v. Board of Education. *Teachers College Record, 107*(3), 389–423.

Valencia, R. R., & Aburto, S. (1991). The uses and abuses of educational testing: Chicanos as a case in point. In Valencia, R. R. (Ed.), *Chicano school failure and success: Research and policy agenda for the 1990s* (pp. 203–251). New York: Falmer Press.

Valencia, R. R., & Bernal, E. M. (eds.). (2000). The Texas assessment of academic skills (TAAS) case: Perspectives of plaintiffs' experts. [Special issue]. *Hispanic Journal of Behavioral Sciences, 22*(4).

Valencia, R. R., & Black, M. S. (2002). "Mexicans don't value education!": On the basis of the myth, mythmaking, and debunking. *Journal of Latinos and Education, 2*(2), 81–103.

Valencia, R. R., Menchaca, M., & Donato, R. (2002). Segregation, desegregation, and integration of Chicano students: Old and new realities. In R. R. Valencia (Ed.), *Chicano school failure and success: Past, present, and future* (2nd ed, pp. 70–113). London: Routledge.

Valencia, R. R. & Solórzano, D. G. (1997). Contemporary deficit thinking. In R. Valencia (Ed.), *The evolution of deficit thinking in educational thought and practice* (pp. 160–210). Washington, DC: Falmer Press.

Valencia, R. R., Villareal, B. J., & Salinas, M. (2002). Educational testing and Chicano students: Issues, consequences, and prospects for reform. In R. R. Valencia (Ed.), *Chicano school failure and success: Past, present, and future* (2nd ed., pp. 253–309). New York: Routledge.

Valenzuela, A. (1999). *Subtractive schooling: U.S.–Mexican youth and the politics of caring.* New York: State University of New York Press.

Valenzuela, A. (2000). The significance of the TAAS test for Mexican immigrant and Mexican American adolescents: A case study. *Hispanic Journal of Behavioral Sciences, 22*(4), 524–539.

Valle, V., & Torres, R. (1994). Latinos in a 'post-industrial' disorder: Politics of a changing city. *Socialist Review, 23,* (4), 1–28.

Vasquez, M. (1982). Confronting barriers to the participation of Mexican-American women in higher education. *Hispanic Journal of Behavioral Sciences, 4,* 147–165.

Vasquez, R. (2004, February 26). School progress in eastside too slow. *Mexican American Sun.*

Velez-Ibañez, C. G. (1980). Mexicano/hispano support systems and *confianza*: Theoretical issues of cultural adaptation. In B. Valle & W. Vega (Eds.), *Hispanic natural support systems* (pp. 45–54). California Department of Mental Health.

Vélez-Ibáñez, C. G., & Greenberg, J. (1992). Formation and transformation of funds of knowledge among U.S.-Mexican households. *Anthropology and Education Quarterly, 23*(4), 313–335.

Vigil, E. B. (1999). *The crusade for justice: Chicano militancy and the government's war on dissent.* Madison: University of Wisconsin Press.

Vigil Laden, B. (2000). The puente project: Socializing and mentoring Latino community college students. *Academic Exchange Quarterly, 4,* 90.

Villalpando, C. M. (1996). *Chicanas and Latinas in higher education: La voz olvidada (the forgotten voice).* Unpublished doctoral dissertation, University of California, Los Angeles.

Villalpando, O. (2003). Self-segregation or self-preservation? A critical race theory and Latina/o critical theory analysis of findings from a longitudinal study of Chicana/o college students. *International Journal of Qualitative Studies in Education, 16*(5), 619–646.

Villalpando, O., & Solórzano, D. G. (2005). The role of culture in college preparation programs: a review of the literature. In W. Tierney, Z. Corwin, & J. Kolyar (Eds.), *Preparing for college: Nine elements of effective outreach* (pp. 13–28). Albany, NY: SUNY Press.

Villanueva, M., Erdman, B., & Howlett, L. (2000). World city/regional city: Latinos and African Americans in Chicago and St. Louis. JSRI Working paper #46. The Julian Samora Research Institutte Michigan State University, East Lansing, Michigan.

Villaseñor, V. E. (1991). *Rain of gold.* Houston, TX: Arte Publico Press.

Villenas, S., & Deyhle, D. (1999). Critical race theory and ethnographies challenging the stereotypes: Latino families, schooling, resilience and resistance. *Curriculum Inquiry, 29*(4), 413–445.

Villenas, S., & Moreno, M. (2001). To *valerse por si misma* between race, capitalism, and patriarchy: Latina mother-daughter pedagogies in North Carolina. *International Journal of Qualitative Studies in Education, 14*(5), 671–688.

Wakatsuki Houston, J., & Houston, J. D. (1973). *Farewell to Manzanar: A true story of Japanese American experience during and after the World War II internment*. Boston, MA: Houghton Mifflin.

Ward, J. (1996). Raising resisters: The role of truth telling in the psychological development of African American girls. In B. Leadbetter & N. Way (Eds.), *Urban Girls: Resisting Stereotypes, Creating Identities* (pp. 85–99). New York: New York University Press.

Watford, T., Rivas, M. A., Burciaga, R., & Solórzano, D. G. (in press). Latinas and the doctorate: The 'status' of attainment and experiences from the margin. In J. Castellanos & A. Gloria (Eds.), *Journey to a Ph.D.: The Latina/o experience in higher education*. Madison, WI: University of Wisconsin-Madison Press.

Weill-Greenberg, E. (2005, February 24). Calling all soldiers: Military recruiters face resistance from young anti-war activists. *New York Amsterdam News*. Retrieved June 25, 2005, from http://www.amsterdamnews.org/news/Article/Article.asp?NewsID=54103&sID=4

Wells, A. S., & Crain, R. L. (1997). *Stepping over the color-line: African American students in White suburban schools*. New York: Teachers College Press.

Wells, A. S., & Serna, I. (1996). The politics of culture: Understanding local political resistance to detracking racially mixed schools. *Harvard Educational Review, 66*(1), 93–118.

West, C. (1993). *Race Matters*. Boston: Beacon Press.

White, M. A. (2002, Spring). Paradise lost? Teachers' perspectives on the use of cultural capital in the segregated schools of New Orleans, Louisiana. *The Journal of African American History*, 269–281.

Williams v. State of California, (2000). Superior Court of the State of California for the County of San Francisco. Case No. 890221 (Plaintiff Complaint).

Williams v. State of California, (2004). Superior Court of the State of California for the County of San Francisco. Case No. 312236 (Settlement Agreement).

Williams, N. (1988). A Mexican American woman encounters sociology: An autobiographical perspective. *American Sociologist, 19*, 340–346.

Williams, P. (1987). Spirit-murdering the messenger: The discourse of finger pointing as the law's response to racism. *University of Miami Law Review, 42*, 127–157.

Williams, P. (1991). *The alchemy of race and rights: Diary of a law professor*. Cambridge, MA: Harvard University Press.

Williams, P. (1997). Spirit-murdering the messenger: The discourse of fingerprinting as the law's response to racism. In A. Wing (Ed.), *Critical race feminism: A reader* (pp. 229–236). New York: New York University Press

Williams, R. A. (1995). Foreword. In R. Delgado. *The Rodrigo Chronicles: Conversations about America and Race*. (pp. xi–xv). New York University Press.

Williams, R. A. (1997). Vampires anonymous and critical race practice. *Michigan Law Review, 95*(4), 741–765.

Willig, A. (1985). A meta-analysis of selected studies on effectiveness of bilingual education. *Review of Educational Research, 55*, 269–317.

Winfield, L. F. (1997). Multiple dimensions of reality: Recollections of an African American woman scholar. In A. Newmann & P. L. Peterson (Eds.), Learning from our lies: Women, research, and autobiography in education (pp. 194–208). New York: Teachers College Press.

Wing, A. K. (Ed.). (1997). *Critical race feminism: A reader*. New York: New York University Press.

Wing, A. K. (Ed.). (2000). *Global critical race feminism: An international reader*. New York: New York University Press.

Wolf-Wendel, L. E. (1998). Models of excellence: Baccalaureate origins of successful European American women, African American women, and Latinas. *Journal of Higher Education, 69*(2), 141–186.

Wolf-Wendel, L. E. (2000). Women-friendly campuses: What 5 institutions are doing right. *Review of Higher Education, 23*(3), 319–345.

Wollenberg, C. M. (1976). *All deliberate speed: Segregation and exclusion in California schools, 1855–1975.* Berkeley: University of California Press.

Wollenberg, C. M. (2004). The Relationship of the *Mendez* Case to Brown v. Board of Education. Paper presented at Haro, C., & Bermudez, N. "Symposium: *Mendez v. Westminster School District*: Paving the Path for School Desegregation and *Brown v. Board of Education*." March 14, 2004. University of California, Los Angeles Chicano Studies Research Center.

X, M. (1972). Who taught you to hate yourself? On *music and dialogue from the original motion picture Malcom X* [Track No. 6]. A Marvin Worth Production.

X, M. (1992). *By any means necessary* (2nd ed.). New York: Pathfinder.

Yamamoto, E. K., Serrano, S. K., Fenton, M. S., Gifford, J., Forman, D., Hoshijo, B., & Kim, J. (2000/2001). Civil right in the new decade: Dismantling civil rights: Multiracial resistance and reconstruction. *Cumberland Law Review, 31*, 523–567.

Yosso, T. J. (2000). *A critical race and latcrit approach to media literacy: Chicana/o resistance to visual microaggressions.* Unpublished doctoral dissertation, University of California, Los Angeles.

Yosso, T. J. (2002a). Critical race media literacy: Challenging deficit discourse about Chicanas/os. *Journal of Popular Film and Television, 30*(1), 52–62.

Yosso, T. J. (2002b). Toward a critical race curriculum. *Equity and Excellence in Education, 35*(2), 93–107.

Yosso, T. J. (2005). Whose culture has capital? A critical race theory discussion of community cultural wealth. *Race, Ethnicity, and Education, 8*(1), 71–93.

Zavella, P. (1991). Reflections on diversity among Chicanas. *Frontiers: A Journal of Women Studies, 2*(2), 73–85.

Zentgraf, K. M. (1989). Gender, immigration, and economic restructuring in Los Angeles. *California Sociologist, 12*(2), 111–136.

Zinn, H. (1995). *A people's history of the United States: 1492 to present* (revised and updated ed.). New York: Harper Collins.

Zuckerman, H. (1977). *The scientific elite: Nobel laureates in the United States.* New York: Free Press.